Biopolitics as a System of Thought

Also Available from Bloomsbury

Biopolitics and the Philosophy of Death, Paolo Palladino
Biopolitics After Neuroscience, Jeffrey P. Bishop, M. Therese Lysaught
and Andrew A. Michel
Global Governance and Biopolitics, David Roberts

Biopolitics as a System of Thought

Serene Richards

BLOOMSBURY ACADEMIC
LONDON • NEW YORK • OXFORD • NEW DELHI • SYDNEY

BLOOMSBURY ACADEMIC
Bloomsbury Publishing Plc, 50 Bedford Square, London, WC1B 3DP, UK
Bloomsbury Publishing Inc, 1359 Broadway, 12th Floor, New York, NY 10018, USA
Bloomsbury Publishing Ireland, 29 Earlsfort Terrace, Dublin 2, D02 AY28, Ireland

BLOOMSBURY, BLOOMSBURY ACADEMIC and the Diana logo
are trademarks of Bloomsbury Publishing Plc

First published in Great Britain 2024
This paperback edition published in 2026

Copyright © Serene Richards, 2024

Serene Richards has asserted her right under the Copyright, Designs and
Patents Act, 1988, to be identified as Author of this work.

For legal purposes the Acknowledgements on p. vii constitute
an extension of this copyright page.

Design by Charlotte Daniels
Cover image: © photo agence IM'média

All rights reserved. No part of this publication may be: i) reproduced or transmitted in
any form, electronic or mechanical, including photocopying, recording or by means of
any information storage or retrieval system without prior permission in writing from
the publishers; or ii) used or reproduced in any way for the training, development or operation
of artificial intelligence (AI) technologies, including generative AI technologies. The rights
holders expressly reserve this publication from the text and data mining exception as per
Article 4(3) of the Digital Single Market Directive (EU) 2019/790.

Bloomsbury Publishing Inc does not have any control over, or responsibility for,
any third-party websites referred to or in this book. All internet addresses given
in this book were correct at the time of going to press. The author and publisher
regret any inconvenience caused if addresses have changed or sites have
ceased to exist, but can accept no responsibility for any such changes.

A catalogue record for this book is available from the British Library.
Library of Congress Cataloging-in-Publication Data
Names: Richards, Serene, author.
Title: Biopolitics as a system of thought / Serene Richards.
Description: 1. | London : Bloomsbury Academic, 2024. |
Includes bibliographical references.
Identifiers: LCCN 2023053557 (print) | LCCN 2023053558 (ebook) |
ISBN 9781350412088 (hardback) | ISBN 9781350412125 (paperback) |
ISBN 9781350412101 (epub) | ISBN 9781350412095 (ebook)
Subjects: LCSH: Life. | Biopolitics.
Classification: LCC BD435 .R53 2024 (print) | LCC BD435 (ebook) |
DDC 128–dc23/eng/20240318
LC record available at https://lccn.loc.gov/2023053557
LC ebook record available at https://lccn.loc.gov/2023053558

ISBN: HB: 978-1-3504-1208-8
PB: 978-1-3504-1212-5
ePDF: 978-1-3504-1209-5
eBook: 978-1-3504-1210-1

Typeset by Deanta Global Publishing Services, Chennai, India

For product safety related questions contact productsafety@bloomsbury.com.

To find out more about our authors and books visit www.bloomsbury.com
and sign up for our newsletters.

Contents

Acknowledgements		vii
Preface: Smart Being		viii
Introduction: Biopolitics as a system of thought		1
1	Knowledge and politics	15
	Knowledge and exchange value	17
	People think	21
	Anthropology and the science of man	24
	Life and knowledge	30
2	Government of the living	41
	The laws of social statistics	42
	Biopolitics and state racism	49
3	Life: A fragile threshold	65
	Life-distilling machine	69
	Life and politics	76
	Absolute immanence	81
	In the real world	83
4	Juridical artifice	87
	Life and law	95
5	Destituent politics	107
	Subject-to-subject cycle	110
	Constituent power and life	113
	On the manner of being	120
	The possible is unrealizable	126

6	Collective intellect	131
	Immobility and expression without world	131
	To phantasm	139
	Through the looking glass	144

Conclusion: Sobriety — 151

Notes — 155
Bibliography — 180
Index — 191

Acknowledgements

Throughout the time thinking through the ideas presented here I have been accompanied by warmth, support and encouragement. I am filled with gratitude and wish to thank Peter Goodrich, Nathan Moore, Maria Aristodemou, Jeremy Pilcher and Olivier Boulnois. Thanks to Connal Parsley and Maria Drakapoulou for organizing the University of Kent Law and the Human conference in 2022 where I first presented the idea of Smart Being. All my thanks and gratitude to Mogniss H. Abdallah and agence IM'média for the cover image of the *Mouvement des travailleurs arabes*. Thank you also to my editors at Bloomsbury: Liza Thompson, Katrina Calsado and Ben Piggott. To Adam Bartlett, Justin Clemens, Bryan Cooke, Lucas Marvel and Rory Mullan whose presence on the other side of the world was felt in the closest proximity in shared humour and a collective thought. Thank you to the Melbourne School of Continental Philosophy for the opportunity to teach a course on some of the main themes of this project and to the brilliant students whose engagement was invaluable. Thank you also to Leticia Paes, Luiz Valle Junior, Sara Paiola, Ceylan Begüm Yildiz, Alper Ral, and Oliver Davis. My loving thanks to Riccardo Giusti for arriving in the middle of things. My thanks also to Susan and David Walden, and to my brother Sinan Richards whose encouragement kept me going.

Preface

Smart Being

Little, if anything, phases Smart Being. Professional, ambitious, educated, a citizen of the world. Inheritor of enlightenment ideals, a rational actor with a teleological belief in humanity's self-fulfilment and progress, where this progress leads to, however, is anybody's guess, Mars perhaps? Or the annihilation of the living all together. For Smart Being, a necessarily linear trajectory awaits – certainly composed of ups and downs, though tending unmistakably upwards, thanks to hard work, a sprinkle of resilience, and the warm embrace of modernity's finest tools.

Of the seven deadly sins, only envy remains, so Guy Debord tells us, becoming 'an exclusive and universal motive'.[1] The Tesla, not without its faults including spontaneous self-combustion, fulfils this function. A symbol of our times perhaps, though lacking in ubiquity. For this, the smart meter provides the answer; ecological and efficient, though there is no free lunch, should the demand for energy to become too high, the supply to Smart Beings could be cut off. Appliances deemed to be of 'high usage' could be turned off, including electric vehicle chargers. Smart Being's central heating could be adjusted without notice, no doubt for their long-term safety and security. To control after all does not mean merely to regulate behaviour under pain of force or violence but to check, to verify, to inspect, to surveil with the aim of maintaining a proper order. And the proper is to Smart Being what water is to fish.

The dazzling lights of the cityscape illuminate desires, dreams, disappointments, appointments. Smart Beings circulate, busying one another with notifications, a tap away from that promotion, massage, lover, dinner reservation; an experience to suit any need and want even for their invention.

Always short on time, Smart Being's patience for small talk has worn thin, thus, Google's Duplex AI voice synthesis system goes some way to alleviating the inconvenience of addressing a service worker over the telephone. Duplex AI promised to offer artificial intelligence capable of making appointments for Smart Beings, making calls mimicking the voice of the user. One would simply instruct the software of one's desire to dine out one evening and a reservation would be made by the software who would ring up the restaurant. A surprise then when it was discovered that it was, in fact, a human being behind the software all along, on the other side of the telephone, who was pretending to be an AI voice and in turn imitating the voice of a human being.[2]

When asked about the human beings impersonating an AI to mimic a human voice, Google claimed that these human beings were merely training the AI in real time. The problem was that automated phone systems were still struggling to recognize simple words and commands, as Google Duplex's developer laments, 'they don't engage in a conversation flow and force the caller to adjust to the system instead of the system adjusting to the caller.'[3] Google Duplex promised to do things differently, to 'make the conversational experience as natural as possible'. And what could be more natural than an ordinary person speaking over the telephone to another person? This being too simple and old fashioned for Smart Beings, however, Google Duplex's smart solution appears to be able to mimic communicability in such a way that it has the appearance of an ordinary exchange. For this reason, Google Duplex's developer says that the aim of the conversations is to 'sound natural' by incorporating what is termed disinfluencies like: hmmm's and uhhh's. These 'hmmm's and uhhh's', then, are added to the AI's conversations to sound more familiar and natural.

The infinite potentiality in language is precisely what puzzled linguists and grammarians long before Silicon Valley technologists. Not simply the fact that not-All can be said, but that not everything said has a meaning, that is, that not everything said serves to communicate this or that message. In endeavouring to render the discipline of linguistics a legitimate science, Ferdinand de Saussure aimed to construct a so-called 'ideal form' based on the concept of the sign. The consequence was that in introducing the sign, that which could not conform to its representation fell out of reference, the not-all, or babble and sounds. This so-called not-all, is incapable of representation. Just like Silicon Valley technologists before them, linguists and grammarians strived to construct and give rise to a real of language, necessarily excluding the incorrect or that which it deemed impossible to say. But this impossibility is precisely part of language, since it is only through language that the incorrect for instance can be considered as such. It forms an intricate part of our own capacity for expression. *Lalangue*, the not-all of language which it is impossible to extricate serves a different purpose to communication, as Mladen Dollar says 'it is the stuff that enables the flash of appearance of the unconscious' 'there is a sound surplus which does not make sense, it is there just like that, for the fun of it, for the beauty of it, for the pleasure of it.'[4] It is, to think of Simone Weil, the tonality and sound of the universal cry of hurt that the language of law and power cannot hear nor understand. The not-all, that which it is impossible to represent, haunts Smart Being as a shadow, it is that which lies perilously closest to it, and for this reason is driven to expulsion, as that which is incomprehensible, absurd, unnatural to the natural proclivity of Smart Being to reason, and enlightenment.

Smart Being's fixation with the idea that its artifice ought nonetheless be 'natural' as though this were not always invented historically, and invested with a plethora of meaning, is a curious phenomenon given such intelligent systems self-define as already being artificial. Yet, perhaps the point is that it is precisely the lack of any artifice that characterizes it, as Jean Baudrillard writes:

> Artificial intelligence is devoid of intelligence because it is devoid of artifice. True artifice is the artifice of the body in the throes of passion, the artifice of the sign of seduction, the artifice of ambivalence in gesture, the artifice of ellipsis in language, the artifice of the pithy remark that completely alters meaning.[5]

Instead, the artificial machines deploy artifice meekly, only breaking cognitive acts down to their simplest elements with the aim of turning them into models of the representable. This striving for authenticity for want of insufficiency in the meek artifice is not novel, and not limited either to technological enterprises. In an advertisement brochure for HafenCity, a smart city in Hamburg, Germany, urbanists expressed delight at the arrival of the city's first homeless migrant, apparently a sign of authenticity, saying 'Kossakowski's presence is a sign that the developers have long yearned for, although no one will admit it . . . a sign of normality.'[6]

This impulse to expel the human being from the ideal of the thing itself, only to formally include through abandonment, in other words to conceal the sweat and bodily investments that go into the making of tools and ever inventive dispositives, is characteristic of Smart Being's mode of being in the world. Torments are freely shared into the Google search engine, worries about high energy bills, making rent payments, going after that job, diagnosing an illness, how to cope with depression, dream travel destinations, daily horoscopes, a list of the best pizza in London. The list is endless, this is the place where the psyche and decipherability collide to provide answers to problems, to shed a light on ignorance. Three billion Google searches a day contribute to our digital psychosphere. All the while, powering Smart Being's less than adequate search for meaning in the world is the work of so-called click workers, many in refugee camps from Dabaab to Shatila.[7] These refugees are powering machine learning for Microsoft and Google and spend their nights labelling footage of urban areas: 'house', 'shop', 'car', labelling videos, transcribing audio, all to meet the ostensible needs of firms and Smart Beings on the other side of the planet. This is the positive biopolitics of techno-capital, assigning a value to life with some lives necessarily considered less valuable than others, made to work in service of those whose lives are deemed more worthy, until this stratification reaches the worthy Smart Beings who do not escape valuation as we well know, where the likelihood of one's exposure to death depends on race, class, disability and so on.

The belief in techno-capital's ability to resolve and provide answers to worries and torments is offered up as Smart Being's best chance of survival and prosperity, submission, in a sense to an economic logic that promises a distant future in which, as Tari put it, everyone is better off, working the right amount for the correct sum, and where the law will always be on their side. This mystification is a promise of a future that does not exist. Smart Being is a resilient being precisely because the possibilities of creating a habitable world seem out of reach. This is the capitalist religion, having neither ideal nor dogma, deriving its sense only in relation to itself. It guarantees its meaning with reference to itself, as Walter Benjamin says.[8] We can think here of the attribution of economic indices to every detail of conduct, in the gathering of information and data over the minute details of the social fabric, human beings and the planetary environment. Everything in the cult is the means to an end, a purpose or value. Capitalist religion also makes guilt pervasive, creating guilt without atonement, in Benjamin's words, 'it is a religion which offers not the reform of existence but its complete destruction. It is the expansion of despair, until despair becomes a religious state of the world in the hope that this will lead to salvation.'[9] Caught up within the dynamics of techno-capital, Smart Being looks to the tools of techno-capital as a means to end worries, torments and restlessness. Believing in the very thing that conjures and organizes deficits without any escape. Smart Being is invested in its own production, quantifying the becoming of its own self – at once an invitation to be the best one must become and a commandment, an injunction to participate, since living itself is always at stake. One's conditions of life and living conditions, one's being and acting, what one is and how one is, collapse into one, directed to survival, experiencing power's positivity and its absolute domination applied through the body and psyche, organizing the possibility and impossibility of encounters, and the scope of political action.

Much has been made of late of Francis Fukuyama's proclamation three decades ago of an end of history.[10] Though we would be better served pondering a lesser-known thesis. A few years after Fukuyama, Paul Virilio would write that we are not seeing an end of history at all but rather an end of geography. The current transmission revolution, as Virilio put it, based on the ceaseless feedback of human activities is generating the 'invisible threat of an accident befalling this generalised interactivity'.[11] That is, there is no longer any distinction between the outside and the inside; the interactivity in question heightened today through the infinite reel of the social media timeline produces a synchronic experience of affective experience, the synchronicity of emotion, thought, rage and celebration, indignation and opinion, no matter the binary choices on offer. What would it mean to struggle with our thoughts, experiment with a different mode of conceiving certain problems and questions? A horror, Antonin Artaud knew very well, as Deleuze points out. Deleuze states that 'the problem for [Artaud] was not to orientate his thought, or to perfect the expression of what he thought, or to acquire application and method or to perfect his poems, but simply to manage to think something'.[12] Managing to think something is difficult, one must be open to it occurring to us, interrupting us, transforming us, being open to what Deleuze says could put our own coherence in peril. So that there is a displeasure, a suffering, in thinking. Smart Being is the being who by definition avoids thought, avoiding the potentially hazardous or disruptive in an effort to preserve itself, within the shelter of convenience, of picking and choosing between already established choices.

And yet, hard as it may try, Smart Being cannot hide its existential angst. For one thing its etymological history already betrays it and offers us a clue. Smart from old English smeortan meaning 'causing sharp pain', tells us that smarting besieges being, the being that lies beneath the shell of Smart Being, a sharp stinging and sense of impending doom testifies for the unattainability of pleasure, and the unfulfilled promises of a future that is uninhabitable. Rather than confront its own insufficiency, or its own fallibility, Smart Being makes the world conform to its delusions, setting benchmarks of knowledge production, of educational attainment, of the proper mode of doing things, of the mode of the habitable, of language, of expressions, of the proper use of tools, of its relation to the environment and the physical world; it obliges the world to be caught up in its dream that only it believes in for it appears as a nightmare for the clear sighted. This epistemological arrogance prevents Smart Being and the rest of us from conceptualizing thought as a mode within which conditions of the possible are realized. A collectivity of thought is lacking that would enable us to see that the door is closed, that only a politics worthy of the name can transform the present into a habitable world. For Sylvain Lazarus the thought of the people, not with a capital P, stands in contrast to scientific and positivist thought which can only formulate a given state of affairs, based around, for example, the productive inputs required to achieve economic growth in a given year. On the contrary, politics itself is a thought, it has no object as such, and the aim is to conceive of a politics capable of transforming the given state of things. It is unlikely that the thought capable of producing Smart Beings is capable of the thought required for a politics to come. Virilio proposes a modest suggestion, for him it is necessary for cybernetic and scientific thought to recall its vulnerability and exercise some humility. The accident is the proof of this necessity. As Virilio puts it:

> The innovation of the ship already entailed the innovation of the shipwreck. The invention of the steam engine, the locomotive, also entailed the invention of derailment, the rail disaster .... Each period of technical evolution, with its set of instruments and machines, involves the appearance of specific accidents, revealing in the negative the growth of scientific thought.[13]

So that wisdom means first of all recognizing the accident that accompanies any artefact, rather than concealing its existence. Censoring this necessary truth is, for Virilio, to practice dissimulation and disinformation.

From the incomprehensible utterances of *lalangue*, the shadow of language that contains desires, delusions and emotions, to the so-called click workers in refugee camps, to Smart Being's own dissatisfaction, its own insufficiency, the shadows that sustain our representations of reality and make for the conditions of possibility for Langue, Silicon

Valley entrepreneurs and Smart Beings, persist. Nothing short of a transformation of this ultimately biopolitical relation is required, a renewed sense of perception prioritizing that which initially appears as most distant from us that is in reality perilously and irreconcilably nearest. This is no easy task, embracing a sadness, for instance, that lies deep within us is difficult precisely because of the cruelty of sadness, its limitless range without cause and without the possibility of knowing when or how to end it. Yet, as Anne Dufourmantelle writes, the moment that sadness relinquishes its grasp, 'you write, you dream, and you fall asleep' 'sadness will have left you free, but different. Whence its risk.'[14] This too is the risk of thought, the possible shattering of presupposed assumptions. Dufourmantelle continues, 'to take the risk of sadness would be to understand that sadness is the secret underside of beatitude, and of the enlargement of being unto which it beckons us, it makes us remember another possibility of being toward ourselves and in the world.'[15]

The door is closed, as Agamben reminds us, and yet, and only for this reason can it be forced open. Until then, for those of us yet to be baptized into fully believing ourselves to be Smart Beings, we remain in Dante's Limbo, where, for this lack of baptism, 'and for no other guilt, we here are lost. In this alone we suffer: cut off from hope, we live on in desire'.[16]

Introduction
Biopolitics as a system of thought

'My lucidity is total', Artaud writes, 'keener than ever':

> I would like to get beyond the point of absence, of emptiness . . . I have no life, I have no life!!! My inner enthusiasm is dead . . . I said LIFE. I did not say the appearance of life, I said real life, the essential illumination: being, the original spark from which every thought is ignited. . . . The trouble is always the same. Try as I may, I cannot *think*. Try to understand this hollowness, this intense and lasting emptiness. This vegetation. How horribly I am vegetating. I can neither advance nor retreat. I am fixed, localised around a point which is always the same . . . I have not gone beyond . . . for in order to go beyond . . . I would first have to *live*. And I refuse to live.[1]

If these words by Artaud written in November 1927 to the psychoanalyst René Allendy resonate with us today it is because we too struggle with a similar predicament: an atrophy, an existence that feels fixed, localized and constricted. Our minds and bodies immobile, instrumentalized, and increasingly directed to survival. This is not for a lack of ideas and tools that the ingenuity of mankind has developed over centuries, from discoveries in science to art and medicine. As Artaud writes, in order for him to think, he would first have to *live*. It is no coincidence then that in our world made increasingly *unliveable*, we find ourselves unable to think, too. Why does Artaud associate the ability to think something with the necessity of living, with life? What does it mean for Artaud to say that he would first have to live, and that he refuses to live, when, clearly, he is alive and sharing his thoughts, writing this letter full of emotion, frustration and anger? Artaud knows something that we know, too. That to think is precisely to live, and to live is to *engender* life in living as use of the body, it is power or potential. One must be capable of a life that is engendered, generated, in living itself. That it is not enough to simply be alive, that being alive and not living, perhaps even refusing to live, can trigger a deep suffering, a perpetual torment, this torment and suffering is felt least of all cognitively but sensibly, in the very depth of our soul, at the heart of the body, where the visceral weight of each breath cries out for our attention, heavy and light, light and heavy. Numerous terms can be used to describe this experience: depression, existential angst, lethargy or anxiety. The world over, the possibility of living is conditioned and conditional. From the ravages of war and genocide, poverty to fires and floods, to the emptiness of a metropolis, homelessness and addiction, to the banality of mundane existence and making ends meet. The world over has been engaged, time after time, in objecting to the present state of things, mobilizing in anger and mistrust of the solutions and changes proposed over and over again with little to show for it except broken promises and botched realizations. From Chile to Baghdad, and Paris to Beirut, 2019 saw an overwhelming wave of discontent from every corner of the world, people making demands for life, demands to live, testifying for the desire to learn to live again despite it all. These explosions and expressions of life largely go unheard being instead absorbed into an already existing state of affairs that annihilates life and the living. Though we are not lacking in reasons to transform our present system of social relations something is amiss and not for a lack of effort or want. Nor for a lack of knowing what is to be done; the possibilities and options are numerous. What is perhaps missing is an emphasis and articulation over the 'how' for this is not at all self-evident and would require reformulating our problematics and the articulation of strategies. The aim here is to query this immobility or atrophy in both our thinking and our politics, or mode of acting by thinking through the question: What mode of politics does our present mode of thought make possible?

Our biopolitical horizon is a mode of thought as much as it is a mode of governance. If thought has to do with life, and if governance has to do with the living, then there must be a relation between biopolitics and our capacity to think and to act. For this reason, throughout this book, I articulate the notion of biopolitics as it relates to everyday life. What does biopolitics mean for our capacity of action, of thinking, of living? How does biopolitics shape our manner of life, our emotions and dreams? Are these even related? I argue that they are. While biopolitics has traditionally been conceived as a technique of governance of life with an emphasis on biological life, so that examples from biogenetics to health measures and biometric surveillance have been a key focus, I show how biopolitics intervenes at the level of our manner of living, at the level of conduct and everyday existence. This is not to say that ordinary, everyday existence is somehow apart from biometrics, rather the point is to illustrate that the biopolitical is not a separate sphere of its own with particular sociological or biological characteristics that apply to certain circumstances, but rather a far more pervasive force.

A point of clarification is required here concerning the idea of what I call: biopolitics as a system of thought. Needless to say there is some irony to this since, just like Smart Being, biopolitics does not think, though it has to do with thinking. There are conceptual truths presupposed in the mode of biopolitics' functioning as a technique for the governance of life. First is the assumption of a separation between potential and action, essence and existence, living and living well, so that it becomes a matter of how to bridge the two together. Second, the ascription of value to life that takes place by objectifying it, not to value life and the living as such but to measure it and decide upon its worth whether for the purposes of intervention, abandonment or death. These presuppositions are the silent precursors to any mode of biopolitics, even the so-called positive biopolitics of techno-capital or big state intervention and administration. This is evident in the work of, for example, the theorist of technology Benjamin Bratton and the legal scholar Adrian Vermeule. For Bratton, the proposed vision of a positive biopolitics entails a mode of authoritarian planetary governance through an embrace of technology and science's potential to solve problems such as the climate crisis, described by Bratton as a 'planetary-scale crises of biochemistry'. With little concern over global capitalism's role in precipitating the destruction and annihilation of the living, both human and non-human, Bratton's vision entails a continued objectification of life and the living, a continued instrumentalization of knowledge and life towards means and ends in view of the 'correct' as determined by a specific vision of the world, and a valuation of the living where some lives are necessarily thought to be of more or less value. Vermeule's vision entails a similarly ambitious administrative programme that aims at governing for the so-called common good; a common good grounded in theological principles – an old-fashioned version of Bratton's faith in a modern technocratic fiefdom – with a clear vision of what this might look like, and a clear ascription of an essence to the human being, where it would then be a matter of forcibly ensuring that existence, the manner of living, adheres to it in accordance with an idea of morality.

Biopolitics is incommensurate with the idea of life engendered in living since, from the outset, limits and conditions of thought, action, and life are set up in it as practical realities that are presumed immovable to the extent that it is only by first accepting these presuppositions that any articulation of law, politics or life can be made intelligible and communicable. For this reason, I engage with modes of thinking that attempt to disrupt this mode of problematizing the world in which we live, primarily through the thought of Giorgio Agamben, Michel Foucault and Gilles Deleuze. Agamben's notion of the form-of-life helps us think through what a notion of life might look like that would stand in contrast to the biopolitical. Agamben writes:

> The form-of-life is, in this sense, the revocation of all factical vocations, which deposes and puts in tension from within the same gesture by which it is maintained and dwells in them. It is not a question of thinking a better or more authentic form of life, a superior principle or an elsewhere, which arrives from outside the forms of life and the factical conditions to revoke and render inoperative. Inoperativity is not another work that appears to work from nowhere to deactivate and depose them: it coincides completely and constitutively with their destitution, *with living a life*.[2]

With the 'revocation of factical vocations' Agamben is gesturing towards a different conceptualization of 'needs' which our modern era has developed by way of the human sciences from economics and evolutionary biology to behavioural science and public policy where the human being is conceptualized as always already wanting with scarcity as a given. Where, in order to simply survive one must labour to satisfy these needs expropriated from common use and privatized under global capitalism, thus organized in accordance with the basic tenets of commodification and exchange. The human being's life is continually at stake in this schema, and politics for the most part takes the form of management, that is, it functions to manage this process of the allocation of resources given fixed presumptions about the world. It is this biopolitical mode of thinking that is in question in the present work.

In the *Economic and Philosophical Manuscripts*, Marx states that communism concerns:

> The appropriation of the human essence by and for man; communism therefore as the complete return of man to himself as a social (i.e., human) being. . . . It is the genuine resolution of the conflict between man and nature and between man and man – the true resolution of the strife between *existence* and *essence*, between objectification and self-confirmation, between freedom and necessity, between the individual and the species.[3]

In this brief passage, Marx appears to articulate a vision of communism as non-biopolitical, pointing towards a destituent power that would see a dissolution of the 'strife between existence and essence'. I mention destituent power here as this is precisely what is at stake in our schematization of a non-biopolitical mode of life. In this context, following Agamben, the metaphysical apparatus characteristic of biopolitics has to do with ontology in that it presupposes a split of being between possibility and reality, or essence and existence.[4] With this splitting, the problem for the apparatus, or for government, is how to then intervene into life in such a way that either bridges the two together, shift them further apart or play one against the other. For Agamben, as it is for Marx, a dissolution of the 'strife between existence and essence', would entail the destitution of their separability, between essence and existence, between possibility and reality, a destitution then of the pre-requisite to the state form's mode of intervention, control and governance of the human being, and where life itself is, instead, lived in its acts and is generated in living. For this reason, the knowledges and disciplines of the human sciences are important in the context of biopolitics, since these allow for techniques and modes of intervention, where knowledge is instrumentalized towards means and ends, and plans and projects are to be realized which gives sense to the question: 'What is to be done?' Indeed, in our epoch, the reigning question around which our politics revolves is precisely 'what is to be done?' A necessary question whose answer is by no means self-evident. But how did it come to be both relevant and urgent in our times? As Reiner Schürmann points out, this question is a modern one that would seem out of place in ancient Greece, for whom instead it was necessary to ask 'what is the best life?' and in medieval times the question 'what acts are naturally human?' figured as most relevant.[5]

An essential question for us to pose, then, is: How did we arrive at this question 'what is to be done'? One way of thinking about this might be in what the question itself presupposes – that the possible and the real do not co-exist, so that the possible must be made into a reality. So that when knowledge turned its attention to the human being qua human, giving rise to the plethora of taxonomical references over nature and its evolution, prescribing the essence of the human being as a labouring and speaking animal, in other words transforming metaphysical questions into empirical fact, it also set out to define the conditions of the possible, the thinkable, the impractical and the impossible. With the very idea that the human being requires shelter and nourishment in order to live irrespective of a 'juridical right' to it conceived as impractical given the so-called practical state of affairs and laws of economy, it is evident what gives 'what is to be done?' its sense. The trouble is that, as Lenin remarks in his *What Is to Be Done?* (1902), there is a danger in slipping into economism while relegating the political or social as a secondary consideration. In fact, these 'spheres' of living are inseparable. It is a biopolitical mode of thought that separates and divides them, as I will show.

To this end I proceed through three registers: the dominant articulation of life in the Western philosophical and anthropological tradition, the relation of law to life, and of politics to life with crossovers throughout. This is not a history of the concept of biopolitics but an exercise in working through its mode of functioning, its mode of operation and what problems arise as a result so that different questions might finally be posed. To remain within its existing mode of problematization would be to presume problems are given 'ready-made, and that they disappear in the responses or the solutions' where 'the master sets a problem, our task is to solve it, and the result is accredited true or false by a powerful authority'.[6] The trouble is that the mode of problematization of the image of thought will always find a solution it deserves in proportion to its own sense, a charge on plastic straws is understood to be a solution to the excess use of plastic, for instance, in line with assumptions made of the human being as a rational actor seeking to maximize utility so that the charge on plastic straws would act as a disincentive. While there is nothing objectionable to this necessarily, given the 8 million tonnes of plastic dumped into the ocean each year, chocking marine life and populated communities along the coast of Indonesia among other places, it remains unclear what it is that is being solved. As Deleuze writes: 'the solution necessarily follows from the complete conditions under which the problem is determined as a problem, from the means and the terms which are employed in order to pose it.'[7] Given the practical realities of the insatiable thirst for profit, the charge on straws has its sense. Politics, in accordance with this image of thought, is limited to that which the image determines as sense. Thought, as opposed to doxa, is concerned, on the contrary, with the many manners and ways of living and thinking of social life, that also have their own images and modes of thinking about the world. It is for this reason, Deleuze says, that every society has 'all of its rules at once – juridical, religious, political, economic; laws governing love and labour, kinship and marriage, servitude and freedom, life and death'.[8]

I begin then with a question posed by Foucault: 'what modes of thinking lie behind the practices that we accept?'[9] It is important since it concerns the relation between (1) life, (2) knowledge over life, and (3) the question of how life should or is able to be lived. Most dominant, first of all, is the instrumentalization of knowledge, affixed to exchange, privileging a rationale of means and ends, thereby assigning a value to life and objectifying all living things. Knowledge affixed to power and exchange comes to shape not just what we know about the world and certain phenomena, but what the parameters of life are and how living should look like. In other words, certain postulates are taken as given and presupposed which in turn shape how we articulate our politics, using the same language and frame of reference, accommodating knowledge's findings that are themselves set up in a particular way with certain givens. In this way, what is possible becomes what is practicable to be done, what is permissible to be done. This mode of thinking and proceeding is completely at odds with how people think as is evident in mobilizations and insurrections around the world where it is not a matter of adjusting this or that policy or subjective right, but rather the assertion of *another life*. This is precisely what scientistic and positivist thought cannot entertain or grasp, but only able to formulate an already given state of affairs, this 'academicism' of politics dismisses the idea of a space of intellectuality of people.[10] The human being, as the empirico-transcendental doublet that Foucault describes, is both object and subject of knowledge and the site of intervention and governance, not merely of the individual body but into its tendencies, and what might potentially be at stake or occur in the future before this has taken place. At the same time, finitude haunts the subject, as the tools of calculable probability bring up the known in utmost detail they also conjure and quantify that which we do not know. Statistical knowledge also invites a self-governing of the individual subject, through normalization for instance, and this is a continuous process not fixed once and for all. That is, the individual subject, as a task, never reaches completion. This mirrors the function of the anthropological machine that decides upon the qualities that make up the human being, a life-distilling machine or ontological apparatus, to use Agamben's terms.

In *De anima*, Aristotle defines life through the exclusion of nutritive life, which forms part of numerous faculties or potentials that in the end constitute the living being. This articulation, in turn, makes possible a manner of thinking that thinks the concept of life through the addition or subtraction of these faculties, thereby prioritizing the following question: through what modes or faculties is it possible to belong to a species? In this way, the status of the human being is conceptualized as something that one can *attain*, where the goal post continually shifts, so that one's belonging to a species can be called into question should any qualifying identifier be missing given the cultural or political climate of the day. For this reason, Agamben calls this separation of nutritive life 'immediately political', given that, in the Aristotelian schema, it is excluded from happiness, virtue and politics. From this schema, we glean that there exists something that is *inextricably* and *intimately* part of life that is simultaneously subject to a decision of scission and separation. Where a part of life is considered not truly human and therefore excluded from reason, from the good life, all the while being precisely that which is presupposed. This is the functioning of the anthropological machine that produces the human by capturing the (in)human, while the latter is, in truth, inseparable; it is an artificial separation. As is well known, in Aristotle's conceptualization of politics, natural life or *zoè* is excluded from participation in the *polis*, just as the perfect community is defined by 'opposing the simple fact of living (*to zēn*) to politically qualified life (*to eu zēn*)'.[11] In this sense, Agamben asks how it could be possible that Western politics constitutes itself on the basis of an exclusion, which is at the same time an inclusion?[12] This is a pertinent question given that it touches upon the mode of being of the human being, potentially demarcating a limit between the possible and the impossible.

It would not be unreasonable to level a criticism at this point and to say that this is much too abstract and unrealistic, how does something like the ontological apparatus or machine have any relation to the lives that we live? We will need to recall that the machine in question functions on the basis of the articulation of life, drawing up caesuras and divisions on what constitutes its proper mode, that, together with its forms of knowledge, go on to establish the conditions that define it and how it should be lived, how living should take place. This is a reciprocal process; knowledge can also establish and presuppose what already is in a given state of affairs without questions as to its desirability or use. In *Foucault*, Deleuze comments on the relation between power, the human sciences and our mode of social organization, saying that

> The sciences of man are inseparable from the power relations which make them possible, and provoke forms of knowledge [*savoirs*] which can more or less cross an epistemological threshold or create a practical knowledge [*connaissance*] . . . we are not saying that the sciences of man emanate from prison, but that they presuppose the diagram of forces on which prison itself depends.[13]

The sciences of man 'presuppose the diagram of forces on which prison itself depends' which include a certain conceptualization of the human being, as, for example, a subject of *will* having full mastery over their thoughts, intentions, and actions that can be held culpable within the remit of the criminal law in accordance with the basic tenets of morality – good and evil. Presupposed then is a certain understanding of the will as though it were not an ambiguous descriptor of the manifold reasons for human actions, an understanding that takes as given the transformation of the human being as one who *can* – as was the case for the ancients – to the human being as one who *wills*, which the Christian subject crystallizes and modernity adheres to. In other words, as Agamben writes, a shift in the understanding of human actions as acting 'from the sphere of "potential" (*dynamis*) in to that of will'.[14] Positivism cannot *think* this presupposition, just as linguists cannot think the fact that language as such exists, the *factum loquendi*, on which its science is based. There is no room in it to consider the notion of will as a metaphysical artefact with a plural history.[15] As Lazarus puts it, 'scientistic thought – insofar as we are supposing here that it is a thought – is in the impossibility of thinking what is thought in its thought. If scientistic thought is a thought, it is a thought without thought or, more precisely, without thought in interiority.'[16]

Law follows a biopolitical schematization through the notion of juridical personality that in Roman law had a different conceptualization understood primarily as a fiction or artefact of law. The jurist Yan Thomas reminds us that 'in our legal culture, the person is confused with the human being itself'.[17] In other words, our present is marked by an ever-expanding process of bringing into the fabric of law all aspects of what constitute life with the aim of protecting it; where the juridical notion of the dignity of life can, in a sense, be activated and a form of justice apportioned one way or another. Thomas argues that this is essentially where the notion of biopolitics, as developed by Agamben, can most clearly be elucidated. The shifting limit of legal protection, while including previously excluded elements from the patronage of law, is a simultaneous affirmation of that which lies beyond this limit, beyond the sacredness of life, and therefore unworthy of protection. When, in the early 1970s, the *Mouvement des travailleurs arabes* organized for a transformation of their entire mode of living and the social set-up in which they found themselves, facing daily racism in cafes and on the streets, their hometowns ravaged by the exploits of colonialism, inadequate housing, they were not making demands for this or that subjective right. A demand for life can be understood in the manner formulated by Deleuze as the difference between a right to life and the so-called rights of man.

What is in question is the tension between destituent power and constituent power. The latter, premised on the idea of universal rights, is, in truth, a generalization of a mode of thinking and practice incompatible with the universality of a communism to come, where the demand for life comes to be incompatible with the language of power. This articulation of a minoritarian consciousness is able to grasp the un-actualizable in a particular situation, the element that falls out of the edges of the actual situation – we see in this way that the possible is what is always left to be created. In articulating this minoritarian consciousness, Deleuze says, 'one addresses powers (*puissances*) of becoming that belong to a different realm from that of Power (*Pouvoir*) and Domination.'[18]

This is the realm of destituent power and the collectivity of thought that necessarily involve the dissolution of the present state of affairs, rendering them inoperative, it is a dissolution of the self as self-subject and involves another mode of living and thinking. No longer asking 'what I am' but rather 'how I am what I am', that is, the manner of being. There is no presupposition or hidden essence of being, being simply *is* its mode, it is '*continually engendered from its own manner*'.[19] Agamben relates this to the idea of a 'free use of the self' and thus a way to think being not as a value or a property, but rather as a *habitus* or an *ethos* that *engender* us. In this way, being is displaced on the level of the living and generated by the act of living itself, it is a form-of-life. This modal ontology disrupts the Aristotelian ontological apparatus premised on the opposition between existence and essence, potential and act. This radical thesis, that being is generated by the act of living is a similar manner of thinking through the Spinozist phrase that 'we do not even know what a body can do'.[20] 'What bodies can do' is a direct disruption of the classic ontological presupposition concerning the position of consciousness, or the soul, as having power over the body, that is, directing the course of the body's action. A direct rejection of the idea that the soul must 'command' the body to act, to obey, in accordance with a specific law. It is an ethics principally concerned with the actions and passions that one is *capable* of rather than *what* one, as such, *is*. For Spinoza, essence is power and this is because there is no essence only power of action: it is the aggregate of what one can do and what one undergoes, what one suffers.[21] As manners of being we are then defined by what each one of us is capable of doing rather than by any fixed essence. Essence becomes that which each one of us is capable of doing. In this way, essence is identical to power and identical to *how* one lives, existence. There is no longer any transition between potentiality and actuality; potentiality itself already contains a relation to privation, our own not-being and not-doing. We see resistance contained in potentiality, our doing and not-doing, being and not-being: in Kafka with his world record-breaking swimmer who cannot swim, and F. Scott Fitzgerald as the author who cannot write, inoperativity and counter-actualization, to be worthy of what happens to us – painful, difficult, but a way out of *ressentiment*. The *ressentiment* of loneliness, fear, anger, rage, hostility that we see and hear about every day, manifesting at its best online on what we call the digital commons where our energies and attention are continually mobilized in the service of this saturation which, and this is not without perversion, our productive system increasingly depends on. The result is a synchronization of affective experience irrespective of locality or position that is accompanied by immobility, impotence and therefore expressionless since expression involves movement. In the spectacle, the soul is under siege, subject to the spectacle's vast inaccessible reality that can never be questioned. There is no creative act, no thought in the spectacle; the latter can only impose a mode of appearance, an appearance of life that so offended Artaud, it is 'what must be seen but can never be lived'.[22]

And yet, the multitude *phantasms* cogitates and thinks collectively. As Agamben writes, for the Islamic philosopher Averroës, the intelligence is something that is both unique and supra-individual, that individual persons simply had the shared *use*. So that 'the possible intellect is unique and separate: incorruptible and eternal, it is nevertheless joined (*copulatur*) to individuals, so that each of them may concretely exercise the act of intellection through the phantasms that are located in the internal sense'.[23] The intellection is never a private, individual affair, it can only be realized in common: this is the meaning of *people think*. Thinking, for Agamben, is not simply being affected by this or that thing but also and at the same time being affected by one's own receptivity, such that 'thought is, in this sense, always use of oneself, always entails the affection that one receives insofar as one is in contact with a determinate body'.[24] In this way, just as for Averroës, Dante and Spinoza, before him, for Agamben, the act can never be fully separated from potential, that is, if there is thought, then a form-of-life can become form-of-life. Today, the best that the biopolitical mode of thought can offer is the mode of living of Smart Beings. Risk averse, fearful and impotent, painfully cognisant that the future promised will never arrive. Hence the urgency of asking – what conditions of possibility, today, give *sense* to the question: What would a non-biopolitical mode of politics look like? How did it become necessary to pose this question? In what follows, I trace how I arrived at these questions, and the necessary detours we need to pass through along the way.

1

Knowledge and politics

In a dictionary of philosophers published in 1984, we discover that the entry for 'Michel Foucault' was written by none other than Foucault himself. The editor of the dictionary, Denis Huisman, solicited a contribution from François Ewald who was then Foucault's assistant at the Collège de France. When Ewald informed Foucault of this pending task it turned out to be an opportune moment as Foucault was in the middle of reworking volume two of the *History of Sexuality* and had dedicated a part of the introduction to a retrospective summary of his method, detailing the essential focus of his work. It was this same text that Ewald then submitted to Denis Huisman, it included a short introduction and bibliography which Foucault had signed 'Maurice Florence'. In the entry, Foucault writes that his work can be understood as a critical history of thought.[1] A critical history of thought, Foucault continues, is not critique for its own sake but rather an exercise in teasing out what is hidden in plain sight. A critique, Foucault writes, 'does not consist in saying that things are not right as they are. It is about seeing what kinds of givens [*évidences*], familiarities, acquired and unreflected modes of thinking lie behind the practices that we accept.'[2] That is, the unconscious of knowledge, these naturalized assumptions and presuppositions without which a mode of knowledge and a mode of life would not hold up.

So, what 'modes of thinking lie behind the practices that we accept?'[3] is an essential question to pose and one that has political and ethical consequences. It concerns the connection between (1) life, (2) knowledge over life, and (3) the question of how life itself should be lived. For Foucault, the idea that the social alone represents reality or something real as opposed to the exercise of thought is both an unhelpful binary and one that overlooks the significance of an essential activity: thinking. This is because:

> Thought exists, well beyond, well below, the systems and edifices of our discourse. It is something that is often hidden, but that always animates everyday behaviour. There is always a bit of thought even in the silliest institutions, there is always thought even in mute habits.[4]

What is this thought that exists and yet remains hidden? It is our task, following Foucault, to flush out this thought, to show that things are perhaps not as self-evident as we might like to believe. This is a mode of critique that aims at disrupting underlying premises, to complicate what might appear self-evident, to question gestures that have a naturalized appearance and consider instead the effort involved in making them appear. This is because 'a transformation that remains in the same mode of thought, a transformation that would simply be a certain way of better adjusting the same mode of thought to the state of things would only be a superficial transformation'.[5] We could say this is all fair and well – the mode of thought in which we live is characterized by neoliberalism, capitalism, setting up the conditions for the exploitation of the living, both human and non-human, on a path of mutually assured destruction. Indeed, it was the intention of Hayek to make of neoliberalism a 'living thought'. As Foucault writes in paraphrasing Hayek: 'Liberalism must be a general thought, analysis, and imagination.'[6] In order to get a clearer sense of what this might mean for the living, both human and non-human, for politics and for our mode of life we need to grasp how this functions, and more precisely, how a biopolitical mode of thought dominates both the conditions of life and the conditions according to which it might be able to be lived. Proceeding in this manner allows us to get at exposed roots and burrows that may appear to be a part of the natural environment and therefore little cause for concern, though whose exposure, barely noticed, could cause us to trip up and tumble.

Ours is in an era of crises, where crises function as the structural necessity of capital, engendering one crisis after another for its own survival, and while profits are reaped by shareholders a generalized anxiety prevails in our daily lives; the reality of precarity makes certain a permanent uncertainty over making ends meet in a mode of social organization privileging an unwavering adherence to the rationale of means and ends. This chronic uncertainty and insecurity is accompanied by a belief in and a certainty over the mode of thought through which the state of affairs is to be analysed, worked through and understood. Good sense being derived from the apparent neutrality of charts and numbers instrumentalized for the so-called common good. Yet, as Axelos writes in *Future Thought:*

> The openness of the world cannot be exhaustively comprehended by one form of thought – as great as it might be, these are realisations denied by historians, ideologues, orthodox or heterodox supporters of 'isms', professors, and journalists.[7]

If 'virtue is knowledge', as Socrates tells us, then an openness as to its *modality* in our present conjuncture is essential to grasp. It is this modality that Lyotard attempted to unravel in his work *The Postmodern Condition: A Report on Knowledge* (1979).

Knowledge and exchange value

Since the publication of *The Postmodern Condition*, Lyotard has been associated with the term 'postmodernism' and is often characterized as one of its chief advocates despite his critique of the term and the epistemic era encapsulated by it. Lyotard's text, framed as a report on the state of knowledge in so-called advanced industrial societies, was written following an invitation by the Universities Council for the government of Quebec. While Lyotard expressed his discomfort with the work, which in many ways can appear self-evident and perhaps naïve, the consequences of the problems brought to light in it have been under-appreciated at best and taken as inevitable at worst. The *Postmodern Condition* captures the essential problem of the instrumentalization of knowledge, articulating philosophical problems at the level of everyday life to show how knowledge is put to use, from where it derives its authority or legitimation, and how it proliferates.

At the outset, Lyotard makes clear that the term 'postmodern' had already been in wide circulation at the time of his writing, particularly in the field of sociology in the United States. Principally, Lyotard assesses the state of culture given the transformations of the rules of the game in science, literature and the arts in the nineteenth century. A similar concern motivated Foucault in *The Order of Things* published over a decade earlier in 1966, which I'll return to. For Lyotard, the turn to positivism as the only mode of knowledge conducive to the organization of the social is problematic and symptomatic of the decline in faith in the idea of grand narratives. One effect of this shift is that we no longer know for the sake of knowing, 'knowledge is and will be produced in order to be sold, it is and will be consumed in order to be valorised in a new production: in both cases, the goal is exchange'.[8] A cyclical relation is in play where this knowledge is also produced in order to govern and governing as such can only take place or 'govern' through this knowledge. Very different, then, from the Enlightenment where a so-called hero of knowledge would work towards an ideal good, an ethics or political happy ending. Rather, as is well known, postmodern societies hold meta narratives in disdain, favouring instead a prioritizing of means and ends; an instrumentalization of knowledge, an objectification of men and things, and a valuation of the living. To be clear, this is not to *value* all living things as being necessarily valuable or precious, but to assign the living a value commensurate with exchange, a majestic abstraction known colloquially as the invisible hand of the market.

Lyotard attributes this move away from grand narratives to the triumph of techniques and technologies since the Second World War, which has shunned the 'ends of action' in favour of its means, where the effectiveness of 'advanced liberal capitalism' has 'eliminated the communist alternative and valorised the individual enjoyment of goods and services'.[9] Under these conditions the goal is no longer truth as such but rather power; as Lyotard describes 'scientists, technicians, and instruments are purchased not to find truth, but to augment power'.[10]

This relationship to knowledge in turn has practical effects on the organization of social life, setting out the parameters of what is possible to effectuate in the context of government and public policy, and what is more broadly 'practical' to set out to do in the context of a so-called modern, liberal democracy. Any knowledge or thought that does not conform to the modality of augmenting power or profit maximization is necessarily discarded, or de-valued. As Lyotard writes: 'we can predict that anything in the constituted body of knowledge that is not translatable in this way will be abandoned and that the direction of new research will be directed by the possibility of its eventual results being translatable into computer language.'[11] That is to say, 'smart language,' in the language of 'instrumentalization'; where a rationale of means and ends comes to dominate with a view not of human flourishing but rent seeking and profit maximization. This is coupled to the fact that knowledge no longer derives its validity for its own sake but is rather displaced onto what Lyotard describes as a 'practical subject – humanity'.[12] Where knowledge comes to be associated with the subject's self-mastery and self-governance. In the context of law, for example, this results in an assumption of justice in and through law, not because of an external guarantor such as God but by virtue of the legislators bound by law as citizens, whose will is that laws be just, and that this will coincides too with the will of the citizens. This association of legitimacy together with the willing subject is a privileging of the imperative, or in today's terms the prescriptive. As Lyotard writes:

> The important thing is not, or not only, to legitimate denotative utterances pertaining to the truth, such as 'The earth revolves around the sun', but rather to legitimate prescriptive utterances pertaining to justice, such as 'Carthage must be destroyed' or 'The minimum wage must be set at x dollars'. In this context, *the only role positive knowledge can play is to inform the practical subject about the reality within which the execution of the prescription is to be inscribed.*[13]

In other words, the parameters within which what is able to be done appear to already be fixed *in advance*, one that already thinks the terms and conditions of a minimum wage and its conceptual necessity. While these are worthwhile policy initiatives, the question as to what conditions of life make it necessary to set a minimum wage in the first place is not able to be thought or posed. As Lyotard describes, this set-up 'allows the subject to circumscribe the executable, or what is possible to do' whereas 'it is one thing for an undertaking to be possible and another for it to be just'.[14] So that what appears to be possible, permissible to articulate and organize around, does not mean that this would be desirable or just. Within this set-up, knowledge has a specific relation to the state and society primarily in the form of means and ends, or instrumentalization.

Knowledge, affixed to exchange value, comes to actively shape and define how life as such should be lived, setting out the conditions of life and its living conditions. The word 'condition' is instructive here. In Roman law, *condicio* denoted the 'legal or social status of a person', so that an appropriate sanction could be applied. Additionally, a *condicio* was often attached to 'a transaction or a testamentary disposition' one whose fulfilment depended on the latter. Which is to say, 'until the fulfilment of the condition' the transaction's coming into force remained uncertain.[15] *Condicio*'s meaning evolved from this primarily juridical sense, as a stipulation on condition that terms are fulfilled prior to its realization, to one which also means 'mode of being' or situation.[16] 'Condition' also came to refer to one's 'mental disposition, cast of mind; character, moral nature; disposition, temper' including also one's general state of health, 'especially one which is poor or abnormal', as well as the state of one's circumstance, wealth, and 'social position'.[17] While these two general meanings, as stipulation on the one hand, and as mode of being on the other hand, appear to be distinct, there is, nonetheless, a connection between them. That is, that our mode of being is predicated on stipulations, that our *condition* could be said to depend on certain *conditions*. It is this relationship to one's very mode of being and acting in the world that is at stake and remains elusive. If a knowledge that is not able to be translated into the language of power is simply discarded or dismissed, then what does this mean for the transformation of our mode of life? It has been the case that political demands for change and alternatives have had to be translated into a mode intelligible for the language of power and exchange to understand, which seems only to perpetuate existing deadlocks. For Sylvain Lazarus, this concern over the relation between thought and politics was crucial to understand, particularly as it relates to the possibility of transforming our system of social relations.

People think

In *Anthropology of the Name* (1996), described by Badiou as 'the most radical critique of the very grounds of social science', Lazarus gestures towards similar inquiries concerning both the limits of politics and of knowledge in our so-called 'postmodern society.' That is, concerning the question of knowledge and its legitimation, the notion of the problem and how it comes to be solved. More precisely, this concerns the relation between knowledge and the state or society, knowledge affixed to exchange value, and, most importantly, the role of knowledge in setting up the conditions of life, the conditions within which a certain mode of life is made possible, deciding therefore on the frame of what a possible politics might look like or allow.

In opposition to the idea of scientism, Lazarus proposes the Anthropology of the name. Scientism can be described as a category of science commonly found in the social sciences. As Lazarus puts it:

> The terms of 'scientistic thought' characterise the conception of science at work in sociology, economics and history. The theory that it proposes of science is that of exteriority, law, causality and the universal. I am challenging it because it presents itself as the sole paradigm of knowledge, and calling into question the theory of science that it develops.[18]

For Lazarus, this mode of 'scientistic thought' or positivist thought only ever formulates an already given state of affairs – based on, for example, the productive inputs required to achieve economic growth in a given year – akin to State discourse, that is then diluted 'in articles by those journalists who pick them up'.[19] In contrast, an Anthropology of the name posits the simple notion that people think, which instead functions on the level of the *possible*, such as the transformation of economic and social relations so that basic material needs for living, like housing and food, are available universally across the world, ceaselessly reminding us of an *elsewhere* than the given state of things. The term 'people' that Lazarus deploys refers to the names that are *indistinct*, or *impersonal*. This is not the people with a capital P that are presupposed in the disciplines of political science and theory. Here Lazarus is indifferent to the classist view that sticks to representations. Instead, the people are 'whatever'[20] – impersonal and indistinct, where nothing is presupposed or pre-judged. This marks a radical separation from established disciplines and discourses from sociology to history and philosophy. The 'academicism' of politics, as Lazarus describes it, dismisses the idea of a space of intellectuality of people.[21] While we do not know what 'people' are nor do we know what thought is, that people think remains 'a relation of the real, and not a relation to the real'; where the latter concerns the connection between subject and object leading to what Lazarus calls an 'objectal thought'.[22] An anthropology, as Lazarus describes it, on the contrary, is able to grasp the subjective rather than confining thought to a so-called objective reality that, as we have seen and will elaborate on in more detail, already comprises a given set of presuppositions and postulates always thought in view of exchange or market efficiency, such that the rights of people are subjected to them.

That people think is not the equivalent of saying that it is a matter of giving a voice to 'unheard voices' or, as Lazarus puts it, to the 'wretched'.[23] Rather, 'it is a matter of organising people by building a different space together, a genuine space where dogmatism and exhausted Marxism are left behind and possibilities can be formulated'.[24] This is because, for Lazarus, there is a modal relation to politics – politics as such does not exist in a constant fashion:

> Politics is not a permanent instance of societies; it is rare and sequential, and is manifested in historical modes. The mode, which is the relation of a politics to its thought, characterises the lacunary existence of politics and permits a grasp of politics through its thought.[25]

This is a vital point, that there exists a relation between politics, thought and space, that each engender and conjure in each other certain modes of being. Reiner Schürmann posed this problem in a similar way in thinking the relation between knowledge and action. Schürmann asks how, within certain epochal periods such as the 'Middle Ages' or the 'nineteenth century', certain practices were possible and even necessary and others not? How is it that 'a revolution was impossible in the Middle Ages' or 'a Cultural revolution during the First International?'[26] In other words, Schürmann asks, how is it 'that a domain of the possible and of the necessary is instituted, lasts for a while, and gives way under the effect of a mutation?'[27] Schürmann argues that the causal explanations offered up, whether these are speculative or to do with economism, leave us dissatisfied as these leave the presupposition of causality unquestioned. Indeed, for Lazarus, the space of politics as such is ephemeral and cannot be analysed from an objectal position largely conceived as being the space of the State. As Lazarus writes:

> Politics in the field of the State has the noteworthy characteristic of not presenting itself as thought. Quite the contrary – for it presents itself instead as an objectivity, or, otherwise put, as an objectivist reality. It merges the politics it conducts, politics in general and the State; and, in order to do so, it asserts the complex character of the whole. Only by way of law, political science and economics can one have access to what is, in this view, an intellectually composite whole.[28]

Thought and politics merge into the field of the State that presents itself as an objectivity, defining not simply what thought is, or what the political is and ought to be, but how life as such should be lived. Yet, as Lazarus points out, the very thing that makes knowledge as such possible is that it is never total, that there is always 'something left over, a residue that escapes thinkability'.[29] Just as there is no fixed mode of life, there is nothing necessary or predetermined in the social set-up in which we live. In our epoch, the reigning question around which our politics revolves is 'what is to be done?' An essential question whose answer is by no means self-evident. How did it come to be both relevant and urgent in our times? As Schürmann points out, this question is a modern one that would seem out of place in ancient Greece, for whom instead it was necessary to ask 'what is the best life?' and for the medieval period the question 'what acts are naturally human?' figured as most relevant.[30] An essential question for us to pose, then, is how did we arrive at this question: What is to be done? Alongside the question of class struggle and its organization it will be necessary to consider the way in which we conceptualize ourselves in the world, the relation between man and nature, and the role that knowledge plays in determining this. When knowledge turned its attention to the human being qua human and the plethora of taxonomical references over nature and its evolution it also set out the conditions of the possible. In setting out empirical parameters under the guise of neutrality in establishing the conditions of life and how it should be lived. It is our task to attempt to elucidate this hypothesis and weigh up the consequences.

Anthropology and the science of man

That there is a connection between knowledge and politics is nothing new. In Aristotle's *Politics*, for instance, the human being as *zoon logon echon*, the speaking being that has language, is defined as such in being capable of a politics, through the additional capacity of language the human being is able to distinguish between the just and the unjust. That practical philosophy borrows its postulates from first philosophy is also well known. In doing so, practical philosophy shares a fundamental feature, a search for an *arche*, origin or ground.

The Kantian inheritance plays a big part in how we think about philosophy, instrumentality and the human being. Michel Foucault's *The Order of Things* puts these questions in perspective. It is no coincidence that this seminal work was born out of a direct engagement with Kant's *Anthropology from a Pragmatic Point of View* (1798). Indeed, while in Hamburg in 1960, Foucault began work on the translation of Kant's text, as well as preparing an introduction for its publication in French. In 1961, Foucault submitted an early version of his thesis, 'Madness and Civilization', and a second thesis entitled 'Kant: Anthropology. Introduction, Translation, Notes' – supervised by Jean Hyppolite. Interestingly, the advice from the jury noted that the introduction to Kant should be developed and published as a separate work. So that when, in 1964, Foucault's translation of Kant's *Anthropology* was published, only 6 out of a total of 128 pages appeared in the introduction.[31]

It seems that, during this period of his work, Foucault was picking up an old debate, an intellectual quarrel between two German thinkers, Heidegger and Cassirer, which took place in Davos, Switzerland in 1928 and 1929. Part of the debate between Heidegger and Cassirer concerned Kant's *Critique*, animated on one hand by the neo-Kantians and the newly emerging phenomenologists on the other.[32] At the time, both schools of philosophy were being challenged by emerging theories in evolutionary biology, combined with the crises following the First World War and Socialist revolutions. Indeed, as Étienne Balibar writes, the growing secularization that began in the sixteenth century of the so-called Image of the World, that subsequently invited novel formulations over the nature and question of the human being and 'Man', also shaped the developments of these debates.[33] According to the intellectual historian Peter E. Gordon, this debate became a turning point in philosophical circles between so-called analytic and continental philosophy.[34] This debate, Gordon explains:

Frequently plays a divisive and allegorical function in the history of Continental philosophy. Scholars from a variety of disciplines and ideological camps are tempted to regard it as a final moment of rupture – between humanism and anti-humanism, enlightenment, and counter-enlightenment, or rationalism and irrationalism – as if the defining struggles of twentieth century thought were crystallised within this single event.[35]

However, the concern here is not the divide between these different schools of philosophy, but rather to examine a key theme concerning the differing approaches to developing an understanding of 'Man' or the human being, which, as we will see, then has consequences on the way in which we articulate our politics.

According to Balibar, what concerned the two main protagonists of the debate, Heidegger and the post-Kantian Ernst Cassirer, was a philological dispute concerning a passage from Kant's course on *Logic*. More precisely, what would come to have a profound impact on the human sciences, the law and philosophy, is Kant's addition of a fourth question to his original three in the *Lectures on Logic*. Here, Kant seems to assign two separate methods or approaches to philosophy; one he describes as scholastic: to do with skill, where the philosopher would be a kind of 'artist of reason'. Another, he describes as the worldly concept: to do with usefulness, where 'a doctrine *of wisdom*, the *legislator* of reason' is favoured, and the philosopher a legislator.[36] The artist of reason seeks only speculative knowledge, without thinking how this knowledge could serve or contribute to 'the final end of human reason'. For Kant, the practical philosopher is the real philosopher, 'for philosophy is the idea of a perfect wisdom, which shows us the final ends of human reason'.[37] This philosophy, that concerns the 'ends of human reason', is understood to be, for Kant, '*a science of the highest maxim for the use of our reason*'.[38] As Kant explains:

> For philosophy in the latter sense is in fact the science of the relation of all cognition and of all use of reason to the ultimate end of human reason, to which, as the highest, all other ends are subordinated, and in

which they must all unite to form a unity. The field of philosophy in this cosmopolitan sense can be brought down to the following questions:

1. *What can I know?*
2. *What ought I do?*
3. *What may I hope?*
4. *What is man?*

Metaphysics answers the first question, *morals* the second, *religion* the third, and *anthropology* the fourth. Fundamentally, however, we could reckon all of this as anthropology, because the first three questions relate to the last one.[39]

Those three questions along with the addition of the fourth caused great controversy, since, for the first time, 'I' was to denote both a *subject* and an *object*. This Kantian transformation was, until then, left unthought. At the time, concern grew over the fact that the question concerning what it is to be a human being was neglected in philosophy. Therefore, this question, along with the emerging discipline of philosophical anthropology, took on a renewed importance. This work was dominated by philosophers, including Georg Simmel and Max Scheler, and the biologist Jacob van Uexkül.[40] Philosophical anthropology was heavily influenced by evolutionary biology and reliant on it for its empirical research. Evolutionary biology upheld the idea that the human being's capacity for rational reflection and 'wilful' action can be understood through comparative zoology. As Gordon describes, von Uexkül adopted this point of departure, while others shaped their theoretical perspectives on the idea that biological attributes could instead be explained through metaphysical and theological explanations.[41] On the whole, however, the influence from evolutionary biology posed important questions and challenges to purely speculative thinking, to the extent that a new conception of the human being was thought to be essential.[42] Kant's innovation therefore inaugurated a new manner of thinking, a new knowledge: anthropological knowledge, where man would at the same time be both the subject and object of analysis.

The nature of the dispute centred on the question of whether 'anthropology' as such should be used as a framework for analysis in the human and social sciences. Heidegger argued that anthropology simply repeated the same metaphysical deadlocks that would remain ignorant on the question of being. In *Letter on Humanism*, Heidegger shows that metaphysics from Plato onwards had been unable to think being, or the truth of being. Instead, the question of being is related to categorical representation, where the question is not *of* being, but *about* being.[43] Moreover, for Heidegger, it seems that we are not perplexed by the seeming impossibility, and forgetting, of this mode of enquiry.[44] As Jean Greisch explains, we are no longer capable of confronting such a problem, that is to say, the question is no longer relevant for us. And this, not because a definitive answer can be proposed, but, rather, because we dare not consider it given the enormity of the task that such a question necessarily entails.[45] Yet, for Heidegger, the question of being is absolutely necessary, not simply for philosophical knowledge, but also for enquiries into all human preoccupations (the natural, and human sciences for instance). As such, the necessity and the priority of the question of being is essential since it makes possible all investigations into more particular spheres relating to being; the ontological thus precedes the ontic, both in terms of politics and the positive sciences. In other words, while the Being of being is considered (the 'what' of beings), the question of being as such is simply presupposed as always already defined and understood, such that no further enquiries are thought to be necessary.

Metaphysics, in this sense, looks for a common or general ground of beings, as what is most commonly shared among beings.[46] In this way, the question about being remains tied to a representational paradigm.[47] For Heidegger, 'anthropology' remains tied to the same horizon as the human sciences, and thus inherits identical problems of subjectivism and objectivism.[48] According to this schema, the world is 'conceived and grasped as picture', such that everything that is, is found in being, in man, and set up by man whose task is to *represent*.[49] Man, as all-encompassing, situates himself as the ground or foundation of all knowledge; and metaphysics, like philosophical anthropology, is tasked with the relation between empirical subjects and subjectivity, or man's essence. Man is, as it were, put *into the scene*, as the centre of the world, and becomes 'the representative of that which is, in the sense of that which has the character of object'.[50] In this way, the emergence of anthropology posed a number of novel questions concerning the human being. As a new discipline, anthropology claimed both a transcendental and empirical space. A number of intellectual traditions were made to take part in it, from Marxism to psychoanalysis and the social sciences. As Manfred Frank articulates it:

> Anthropology is transcendental: the world is explained from the standpoint of the human being and of the specifically human production or attribution of meaning. At the same time, anthropology is empirical, for it takes human activity, as Marx calls it, as an 'objectified activity' and no longer as purely spiritual or transcendental spontaneity that can only intervene in the realm of the existing world by means of several mediations.[51]

In this sense, the representation of Man as the source and foundation of all knowledge in turn shaped a conception of the human being as *subject*. According to Balibar, this representation of Man has not simply been a means to valorize the human being as the so-called bearer of universality but has also been 'the representation of *Man as* (a, the) *subject*'.[52] In other words, the essence of the human being becomes subjectivity. For this reason, the metaphysical endeavour relies on a particular conception of the human being, which, for Balibar, can be summarized with the following equation: 'Man = (equals) Subject or: The Subject is (identical to) the *Essence of Man*'.[53] What consequences can be drawn from this, and how is 'anthropology' as such relevant in this context?

This is the terrain that Michel Foucault would follow in the time leading up to, and including, the publication of *The Order of Things* (1966). From the 1950s,[54] Foucault was concerned with the growing 'anthropologisation of philosophy'.[55] In one of his first lectures at the

University of Lille in 1952–3 entitled '*Connaissance de l'homme et réflexion transcendentale*', Foucault lays the groundwork for his project on the growing influence of anthropological themes on nineteenth-century philosophy.[56] Marked, as we've seen, by Kant's addition of the fourth question 'what is man?' that denoted, for the first time, the 'I' as both a subject and an object. From this point on, 'Man' is the representation of the subject and understanding situated 'outside'. From the point of view of the world, the essence is at once separable and coincides with subjectivity, which inaugurates, in Foucault's terms, an empirico-transcendental doublet: both the object of knowledge and the subject supposed to know. It is this double bind that would interest Foucault; one that has repercussions for the very idea of a government of men and things. The status of the human being as an empirico-transcendental doublet signifies the emergence of a new episteme, and Foucault is concerned with unravelling the social, historical and discursive arrangements that set up the conditions of possibility for its emergence.

Life and knowledge

The set-up 'Man' rearranged and modified existing conceptions of culture, knowledge, religion and science – life and its meaning, its mode and its habits, substituting the manifold for the 'civilized' and the so-called proper mode of doing things within the schema of what the new science of man ordains to be true for all living things. In a 1973 interview concerning the main themes of this work, Foucault says that Western civilization is quite unique in giving 'Man' as such pride of place, as being 'king of all of creation'. Elsewhere in time and space, man as such holds little importance, being instead caught up in a network or social set-up where he is thought to occupy only a part.[57] Within our modern schema or mode of thought of man as 'king of all creation', all of history is told from the perspective of man's progress, despite the fact that, up to the nineteenth century, man was not the principal concern of our so-called civilization. For the Greeks, for example, it was about the Gods, nature and the cosmos. As Foucault writes: 'his flesh is a glebe, his bones are rocks, his veins great rivers, his bladder is the sea.'[58] By the end of the sixteenth and seventeenth centuries knowledge transforms into examining difference and identity (in terms of order and classification of the species). This, for example, altered the way in which the human being conceptualized notions of kinship, resemblances and affinities, which were intricately connected with language and with things. Foucault names this new conjuncture 'rationalism', which accompanies the disappearance of the belief in magic and superstition, and the entry of nature into the scientific order.[59]

A shift in emphasis, then, prioritizing the notion of evidence and the idea of difference *between* things. This transformation eventually leads to a sense of urgency over the need to construct taxonomies both locally and across the world, a tool in the so-called age of discovery and inseparable from the architectonics of colonialism and empire.[60] The new taxonomies are unlike the one described by Borges that Foucault draws our attention to at the outset of the work. Through Borges' wonderful taxonomy where animals are divided into different categories like 'belonging to the empire', 'fabulous', 'frenzied', 'that from a long way off look like flies' to name just a few, we become aware of the limitations of our own system of thought and mode of relating to the world and cosmos. As Foucault writes:

> In the wonderment of this taxonomy, the thing we apprehend in one great leap, the thing that, by means of the fable, is demonstrated as the exotic charm of another system of thought, is the limitation of our own, the stark impossibility of thinking that.[61]

The impossibility of thinking otherwise means that we cannot conceptualize another mode of living. Indeed, when we think through the question 'what is to be done?' we seldom begin from the position of imagining what form-of-life we would like to live and organize material conditions accordingly. Rather, we proceed in the opposite direction, we assume the social set-up to be fixed such that forms of life must conform to what is already in place, and what is to be done is transformed into what is permissible to be done within our existing rules of intelligibility. Marielle Macé's question in *Styles: Critique of our Form of Life* is all the more pressing, then, when she asks 'tell me what you really want to see, to protect . . . what you really want to imagine in the forms of living, and I will tell you what kind of world you are supporting'.[62] Where the superstructures appear to be in increasing contradiction with all forms of the living – both human and non-human – it is all the more urgent to problematize their mode of operation by fully grasping the system of thought that lays idly behind the practices that we accept.

The modern episteme that Foucault describes is marked by the inauguration of what he calls the 'quasi-transcendentals' of language, labour and life that come to organize how our form-of-life as such can be understood and how it should be lived; that is, new 'positivities' advancing their own rationality and laws, while at the same time defining Man's place within them.[63]

In classical thought, while the human being was situated in a privileged position in the order of the world, 'a subject' of representation[64] as such was impossible. As Foucault explains:

> Before the end of the eighteenth century, *man* did not exist – any more than the potency of life, the fecundity of labour, or the historical density of language. He is a quite recent creature, which the demiurge of knowledge fabricated with its own hands less than two hundred years ago: but he has grown old so quickly that it has been only too easy to imagine that he had been waiting for thousands of years in the darkness for that moment of illumination in which he would finally be known.[65]

Though the natural sciences investigated 'Man' this was primarily from the perspective of man as species. Indeed, as Foucault goes on to say, 'there was no epistemological consciousness of man as such'.[66] There was no clearly articulated and isolated space for man in the classical episteme. Man is now able to include the world in a discourse, which 'has the power to represent its representation'.[67]

Foucault is not saying that 'men' as persons and living beings did not exist prior to this movement within the historical conjuncture that he describes. Rather, in his analysis, Foucault is attempting to connect the appearance of man within a specific notion of humanism, and its coincidence with early biological studies. Therefore, Foucault refers to humanism in the context of the nineteenth century more generally. This perspective can be explained by Foucault's archaeological method that aims to consider the historical *a priori* of the branches of knowledge that make up the human sciences. Within this context, Foucault is keen to show that it is in fact man's representation as *finitude* that for the first time is the 'foundation of all positivities and present [...] in the element of empirical things'.[68] That Man, in his finitude, is taken to be the subject of analysis in accordance with Life, Language and Labour. For this reason, Foucault describes man as a 'strange empirico-transcendental doublet', since, 'he is a being such that knowledge will be attained in him of what renders all knowledge possible'.[69]

Man is thought to be the foundation of his own knowledge, his own laws, his own discourse and his own finitude. This is the contribution that Foucault seeks to highlight, that for the first time man is conceptualized as a being whose nature (or essence) it is to know both nature and himself as a natural being:

> The modern themes of an individual who lives, speaks, and works in accordance with the laws of an economics, a philology, and a biology, but who also, by a sort of internal torsion and overlapping, has acquired the right, through the interplay of those very laws, to know them and to subject them to total clarification – all these themes so familiar to us today and linked to the existence of the 'human sciences' are excluded by classical thought: it was not possible at that time that there should arise, on the boundary of the world, the strange stature of a being whose nature (that which determines it, contains it, and has traversed it from the beginning of time) is to know nature, and itself, in consequence, as a natural being.[70]

The key difference from classical discourse, according to Foucault, is that the conditions of possibility of living were not interrogated or implied by the articulation of the human being as something like Man, Subject or Cogito. Here, life comes to define both life itself and the conditions of possibilities for living:

> When natural history becomes biology, when the analysis of wealth becomes economics, when, above all, reflection upon language becomes philology, and classical *discourse*, in which being and representation found their common locus, is eclipsed, then, in the profound upheaval of such an archaeological mutation, man appears in his ambiguous position as an object of knowledge and as a subject that knows: enslaved sovereign, observed spectator, he appears in the place belonging to the king.[71]

This marks a turning point from the idea of representation as the source or origin of living beings to the idea of human beings now existing 'in accordance with the laws of life, production, and language'.[72] In this context, 'Man' finds himself at the centre, and as the *source* of order. So, what is significant in this mode of thought is the prescription of the essence of man, as a labouring and speaking animal, turning metaphysical questions into empirical facts. Not simply in terms of fact gathering but in engendering what subsequently becomes thinkable and possible, or unthinkable, impractical and impossible.

Yet, Man's position remains ambiguous, being accessible 'only through his words, his organism, the objects he makes', such that

> All these contents that his knowledge reveals to him as exterior to himself, and older than his own birth, anticipate him, overhang him with all their solidity, and traverse him as though he were merely an object of nature, a face doomed to be erased in the course of his history. Man's finitude is heralded – and imperiously so – in the positivity of knowledge; we know that man is finite, as we know the anatomy of the brain, the mechanics of production costs, or the system of Indo-European conjugation; or rather, like a watermark running through all these solid, positive, and full forms, we perceive the finitude and limits they impose, we sense, as though on their blank reverse sides, all that they make impossible.[73]

'Man', in appearing, brings forth the end of his own appearance. The epistemological conditions of possibility that render possible something like 'Man', according to the 'positivity of knowledge' where 'Man', as such, is both the subject and the object, is at once a discovery of the limit, marking the coming to be of Man's finitude – we sense, through these positivities, 'all that they make impossible', with veins never again as great rivers, nor the bladder the sea.

Man's body is his limit, that is, man's 'finitude' is 'marked by the spatiality of the body', so that finitude as such is not an externally determined phenomenon, but rather lies at the source of existence itself.[74] In this sense, Foucault directs our attention to the problem of the origin. That, in the end, at the core of this empirical trajectory, is the call to work backwards, in a sense 'down to' an analytic of finitude to discover Man's foundation.[75] Man's being, in other words, provides the foundation and the knowledge that there is finitude; much like the function of the disease in Xavier Bichat's work, that co-exists with life and with the living, and not as something that comes after life.[76] Life itself carries the disease. As Foucault would say: 'knowledge of life finds its origin in the destruction of life and in its extreme opposite.'[77] 'Man' carries with him the end of man. Knowledge becomes a question of revelation, of revealing the conditions of knowledge in accordance with the empirical contents it allows for. For Foucault, this means that the analysis is limited to one of a positivist nature, where the 'truth of the object determines the truth of the discourse that describes its formation'.[78] Moreover, the discourse itself anticipates an already self-defined truth, so that whatever one seeks is already predetermined.[79] This means that contemporary discourse is limited to either a positivist type, or an eschatological one, where man is produced as a 'truth' within it, both reduced and promised at the same time. Hence, a discourse that is both empirical and transcendental that would enable an analysis of man as a subject and site of knowledge that has been empirically determined, and, at the same time, referred back to an origin.

This discovery is not a stable one, however, since the possibility for both 'infinite understanding' and infinite experience continue, paradoxically, to exist in the form of illusions perhaps but nevertheless as a shadow, and the thought. In being an empirico-transcendental doublet, man is also the site of misunderstanding, erring within a potential discourse that is the 'not-known'.[80] For Foucault, the question is:

> How can man think what he does not think, inhabit as though by a mute occupation something that eludes him, animate with a kind of frozen movement that figure of himself that takes the form of a stubborn exteriority? [...] How can he be the subject of a language that for thousands of years has been formed without him, a language whose organisation escapes him, whose meaning sleeps an almost invincible sleep in the words he momentarily activates by means of discourse, and within which he is obliged, from the very outset, to lodge his speech and thought, as though they were doing no more than animate, for a brief period, one segment of that web of innumerable possibilities?[81]

The modern *cogito* formulates itself as well as the articulation of thought on that which is not thought or unthought. At the same time, this is not altogether foreign or exterior to it. Such that the *cogito* is ceaselessly grappling with the question of how it is possible for thought to reside elsewhere than in itself, and yet so close to it: 'how it can *be* in the forms of non-thinking.'[82] Just as Descartes' dream of the synderesis, and all experiences of thought not yet accounted for – dreams, illusions, phantasms – the *cogito* realizes that these unthoughts emerge as the very site, and necessary accompaniment, of possible experience and thought. The appearance of man in Western culture gave rise to the simultaneous appearance of the unthought, such that when man became an object of investigation, man risked himself in this knowledge to discover that which is impossible to investigate and know directly, or even indirectly – the unconscious of man, of knowledge and of thought.[83] As Foucault explains:

> Man has not been able to describe himself as a configuration in the *episteme* without thought at the same time discovering, both in itself and outside itself, at its borders yet also in its very warp and woof,

an element of darkness, an apparently inert density in which it is embedded, an unthought which it contains entirely, yet in which it is also caught.[84]

The unthought, or the unconscious, both external but necessarily linked to Man, this space 'is in one sense, the shadow cast by man as he emerged in the field of knowledge; in another, the blind stain by which it is possible to know him.'[85] Man, in its construction, carries with it its shadow; that for the human sciences it is a matter of unveiling, of knowing, of transcribing it.[86] This is why, for Foucault, psychoanalysis, along with ethnography, emerges as *counter science*, since they flow in the opposite direction. Unlike the human sciences that look backward and tirelessly make or construct man as he appears, psychoanalysis and ethnography 'ceaselessly "unmake" that very man who is creating and re-creating his positivity in the human sciences'.[87] There is no attempt to construct a general concept called Man, nor is there the attempt to isolate a unique quality, or singular essence *of* Man. According to Foucault, both ethnography and psychoanalysis have access to a multiplicity of experiences, develop concepts and express a continual dissatisfaction of what may otherwise appear to be established knowledge.[88]

Ethnography, for its part, studies a localized culture rather than a series of events, thus suspending a chronological discourse of humanity. Instead of collecting empirical contents in the service of the historical 'positivity' of investigating subjects, ethnography considers the forms and limits of each culture; not for a general science of Man, but for a *knowledge*, of what, for example, makes man possible within a particular mode or way of life.[89] Psychoanalysis, like ethnography, does not seek a kind of general theory of Man. For Foucault, it is for this reason that a general theory of Man or an anthropology as such is incompatible with psychoanalysis. Instead, like ethnography, it works to 'dissolve man'.[90] Psychoanalysis, instead of approaching the unconscious 'with their back to it' and waiting for it to reveal itself, 'points directly toward it', not in the direction of rendering sayable something which is implicit but rather 'towards what is there and yet is hidden'.[91] In advancing over the space of what is representable, psychoanalysis discovers in it that it is possible for there to be 'system (therefore signification), rule (therefore conflict), norm (therefore function)'.[92] Therefore, challenging what had long been considered to be mythology. Psychoanalysis shows that in the un-representable space lies the very conditions of possibility of knowledge about the living human being. For Foucault, only when these ephemeral elements that escape all signification emerge can we recognize madness in its present form. Not as something 'of another world', as a 'straying of reason', but as something:

> Perilously nearest to us – as if, suddenly, the very hollowness of our existence is outlined in relief; the finitude upon the basis of which we are, and think, and know, is suddenly there before us: an existence at once real and impossible, thought that we cannot think, an object for our knowledge that always eludes it.[93]

Psychoanalysis recognizes itself in this form of madness: that which is closest to it and at the same time appears impossible. When phantasy and the imagination were subsumed under the *ego cogito*, and the phantasm expelled from the subject of experience appearing only in the form of mental alienation and illusion, its presence was transformed as the shadow of Man. The phantasm, or the unthought, having been foreclosed from the constitution of the subject now returns only as symptom. When psychoanalysis is confronted with the *analysand* bearing this symptom, this madness that is all too familiar, it realizes it is all too close, recognizing even itself in it. Such that:

> Psychoanalysis 'recognises itself' when in it is confronted with those very psychoses which nevertheless (or rather, for that very reason) it has scarcely any means of reaching: as if psychosis were displaying in a savage illumination, and offering in a mode not too distant but just too close, that towards which analysis must make its laborious way.[94]

Psychoanalysis is made to confront these psychoses and often finds itself in them. It cannot reach this madness but can only be reminded of its own madness in it, seeing in it only a glimpse of that which it could be, and towards which it 'must make its laborious way'. This is the *arché*, at once the commandment and the beginning, which our analysis now finds itself confronted with. The making of something like 'man' that necessarily excludes that which it is incapable of including, while simultaneously presupposing it; a biopolitical gesture par excellence, that we will continue to examine. The empirico-transcendental doublet, too, knows that all cannot be said, and all cannot be known. Similarly, as we will come to investigate, for Agamben, this can be understood as the anthropogenetic event that ceaselessly and tirelessly divides and articulates something like 'Man', or the human being, with the scission occurring *within* man himself. Man distanced from the animal within, and what is considered to be the irrational phantasm, is expelled from rational consciousness, and the rational subject.

2

Government of the living

We have been developing a sort of genealogy of the emergence of 'man' in philosophy and the human sciences broadly conceived, most significantly in the formulation of the human being as both an object and a subject of knowledge, a *sujet supposé savoir*, which carries with it the assumption of autonomy and reason. Bruno Karsenti examines this antagonism in relation to the specificity of the inheritance of the social sciences in French thought. Three modes of knowledge emerged at the turn of the eighteenth century and into the nineteenth century: sociology, anthropology and philosophy, which, while developing as distinct fields, happened to develop along the same lines.[1] The term 'anthropology', Karsenti tells us, emerged in France soon after its development in the German eighteenth-century thought. The French Revolution (1789–99) precipitated transformations in knowledge epitomized by a novel concern over the 'science of man'. Indeed, the *Institut National* founded a new discipline, the so-called science of man, which was inaugurated in 1796. This new discipline sought to synthesize the physical, intellectual and moral studies of man, in order to provide answers to questions of morality, logic and the physical world more generally.[2] As Karsenti puts it, 'conceived in this way, anthropology is not born from philosophy, but is born *with* it – or, at least, with the renaissance of the latter, on new terms, the novelty of which we would have to investigate'.[3] This led to the emergence of numerous fields of thought from the study of human anatomy to comparative linguistics, and the production of knowledge of so-called primitive peoples. The key, however, is that irrespective of the particular domain, the questions continued to be philosophically informed, that is, 'to know, in all its constitutive complexity, the phenomenon of the human being'.[4]

The laws of social statistics

A pertinent question to pose is the following one: what does this new knowledge make possible? It is argued here that this new knowledge made possible the administration of life and a government of the living. It would be misleading to presume that the government of men and things as such is a new or modern phenomenon. On the contrary, an essential problem that continually preoccupied theologians, philosophers and sovereigns has always been the perceived unpredictability of the behaviour of the human being: the irrational being always already present. Numerous artefacts and apparatuses have been thought up precisely to manage the potential for errancy, irrationality and the unexpected exercise of free will not least God's, hence the separation between God and his office, or God and his works through the idea of Opus Dei.[5]

So what is different with the emergence of 'Man' as subject and object, with a mode of knowledge concerned with instrumentatilization and affixed to power and exchange? The difference lies in both the extent of the exercise of power, the expectations of the individual and a temporal shift in that the government of the present spatio-temporal given is no longer enough. As we will develop, the individual exercises power over and against itself and manages itself biopolitically in the present, in and for the future. Moreover, the exercise of power is not simply one of prohibition but of active, positive, administration; life is fostered and encouraged to guide itself to what is thought to be a proper disposition.

The influence of Newtonian physics inaugurated a particular ethos and drive towards the establishment of 'certainty' in human endeavours, thus encouraging the development of empirically falsifiable truths. Science, during this period, was confronted by the problem of what it called 'indeterminacy' at the level of the individual.[6] The problem of 'free will' and medieval themes of magic, mythology and astrology came to be considered with suspicion given their incompatibility with accurate prediction. The English philosopher, scientist and jurist Francis Bacon was among those suspicious of these forms of knowledge and human experience, calling for the 'maze' or 'forest' of experience to be organized. In this vein, intellectual tools were developed to establish certainties at the level of human experience and human action. Though successful in many respects, this new knowledge simultaneously gave rise to new uncertainties. While the scientific method of verification serves to perform experience into experiments, so that a quantitative result can be induced with the aim of providing a predictive capacity, thus ensuring a kind of certainty of the future; it also brings to light the uncertain in a manner that had previously not been possible to conceptualize, turning the unknown into an object of knowledge to be governed, which over the last two decades has followed what Patrick Zylberman calls the logic of the worst case scenario in accordance with a securitarian paradigm.[7] The new tools in question include the development of statistics, and in particular calculable probability, as the calculation of risk in an effort to determine likelihoods as what is more or less likely to happen, thus apparently giving precision to foresight.[8] The aim is to mathematize the social world resulting in, among other things, a new conceptualization of what it means to govern. As Agamben puts it:

> Just as the probabilistic laws of quantum mechanics aim not at knowing but at 'commanding' the state of atomic systems, so the laws of social statistics do not aim at the knowledge of social phenomena but at their very 'government'. . . . Science no longer tried to know reality, but – like the statistics of social sciences – only intervene in it in order to govern it.[9]

A new field of objects is able to be constructed which 'can function "as if" the field is real for government as much as science itself'.[10] From this desire to mathematize the social world, a new concept emerged, that of 'population' which was thought to have resolved the scientific problem of indeterminacy. Part of the logic of the so-called law of large numbers is believed to be able to foster a greater predictive capacity and ensure a kind of regularity on a mass scale.[11] Population as a statistical construct enabled a form of government that became concerned with the conduct of conduct, the proper conduct of men and things, the proper and efficient circulation of men and things.

The effect of thinking in terms of population as an object of knowledge shifted the focus of governance to one concerned not merely with the present, but perhaps more importantly concerned with the governance of the future; by asking: how to mitigate against certain risks and dangers that are in themselves produced as objects of knowledge through the calculation of probability? So that what is in question is the creation or production of sets of possibilities and acting or intervening in these possibilities independently of their being realized, or not. As Agamben puts it, 'such a possibility tends to replace reality and thus becomes the object of a science of the accidental [. . .] that considers possibility as such, not as a means of knowing the real, but as a way of intervening in it in order to govern it.'[12]

It is this vision of the social world that created the possibility for comparisons, and for the idea of normalization or the 'norm' not only to take on the form of an ideal measure but to actively shape the construction of law. In turn, the law functions to produce the institutions and social realities that at once support these different pieces of knowledge(s), and also make them possible. Foucault posits a transformation in the functioning of power from the territorially focused mode of the seventeenth and eighteenth centuries to one concerned with the life of the population. This new power was only made possible through 'constant surveillance'.[13] For Foucault, the difference can be conceptualized thus: 'the theory of sovereignty is, if you like, a theory which can found absolute power on the absolute expenditure of power, but which cannot calculate power with minimum expenditure and maximum efficiency.'[14] This new power that Foucault refers to, emerging alongside the advent of industrial capitalism, is characterized by the notion of 'discipline'.

There is a difference between outright banishment or confinement and discipline, this is illustrated by contrasting the experience of leprosy and the plague. Where the leper was simply rejected and separated from the social fabric, the plague victims formed part of a mechanics of tactical management. As Foucault describes, 'rather than the massive, binary division between one set of people and another, it called for multiple separations, individualising distributions, an organisation in depth of surveillance and control, an intensification and a ramification of power.'[15] We can get a better sense of the notion of discipline by thinking of it in terms of a technology of power that is not necessarily limited to a particular institution. While Foucault illustrates disciplinary societies through the paradigm of Bentham's panopticon, for instance, or schools and prisons, it would be more exact to conceptualize this in terms of a means through which power is able to distribute itself. That is, a type of power where discipline as such is the *mode* of power's exercise, 'comprising a whole set of instruments, techniques, procedures, levels of application, targets; it is a "physics" or "anatomy" of power, a technology.'[16] Under this mode of power, there is a continuous surveillance of the population, as well as continual assessment and classification, the results of which form the basis of self-governing from the individual subject's point of view. However, this is not to say that sovereignty has altogether disappeared in this schema; indeed, sovereignty continued and expanded its role in terms of the organization of juridical codes. The latter were superimposed on disciplinary mechanisms that, for Foucault, had the effect of erasing elements of domination involved in disciplinary techniques.[17] Therefore, the aim was for each individual to exercise a form of sovereignty over themselves. In other words, disciplines, as such, served to guarantee the cohesion of the social body that constitutes sovereignty, so that in this sense the two forms are interdependent. Crucially, statistics were the significant technology for achieving this and ensuring the interdependence of the individual and the social body. Foucault describes this process as the 'dark side' of juridico-political structures presented on the surface as egalitarian juridical frameworks:

> The general juridical form that guaranteed a system of rights that were egalitarian in principle was supported by these tiny, everyday, physical mechanisms, by all those systems of micro-power that are essentially non-egalitarian and asymmetrical that we call disciplines. And

although, in a formal way, the representative regime makes it possible, directly or indirectly, with or without relays, for the will of all to form the fundamental authority of sovereignty, the disciplines provide, at the base, a guarantee of the submission of forces and bodies. The real, corporal disciplines constituted the foundation of the formal, juridical liberties.[18]

In this way, the disciplines concern the particular mode of behaviour of individuals, in accordance with given expectations dependent on the context, which effectively regulate or coerce bodies to comply with the generalized legal framework. Disciplines therefore function differently to the 'law' as derived from sovereignty, and instead concern the idea of the norm: 'disciplines will define not a code of law, but a code of normalisation, and they will necessarily refer to a horizon that is not the edifice of law, but the field of the human sciences.'[19] This is the crucial point, Foucault reminds us that the disciplines create their own discourse, their own apparatuses of knowledge, across a variety of fields of expertise.[20] For example, the aim of disciplinary societies was not confinement, but rather to ensure a form of attachment for individuals. In the factory, the panoptic model served to attach workers to an apparatus of production. Similarly, for the psychiatric hospital the point was to attach individuals to 'an apparatus of correction, to an apparatus of normalisation'.[21] So that the defining characteristic of discipline and panopticism is the idea of the conformity, or attachment, of individuals to apparatuses of knowledge, or a set of norms. As François Ewald formulates it, 'discipline tends not to divide or compartmentalise society but works instead to create a homogenous social space.'[22]

This is evident too in the ascription or attachment of man to production or labour. Foucault reminds us that labour has been said to define man's very essence, that Marx, Hegel and Locke proposed this idea. However, as Foucault explains, labour as such cannot function as man's essence, instead the attachment of man to labour was made possible through a series of operations that bind individuals to the apparatus of production; and all that the apparatus entails. In this way, according to Foucault, it is not capitalism as such which transforms labour, as man's essence, into profit or surplus value. Rather:

> The fact is, capitalism penetrates much more deeply into our existence. That system, as it was established in the nineteenth century, was obliged to elaborate a set of political techniques, techniques of power, by which man was tied to something like labour – a set of techniques by which people's bodies and their time would become labour power and labour time so as to be effectively used and thereby transformed into hyperprofit. But in order for there to be hyperprofit, there had to be an infra-power [*sous-pouvoir*]. A web of microscopic, capillary political power had to be established at the level of man's very existence, attaching men to the production apparatus, while making them into agents of production, into workers. This binding of man to labour was synthetic, political; it was a linkage brought about by power.[23]

The attachment to labour is not a natural given, nor an operatively neutral set-up, given that the production apparatus to which workers are attached are configured in relation to a set of norms. The infra-power that Foucault mentions functions on the basis of the production and organization of a series of knowledges concerning correction as well as knowledge of the individual. Moreover, these also operate within institutions thereby making man or the individual the subject and object of knowledge, an object of science.[24] So that any attempts at critiquing hyperprofit necessitates a challenge of infra-power, and equally demands questioning the human sciences, as necessarily connected to the latter, including the privileged position granted to man as the central object of this form of knowledge.[25] This is, of course, easier said than done. As Foucault notes:

> When we want to make some objection against disciplines and all the knowledge-effects and power-effects that are bound up with them, what do we do in concrete terms? What do we do in real life? What do the Syndicat de la magistrature and other institutions like it do? What do we do? We obviously invoke right, the famous old formal, bourgeois right. And it is in reality the right of sovereignty. And I think that at this point we are in a sort of bottleneck, that we cannot go on working

like this forever; having recourse to sovereignty against discipline will not enable us to limit the effects of disciplinary power.[26]

This is because of the interdependence of discipline and sovereignty which rely on one another for the cohesion of the social body.

Infra-power and the norm are, therefore, to be distinguished from the juridical: the institutions of law traditionally understood as sovereign power. The norm, while undoubtedly related to power relies on an implicit logic that enables power to self-reflect upon its strategies and define its objects: 'This logic is at once the force that enables us to imagine life and the living as objects of power and the power that can take "life" in hand, creating the sphere of the bio-political.'[27] The significance of the norm cannot be confused with the notion of rule. Indeed, the norm, understood in the particular meaning it acquired at the beginning of the nineteenth century, can signify numerous rules and the means by which to produce them, and, importantly, as a principle for the ascription of value.[28] The norm serves to make visible the distinction between the normal and the abnormal. This conceptualization of the norm has influenced a number of fields of knowledge including 'the moral, juridical, and political sciences, which at the close of the nineteenth century will establish themselves (particularly in Germany) as "normative" sciences'.[29] Conceived in this way, it is possible to see how the connection between the norm, the normative sciences and discipline engage to produce individuals, to restrain or constrain undesirable or abnormal behaviour, to correct deviancy in relation to a perceived norm, used essentially as a standard of measurement, as 'a means of producing a common standard'.[30]

Moreover, statistics have the potential to shape and encourage the self-governing of people's behaviour and selves, where what is at stake is self-reflection with the aim of modifying individual's own conception of their behaviour to suit the 'normal' as determined by statistical abstractions.[31] The norm itself is never fixed in place, indeed the system of norms are flexible and dependent on the continual observation and gathering of information, such that the average produced depends on a number of variables from which the norm itself is derived. In this sense, the norm itself cannot be separated from the abnormal, and is instead formed through its inclusion; the norm is the abstracted average of a series of variations, each potentially abnormal in relation to the fictional average, though to varying degrees.

At this juncture, a moment of reflection is required concerning the problems that we have identified so far. It appears that, in an attempt to know the world and the human being in all its complexity, through the development of evermore sophisticated tools of analysis, which in turn generate further unknowns and generate further complications, that what continues to be at stake is a constitutive impossibility – contingency, unpredictability, the unthought, the future. This impossibility, or crisis, is perpetual, that is, it is at the same time continually produced in the quest of both knowing, and managing, the known and the unknown. It even seems to be a necessary condition for its own perpetuation. The individual subject is never accomplished, but a work in progress: in a continual process of development. The contemporary subject, governed by the imperative 'to be who one must become', lives according to the authority of a different life that is promised to be within reach in this lifetime.[32] The status quo, whatever it may be, is always already insufficient, the imperative is to be what one must become. A process that, by its very essence, is necessarily without end. What is in question is a particular mode of being of the human being, which, as both subject and object of the analysis is at the same time the knowledge that constitutes it.

Biopolitics and state racism

It is no coincidence that the subtitle to the first volume of Foucault's *History of Sexuality* (1976) is 'The Will to Knowledge'. Here, Foucault introduces the notion of biopolitics and develops a preliminary analysis of its functioning as the primary technique of government; connecting knowledge from the human sciences like psychiatry to the exercise of power. Foucault writes:

For millennia, man remained what he was for Aristotle: a living animal with the additional capacity for a political existence; modern man in an animal whose politics places his existence as a living being in question.[33]

This sentence is significant, and it appears in Agamben's introduction to *Homo Sacer I: Sovereign Power and Bare Life* (1995). In a sense, it succinctly captures the difference between Foucault's and Agamben's approaches and understandings of biopolitics. Whereas, for Foucault, the emphasis lies in the clause following the semi-colon, that 'modern man is an animal whose politics places his existence as a living being in question', for Agamben, the key lies in the clause immediately preceding it: that man is 'a living animal with the additional capacity for a political existence'. However, both Foucault and Agamben agree with the premise of the entire sentence. And yet, the slight variation that does exist has given rise to different interpretations which draw different aspects, of what is essentially a shared problem. For Agamben the definition of man as one defined as a living animal with an 'additional capacity' is in itself taken to be problematic. However, for now, how are we to understand the fact that 'modern man is an animal whose politics places his existence as a living being in question'? In tackling this question, the concept of biopolitics will become clearer, and we will see the important influence this will have on Agamben's own conceptualization of the term.

As we have seen, by developing the notion of biopolitics, Foucault is primarily concerned with the notions of power and sovereignty, and how these in turn function in relation to the emergence of a new object of knowledge: population. As Judith Revel explains, the notion of biopolitics implies a historical analysis concerning the idea of political reason, or state rationality, that began with the emergence of liberal political and economic thought in the mid-eighteenth and early nineteenth centuries. Revel suggests that 'by liberalism, one must understand an exercise of government that does not simply tend to maximise its efforts while reducing its costs on the model of industrial production, but rather affirms that we always risk governing too much'.[34]

What becomes apparent within a system of biopower is the emergence of a new type of governmentality that is not reducible to a juridical or economic analysis, but rather one that gives rise to a new object of knowledge: population.

Foucault is interested in the 'how' of power,[35] so as to 'understand its mechanisms by establishing two markers, or limits; on the one hand, the rules of right that formally delineate power, and on the other hand, at the opposite extreme, the other limit might be the truth-effects that power produces, that this power conducts and which, in their turn, reproduce that power'.[36] In this way, the relations of power that traverse the social body are numerous, and these, in turn, are connected to a discourse of truth. These relations of power function on the basis of the production of a so-called true discourse, such that 'power cannot be exercised unless a certain economy of discourses of truth functions in, on the basis of, and thanks to, that power'.[37] The relationship between power and discourse can be more generally understood in juridical terms, such that power is always already tied up with law. More specifically, as Foucault points out, Western societies' elaboration of legal and juridical thought has been intimately tied up with royal power since the Middle Ages; jurists were charged with the organization of royal power, with the rights of the king and the potential limits of his power.[38] As Foucault explains it:

> From the Middle Ages onward, the essential role of the theory of rights has been to establish the legitimacy of power; the major or central problem around which the theory of right is organised is the problem of sovereignty. To say that the problem of sovereignty is the central problem of right in Western societies means that the essential function of the technique and discourse of right is to dissolve the element of domination in power and to replace that domination, which has to be reduced or masked, with two things: the legitimate rights of the sovereign on the one hand, and the legal obligation to obey on the other. The system of right is completely centered on the king; it is, in other words, ultimately an elimination of domination and its consequences.[39]

So that rights are not merely tied up with a relation to sovereignty but also with a relationship of domination, and these are in turn not limited to a direct link to the central position of a sovereign figure, but instead include the forms and mechanisms of subjugation present across the social body as a whole. The emphasis on juridical prohibition in the classical sense is not enough, it is necessary to consider power's so-called positive potential, as a technology or technique. This aspect of power's 'positive' potential can be found not only in Jeremy Bentham's political philosophy but also in Marx. Indeed, in *Capital: Volume II*, Marx appears to suggest that power is more than a central mechanism; instead, intimating that power is multiple. As Foucault writes: 'Powers, this means forms of domination, forms of subjection, that function locally, for example in the workshop, in the army, in a property of slaves or in a property where there are relations of servitude.'[40] Such that, for Marx, the power exercised by the shop manager is a different kind of power to a typically juridical power present in society as a whole, so that society can be understood as an 'archipelago of different powers'.[41]

In order to elucidate a theory of power that takes into account modes of subjugation present across the social field, Foucault begins his analysis with the question of sovereignty. In this respect, Foucault notes an essential change or shift in the manner in which sovereignty as such was said to function. Foucault draws from Thomas Hobbes' conceptualization of sovereignty, where, put simply, in order for 'a State' to be established, a transfer of right occurs so as to facilitate the rights of so-called decision-making representatives. As Foucault explains: 'they do not even decide, basically, to transfer their rights. On the contrary, they decide to grant someone – or an assembly made up of several people – the right to represent them, fully and completely.'[42] Therefore, the idea is to establish a kind of equivalence between the sovereign and his people, such that the sovereign's decision will be that of the people, in such a way that 'insofar as he represents individuals, the sovereign is an exact model of those very individuals',[43] and, therefore, that the mechanism of sovereignty relies on the 'interplay between a will, a covenant, and representation'.[44] The notion of 'will' is crucial in this schema, since in order for a relationship of sovereignty to function in this sense, a certain inclination for life and obedience must take place. 'For sovereignty to exist, there must be – and this is all there must be – a certain radical will that makes us want to live, even though we cannot do so unless the other is willing to let us live.'[45] For Foucault, 'will', in this instance, is inextricably tied up with fear – and it is precisely the 'fearing subject' as such that in turn shapes sovereignty. The sovereign can only exercise his 'right of life' by at the same time exercising a right to kill or refraining from it. So that, the sovereign's power could be described as the 'power over life and death'. For Foucault, this power was 'in reality the right to take life or let live. Its symbol, after all, was the sword'.[46] So that the sovereign could grant life, let live and also decide on death. As Foucault explains: 'the very essence of the right of life and death is actually the right to kill: it is at the moment when the sovereign can kill that he exercises his right over life. [. . .] It is the right to take life or let live.'[47]

This form of power can also be conceptualized as one concerned with the seizure of goods, things and even life in order precisely to suppress or put an end to it. According to Foucault, a radical shift in this form of power has occurred. An example can be seen in power's role in levying taxes, which, although still happens, has ceased to play a central function. Instead, such activities appear to be:

> Merely one element among others, rather than one dedicated to impeding them, making them submit, or destroying them. There has been a parallel shift in the right of death, or at least a tendency to align itself with the exigencies of a life-administering power and to define itself accordingly. This death that was based on the right of the sovereign is now manifested as simply the reverse of the right of the social body to ensure, maintain, or develop its life.[48]

The sovereign's concern, in other words, begins to shift to one less concerned with putting to death, as it were, to one focused on 'making live'; a kind of perpetual power focused on the administration and fostering of life as such. A key problem during the classical period was the question of how to govern, how to establish a relation between politics and strategy, essentially, a problem of management over the relations of force. This classical model of sovereignty was based on territory, reliant on spectacular displays of violence to demonstrate its power and force and defined by the sovereign's right to kill and let live in defence of the territory and principality. Here, the sovereign acts on behalf of the people, represents the people and enacts law on their behalf. The law, in this sense, demands obedience such that any transgression is met with severe punishment. For Foucault, sovereign power, or the mode of power which characterized the classical period, has undergone a transformation. That is not to say that it has been replaced entirely, but rather that it is now complemented by a different mode of power: one less concerned with the territory and instead, as we mentioned earlier, with life and population, precisely in order to both understand its tendencies and intervene in them.

Under this new mode of power, the manner in which sovereignty can be said to 'conduct' itself is rather different. At the outset, it can be briefly described as one not limited to a strictly *negative* display of force but effectuates a kind of '*positive*' influence; where obedience is strongly encouraged, and direct commands take on the guise of invitations. More specifically, Foucault refers to two modes of power: discipline and governmentality. What becomes apparent is a connectedness between sovereignty, discipline and governmentality, where, for Foucault:

> We need to see things not in terms of the replacement of a society of sovereignty by a disciplinary society and the subsequent replacement of a disciplinary society by a society of government; in reality one has a triangle, sovereignty-discipline-government, which has as its primary target the population and as its essential mechanism the apparatuses of security.[49]

In the present context, we will look at Foucault's development of the notion of biopolitics and with a particular emphasis on the functioning of 'governmentality' and leave aside the notion of discipline.[50] In doing so we direct our attention to what it could mean for this new power to *administer* life.

As we have already seen, there has been a shift away from the sovereign rule over territory to one concerned primarily with life, with men and things, and with men in their relations to and with things. As Foucault explains:

> The things, in this sense, with which government is to be concerned are in fact men, but men in their relations, their links, their imbrication with those things that are wealth, resources, means of subsistence, the territory with its specific qualities, climate, irrigation, fertility, and so on; men in their relation to those other things that are customs, habits, ways of acting and thinking and so on; and finally men in their relation to those still other things that might be accidents and misfortunes such as a famine, epidemics, death, and so on.[51]

This form of government does not do away with notions of property and territory, rather these become one or two variables; there is an entire ecosystem which now necessitates, at least, equal attention. Foucault gives us the example the governing of a ship, which might entail taking charge of the boat and its navigation, as well as responsibility over the sailors, the environment, establishing relations with crew and managing cargo. Government is distinguished from sovereignty in this context in that government acts towards particular ends, and is not simply an end in itself, or at least a form of general common good (obedience of divine law or laws of nature). According to a system of governmentality, the correct disposition of men and things implies more than the idea of a 'common good', that things are put to convenient or economic use. With governmentality, a multiplicity of aims and specific goals emerge and proliferate, thus necessitating a so-called correct disposition of things. It is no longer sufficient to ensure obedience to laws (although this continues to be important), but rather laws as such are put to a new *use*. As Foucault articulates it, it is a matter 'of employing tactics rather than laws, and even using laws themselves as tactics – to arrange things in such a way that, through a certain number of means, such-and-such ends may be achieved'.[52] Within this schema, the role of the sovereign changes from violent and spectacular displays of power to embodying patience and wisdom; it is no longer a display of force and the right to kill which is important. The sovereign must instead show wisdom and *knowledge*. Here, it is a question of what Foucault identifies to be a particular 'art of government', which, despite appearances, is not an entirely abstract idea. Rather, the notion can be understood as having emerged alongside key developments in the domain of knowledge, broadly speaking. We saw earlier how man as such began to be the bearer and source of all knowledge, of all law, even retroactively re-situating a history of himself to a degree that had previously been unimaginable. Similarly, in the sixteenth century, the idea of government, and governing as such, drew interest from more than those explicitly engaging in it. The 'art of government' that developed is inextricably tied up with the development of a kind of administrative apparatus of the state. As Foucault explains:

> It was connected to a set of analyses and forms of knowledge that began to develop in the late sixteenth century and grew in importance during the seventeenth. These were essentially to do with knowledge of the state, in all its different elements, dimensions, and factors of power, questions that were termed precisely 'statistics', meaning the science of the state. [. . .] the art of government finds its first form of crystallization, organised around the theme of reason of state [. . .] the state is governed according to rational principles that are intrinsic to it and cannot be derived solely from natural or divine laws or the principles of wisdom and prudence. The state, like nature, has its own proper form of rationality, albeit of a different sort.[53]

The emergence of statistics and classical probability opened up the possibility for the investigation of a new set of problems, thus giving rise to new objects of study, not only the creation and development of the concept of 'population', but also enabling the observation of more precise delineations within it. That is to say, delineations of segments of the population thus inviting, soliciting, key interventions within it. In other words, this new schema is less reliant on transcendental rules or grand moral or ethical claims for its own rationality, and instead finds 'the principles of its rationality in that which constitutes the specific reality of the state'.[54] Population as such, and its necessary counterpart, statistics, re-orients the question of government and enables the emergence of new problems defined and understood, for the first time, in scientific terms, so that statistics now enabled the construction of a societal topology, enabling the state to gaze into a mirror of itself. As Alain Desrosières explains, what was previously thought to have been unknown (and even inconceivable) became an object of knowledge, and, inevitably, a cause of intervention and modification. Specialized administrative bureaus that would emerge as a result 'allowed the new objects created by this state practice to be grasped and compared at a single glance'.[55] The family, transformed from the model of government of the household, now becomes a key aspect internal to the population as such, a segment, and a key instrument of governmental intervention.

In terms of management of the population, the role of government is transformed from one of 'good government' for the 'common good' to one concerned with the welfare of the population:

> The improvement of its condition, the increase of its wealth, longevity, health; and so on; and the means the government uses to attain these ends are themselves all, in some sense, immanent to the population; it is the population itself on which government will act either directly through large-scale campaigns, or indirectly, through techniques that will make possible, without the full awareness of the people, the stimulation of birth rates, the directing of the flow of population into certain regions or activities, and so on.[56]

Together these form part of a new tactic or art of government; the intricacies and details of which had previously been not simply unknown, but beyond the remit of sovereignty entirely. It is in this sense that we should understand what Foucault meant by 'modern man is an animal whose politics places his existence as a living being in question'. This new state rationality begins to occupy, or 'capture', all aspects of man's conduct and relation to things: aptitudes, attitudes, beliefs and essentially aspects to do with processes of subjectification and desubjectification.

Additionally, the knowledge of the population that statistics gives rise to produces a new understanding of the whole concept of economy, more specifically developing what we now understand to be issues of political economy. The latter will come to take its form as the particular technique through which the government will explain its intervening processes within a particular field of reality.[57] Where, 'this state of government, which is grounded in its population and which refers and has resort to the instrumentality of economic knowledge, would correspond to a society controlled by apparatuses of security'.[58] This new power that Foucault describes emerged during the eighteenth century to take life itself as the primary object of both political and economic activity: a focus, then, on making life itself productive and a new emphasis of care over the biological life of the species emerged. This new power is concerned not only with the population as a whole but also with the individual body; concerned with how it should behave and be disciplined. The old sovereign emphasis on regimes of territory and land now shifts to one concerned with the security of population from potential contamination. This new power, less concerned with the right of death, now comes to be understood as being concerned with 'making live, and letting die', drawing from a new domain of knowledge, knowledge of the population as such.

In the final seminar of *Society Must Be Defended*, on 17 March 1976, Foucault makes more explicit the link between state racism and biopolitics. Foucault begins by revisiting the premise of his theory of biopower, which is understood within the particular historical context of the nineteenth century. Here, Foucault says that power's particular novelty was the interest over life in a way that had been unprecedented. Such that 'power over man' focused on man as a living being, where 'the biological came under State control, that there were at least a certain tendency that leads to what might be termed State control of the biological'.[59]

This gives rise to the problem of the relationship between racism and the question of State sovereignty, which is of interest to us here. Fundamentally, how did it become possible to think these two together? Foucault goes further and asks:

What does it mean to say that racism takes off in the sixteenth or seventeenth century, and to relate racism solely to the problems of the State and sovereignty, when it is well known that, after all, religious racism (and religious anti-Semitism in particular) had been in existence since the Middle Ages?[60]

For Foucault, the basic problem is a matter of examining Western institutions, the State, and the mechanisms of power that elicit a kind of permanent war in a peaceful form. As we saw, to understand these mechanisms Foucault relies on Hobbes' theory of sovereignty: 'who said that war is both the basis of power relations and the principle that explains them.'[61] We should recall that in the classical theory of sovereignty, the sovereign's role could be understood as one privileged with the ability to grant the right of life and death; however, this right is always unbalanced, and 'the balance is always tipped in favour of death'.[62] A gradual transformation occurred that Foucault traces through changes in technologies and *techniques* of power. In the seventeenth century, these new powers saw the emergence of a new object of interest, that of the individual body, and the techniques of power were mobilized to ensure their proper spatial distribution: their surveillance.[63] Therefore, the Reason of State power begins to be complemented by a new power emerging in the mid-eighteenth century, one applied to man as living being, and as species. As Foucault explains:

> After a first seizure of power over the body in an individualising mode, we have a second seizure of power that is not individualising but, if you like, massifying, that is directed not at man-as-body but as man as species. After the anatamo-politics of the human body established in the course of the eighteenth century, we have, at the end of that century, the emergence of something that is no longer anatamo-politics of the human body, but what I would call a 'biopolitics' of the human race.[64]

This new technology of power, or 'biopolitics', examines various trends belonging to segments of the population (e.g. birth rates, death rates, the ratio between them, among others), and in turn gives rise to a new set of political and economic problems, each demanding solutions and differing modes of intervention within these populations. Demographers begin to measure and mathematize these 'problems' in statistical terms, and for the first time it becomes possible to quantify and measure 'progress'. Assigning a value to life not to value life and the living as such but precisely to decide upon the *dispensable*. Foucault points out that it is at this moment that something like 'natalist' policies become possible, and, in many ways, become the focal point of political life. At this point, at the end of the eighteenth century, a new approach to biological threats begins to emerge, where it is no longer the threat of epidemics that is at issue but rather potential for endemics, such that it was the:

> Permanent factors which [. . .] sapped the population's strength, shortened the working week, wasted energy, and cost money, [. . .] In other words, illness as phenomena affecting a population. Death was no longer something that suddenly swooped down on life – as in an epidemic. Death was now something permanent, something that slips into life, perpetually gnaws at it, diminishes it and weakens it.[65]

This new form of power begins to function through, and alongside with, new knowledges like medicine and concerns over environmental health to, for instance, manage issues of public hygiene in a particularly urban context: a collaboration between the biological health of the population and the management of poverty as such. In this sense we see how power exercises an ostensibly 'positive' influence over the care and management of the life of the population. For Foucault, the key questions to consider within this schema are:

> If it is true that the power of sovereignty is increasingly on the retreat and that disciplinary or regulatory disciplinary power is on the advance, how will the power to kill and the function of murder operate in this technology of power, which takes life as both its object and its objective? How can a power such as this kill, if it is true that its basic function is to improve life, to prolong its duration, to improve its chances, to avoid accidents, and to compensate for failings? [. . .] *Given*

that this power's objective is essentially to make live, how can it let die? How can the power of death, the function of death, be exercised in a political system centered upon biopower?[66]

If power's role is essentially one of care over the population, to 'make live, how can it let die?' For Foucault, the answer to this can be found in the newly emerging complicity between biology and the state, the insertion or capture of the biological into the political; such that 'modern man is an animal whose politics places his existence as a living being in question'. Foucault's analysis develops into an enquiry into 'state racism', that is, though racism as such has always been said to exist, it is the first time that racism is 'inscribed in the mechanisms of the state'.[67] That is to say that biopolitics is also concerned with the relation between the human race, 'or human beings insofar as they are a species, insofar as they are living beings, and their environment, the milieu in which they live'.[68] How can racism as such be said to function in this context? Put simply, biopolitics works on the basis of the insertion of breaks into the domain of life, delineating and arranging segments within the population so as to distinguish 'between what must live and what must die. The appearance within the biological continuum of the human race of races, the distinction among races, the hierarchy of races, the fact that certain races are described as good and that others, in contrast, are described as inferior'.[69] Such that the function of racism is one of delineation, fragmentation and of creating breaks within the population. The relation, in other words, is a biologically determined one, with the aim of facilitating a distinction between the normal and the abnormal, the healthy and the sick and those who must live and those who must die in order for others to live.

Racism, then, appears to be the pre-condition upon which the idea of state sanctioned 'elimination' becomes acceptable. And the idea of 'normalization',[70] for its part, becomes inseparable from techniques of state racism, so that from biopolitics a normalizing of the techniques of exposure to death emerges. As Foucault writes:

> Racism first develops with colonisation, or in other words, with colonising genocide. If you are functioning in the biopower mode,

how can you justify the need to kill people, to kill populations, and to kill civilisations? By using the themes of evolutionism, by appealing to racism.[71]

For Foucault, a biopolitics of this kind would not be possible without the collaboration between power and particular domains of knowledge, more specifically, between biological theory, evolutionism and the discourse of power. During the nineteenth century, theories of evolution popularized notions of hierarchy and natural selection which became easily transcribed into political terms, where the two would eventually become indistinguishable. These became normalized in discussions over:

> The relations of colonisation, the necessity for wars, criminality, the phenomena of madness and mental illness, the history of societies with their different classes and so on. Whenever, in other words, there was a confrontation, a killing or the risk of death, the nineteenth century was quite literally obliged to think about them in the form of evolutionism.[72]

Most notably, we see the emergence of these techniques in the attempt to transpose scientific knowledge onto the sphere of the social. The Eugenics of the nineteenth century functioned in close collaboration with liberal political economy and statistics to develop a so-called social Darwinism; normalizing, for example, the idea that 'poverty, crime and stupidity arose from the hereditary weakness of the poor, the criminal and the mentally-defective'.[73] So that the transcription of political discourse onto the terrain of evolutionary biology and biological terms broadly conceived transformed the way in which societal and historical questions came to be understood.[74]

As Foucault explains, 'by using themes of evolutionism' it became possible to justify 'the need to kill people, to kill populations, and to kill civilisations'.[75] It is in this sense that one can understand the relations between war, racism and the death-function characteristic of the biopolitical mode of power that Foucault sees as intricately connected to discourses of political and economic liberalism. As Foucault articulates it:

The specificity of modern racism, or what gives it its specificity, is not bound up with mentalities, ideologies, or the lies of power. *It is bound up with the technique of power, with the technology of power.* [. . .] We are dealing with a mechanism that allows biopower to work. So racism is bound up with the workings of a State that is obliged to use race, the elimination of races and the purification of the race, to exercise its sovereign power. The juxtaposition of – or the way biopower functions through – the old sovereign power of life and death implies the workings, the introduction and activation, of racism.[76]

In this sense one can make the connection between 'colonizing genocide' and the Nazi Regime; both relied upon the activation of racism and its sanctioning through precise *techniques* and *technologies* of power: both disciplinary power and biopower.[77] It is these ideas that Foucault developed concerning the administration and care for life, and the simultaneous power of death, which Agamben draws on in his own analyses over the significance of biopolitics for our contemporary politics. Where, similarly for Agamben, 'if there is a line in every modern state marking the point at which the decision on life becomes a decision on death, and biopolitics can turn into thanatopolitics, this line no longer appears today as a stable border dividing two clearly distinct zones'.[78] Here, Agamben follows Foucault's insights concerning the fact that sovereignty enters 'into an intimate symbiosis not only with the jurist but also with the doctor, the scientist, the expert, and the priest'.[79] Where it is clear that in the administration of life, a biopolitical power is not only reliant on a sovereign model, but more importantly functions on the basis of key techniques and technologies of power (e.g. juridical, medical, biological, and other knowledge[s]). Today, we see this thanapolitical potential at play in the liberal discourse on assisted dying, particularly with reference to Canada's MAID (medical assistance in dying) programme. This controversial programme allows not only those with terminal illness to apply for the scheme but those with non-fatal conditions and those living in poverty, who the Canadian government describes as potentially dying from 'not naturally foreseeable' consequences.[80] We see the eugenic potential inscribed in liberalism in this schema, not as an outlier, as something that exists outside of the liberal and biopolitical modality, but as something that co-exists with it, functioning as the condition of its own possibility.

Within this schema, it becomes possible to understand Foucault's description of 'modern man', as 'an animal whose politics places his existence as a living being in question'. As Agamben also points out, traditional political distinctions such as Right and Left lose their distinction at precisely this moment, where 'biological life and its needs had become the politically decisive fact' and where 'the only real question to be decided was which form of organisation would be best suited to the task of assuring the care, control, and use of bare life'.[81] It is in this sense that it becomes possible to say that contemporary politics has become biopolitics. Agamben illustrates this in relation to the collaboration of biologico-scientific techniques and the political order, as well as contemporary juridical phenomena such as the declaration of rights. It is a matter of the complete politicization of life, following, crucially, the isolation and capture of something that is impossible to fully grasp. It is this isolation and capture of the inappropriable to which we now turn; our analysis shifts to Agamben's archaeology of politics, which concerns an essentially *conceptual* splitting of the notion of life: into a politically qualified life (*bios*), and biological life (*zoè*).

3

Life
A fragile threshold

It's perhaps not without irony that while Agamben has dedicated a good amount of his writing to outlining the perils of making distinctions between a political life on the one side and a biological life on the other, the main criticism levied against him is that, in articulating this Aristotelian ontological inheritance and how it functions, he in fact endorses this separation. Moreover, that in articulating sovereign power's reduction of life to bare life and life directed to survival, that it is Agamben himself suggesting that life can be described as bare and without qualities. All the while, for Agamben, the opposite is the case.

Unlike Foucault's development of the concept of biopolitics, for Agamben, this is not a recent phenomenon: that is, it is not something that emerges with the advent of liberal and economic thought in the mid-eighteenth and early nineteenth century. As already mentioned, Foucault's analysis connects a mode of power to a novel technique of governance concerned with a new object of knowledge: population. The development of population is inextricably tied up with the emergence of statistics and the human sciences. Without these forms of knowledge, something like the administration of life would not be able to take place to the unprecedented degree that characterizes our present conjuncture, nor would we be able to conceptualize power's ostensibly 'positive' or active exercise over life. An important caveat is to say that it is not a matter of denunciation or praise, but rather to better grasp how it is that we arrived at this mode of social organization, and what implications, if any, this might have on our politics.

While Agamben is largely in agreement with Foucault's understanding of biopolitics, and the latter's delineation of its use as a technique for the administration of life, via discipline and governmentality, the use of statistics and normalization, Agamben's schema is not confined to a particular historical epoch. Rather, for Agamben, biopolitics has always been a characteristic feature of Western philosophy and politics. For this reason, Agamben's *Homo Sacer* project is described as an archaeology of politics: one aimed at unravelling how the idea of living and living well came to be two distinct modes of life, and how political life and biological life came to be thought separately with increasing attempts aimed at their subsequent unifications. As Agamben writes:

> The archaeology of politics that was in question in the 'Homo Sacer' project did not propose to critique or correct this or that concept, this or that institution of Western politics. The issue was rather to call into question the place and the very originary structures of politics, in order to bring to light the *arcanum imperii* that in some way constituted its foundation and that had remained at the same time fully exposed and tenaciously hidden in it. [. . .] The originary structure of Western politics consists in an *ex-ceptio*, in an inclusive exclusion of human life in the form of bare life.[1]

This is the context of Agamben's writings, which seeks to unravel philosophical assumptions of the 'presupposition', the origin or the foundation in the Western metaphysical tradition. Though this challenge is not one that in turn seeks to recuperate an origin, or found this, or that, grounding, since it is this manner of thinking that engenders the need for a presupposition in the first place. Indeed, it is through the structure of the presupposition that the dual articulation between nature and *logos*, body and soul, animality and humanity, that the Western metaphysical tradition has been characterized.[2] Political philosophy, too, has followed this tradition; inasmuch as politics has always been thought in the structure of the relation between two elements, such as bare life and power, the household and the city, that, as we will see, it then seeks to link together.[3] It is for this reason that

Agamben's thought on politics cannot be separated from the question of ontology, such that politics is metaphysical and vice versa. Pertinent for us, therefore, will be to clarify the nature of the presupposition that is at work, and, importantly, to examine how it has come to shape our conceptualization of life and politics.

For Agamben, the notion of biopolitics is connected to the very conceptualization of the living being, including the human being. The conceptualization of the human being is articulated through ceaseless divisions and caesuras. Agamben shows this through the now well-known classical distinction between *zoè* and *bios* – both terms used to refer to life. To sum up this articulation, *zoè* can be understood as that which is common to all living beings, and *bios* describes a life of qualities, a mode of life of individuals or groups. In Aristotle's conceptualization of politics, natural life or *zoè* is excluded from participation in the *polis*, just as the perfect community is defined by 'opposing the simple fact of living (*to zēn*) to politically qualified life (*to eu zēn*)'.[4]

This is the essential question that Agamben is concerned with: how did politics come to constitute itself on the basis of an exclusion, which functions on the basis of an inclusion? To answer this, Agamben illustrates the inheritance of an Aristotelian conceptualization of life that has come to shape our politics and culture. This articulation of life, founded on negativity and the exclusion of what is essentially an inseparable part of life or the living, is what is understood to be the biopolitical gesture. Opposed to this, the point is to conceptualize a notion of life that is free from presupposition and where it is impossible to separate a 'bare' life from life itself.

Originally published in Italy in 1995, *Homo Sacer* both popularized Agamben's political philosophy and led to much confusion over the terms used by Agamben to convey the sense and meaning of his project. Most notably is the confusion over the notion of 'bare life', which some have interpreted as a pejorative term that Agamben uses to connote an 'empty life' that those on the margins of society are seemingly condemned to, apparently 'devoid' of joy, meaning or any qualities. This is not what Agamben means when he employs the term. Rather, 'bare life' is a fictional concept precisely produced by the articulation of the biopolitical machine, or sovereign exception. As Agamben explains:

> There are not *first* life as a natural biological given and anomie as the state of nature, and *then* their implication in law through the state of exception. On the contrary, the very possibility of distinguishing life and law, anomie and *nomos*, coincides in their articulation in the biopolitical machine. Bare life is a product of the machine and not something that pre-exists it, just as law has no court in nature or in the divine mind. Life and law, anomie and *nomos*, *auctoritas* and *potestas*, result from the fracture of something to which we have no other access than through the fiction of their articulation and the patient work that, by unmasking this fiction, separates what it had claimed to unite.[5]

What is produced in the sovereign exception is the simultaneous isolation, exclusion and inclusion of an aspect of human life – where in the kaleidoscope of human life something is captured and isolated as an object, as a result of sovereign decision-making. 'Bare life' in this sense does not precede a sovereign decision, but rather it is its by-product. Life, on the contrary, cannot be said to be bare and without qualities. So, 'bare life' is not a figure of alterity or an 'other' as such who exists in the world, and that it is our task to uncover and make speak or save. Rather, a useful way to conceptualize 'bare life' is through the notion of the incorporeal. Deleuze and Félix Guattari's illustration of the incorporeal transformation that results in the juridical trial is helpful in this context. Indeed, in this case, it is precisely the judge's sentence that transforms the accused into a convict:

> The transformation of the accused into a convict is a pure instantaneous act or incorporeal attribute that is the expressed of the judge's sentence. [. . .] The incorporeal transformation is recognisable by its instantaneousness, its immediacy, by the simultaneity of the statement expressing the transformation and the effect the transmission produces.[6]

This notion of an incorporeal transformation can also be seen in Agamben's exposition of the *Homo Sacer*: that sacred figure of archaic

Roman law. For this, Agamben draws on Pompeius Festus' treatise *On the Significance of Words*, where Festus describes the sacred man as 'the one whom the people have judged on account of a crime'.[7] Festus adds that 'it is not permitted to sacrifice this man, yet he who kills him will not be condemned for homicide'.[8] In other words, following the judgement of the accused person, the person becomes sacred (*sacer esto*) and is *transformed* into a *Homo Sacer*.[9] The accused man in question is rendered *Homo Sacer* following the judgement; the result is an incorporeal transformation of the body.

Life-distilling machine

Originally published in 2002, *The Open: Man and Animal* curiously does not form part of Agamben's *Homo Sacer* project, though it is continually referred to in the project's concluding text *The Use of Bodies* (2016). *The Open* lays out key concepts, including the notion of the anthropological machine and anthropogenesis through which biopolitics can be better conceptualized. The often-formulated distinction between man and animal is marked by ambiguity. If such a division exists, on what basis can the parameters be decided? And, before a distinction can be made between one form-of-life and others, how have we come to decide and define what life is? Though no precise definition can be given to the notion of life,[10] it is not to say that knowledge and life are necessarily at odds with one another. According to Georges Canguilhem, the tension or conflict 'is not between thought and life in man, but between man and the world in the human consciousness of life'.[11] Therefore, the tension lies in the uncertainty human beings find in and amidst life, or a milieu. Indeed, Canguilhem writes: 'from there it follows that man sometimes marvels at the living and sometimes, scandalised at being himself a living being, forges for his own use the idea of a separate kingdom.'[12] For Canguilhem, knowledge as such cannot avoid its search for meaning, and life as such cannot exist independently of knowledge. So that while knowledge of life assists human beings to negotiate a particular milieu, life also *produces* knowledge and is not simply an *object* of knowledge. In this way, an understanding of the notion of life cannot be said to be one of a purely medical understanding, or scientific, but rather to be closely associated with a historical, philosophical and even literary conceptualization. Agamben argues that in the tradition of Western culture, the concept of 'life' has always been philosophico-political rather than explicitly medico-scientific.[13] Agamben employs numerous examples to show this, one of which is through an investigation of the Hippocratic Corpus; a collection of early ancient Greek medical works by the physician Hippocrates and his teachings. A close examination of the Corpus' index reveals that the term '*zoè*' (natural life) occurs just eight times. This indicates, for Agamben, that the authors of this work were more concerned with the details of the human body: for example, nourishment, health and illnesses. The authors were able to pursue their enquiries without endowing the concept of 'life' with any specificities or functions. In fact, the details concerning life imply an emphasis on what can be said to be 'living', such that their analysis seems to have more to do with the eventual characteristics of the living that in the end constitute the notion of 'life' rather than any articulation of what life as such is.

However, while the concept 'life' is undefined, its articulations are boundless. Life is also divided in the manner in which it is articulated, through a number of scissions and oppositions which then form the basis upon which 'life' is subsequently understood in the medical, and biological sciences, as well as in politics, philosophy and theology. According to Agamben, in our culture at least, 'everything happens as if . . . life were *what cannot be defined, yet, precisely for this reason, must be ceaselessly articulated and divided*'.[14] Life, in other words, appears to be understood through an articulation of a *primary* scission, as a way of distinguishing what can be said to be *living*. Agamben shows this notion to have its roots in ancient philosophy, and more precisely in the Aristotelian interpretation of life.

In *De anima*, Aristotle defines life only by way of isolating the nutritive function, or nutritive life – of which it is then a matter of 'adding', along with other faculties or potentials in the living, in order to constitute life.[15] In this way, for Aristotle, the concept of 'living' is articulated through a number of faculties, including 'reason, perception, motion and rest with respect to place, and further the motion in relation to nourishment, decay, and growth'.[16] Such that, when it comes to plants, they belong, according to Aristotle, to a part of the soul (called nutritive potential) that is common to all other living beings. Agamben points out that Aristotle does not in fact define what life is; rather, Aristotle follows:

> His customary strategy [. . .] dividing it thanks to the isolation of the nutritive function, in order then to rearticulate it into a series of distinct and correlative potentials or faculties (nutrition, sensation, thought). One of the ways in which life is said is separated from the others in order to constitute in this way the principle by means of which life can be attributed to a certain being. What has been separated and divided off (in this case, nutritive life) is precisely what permits one to construct the unity of life as a hierarchical articulation of a series of faculties and functional oppositions, whose ultimate meaning is not only psychological but immediately political.[17]

By dividing life and isolating the nutritive function in this way, Aristotle is not necessarily enquiring what 'living' or 'life' as such might mean. Rather, Aristotle inaugurates a way of thinking that privileges the following question: through what modes, faculties or potentials is it possible to belong to a species? This, in a sense, introduces the conceptualization of the human being as something that one can *attain* through a series of identifications or qualifications. The obverse of this also becomes true, so that without a certain set of qualifications someone's belonging to the species might be called into question. For this reason, Agamben argues that this division and separation of nutritive life is 'immediately political', since for Aristotle, part of the soul is in itself nutritive life, and therefore is not thought to participate in reason. Rather, according to this schema, nutritive life represents something that is not *truly* human, and, accordingly, is necessarily excluded from happiness, virtue and politics.[18] In this sense, there always exists something that is inextricably part of life that is at the same time continually subject to a decision of capture, scission and exclusion. Whereas, on the contrary, for Agamben, nutritive life is just as important to the conception of the human being. It is a misconception to suggest that Agamben dismisses nutritive life in favour of something like a political life. In fact, Agamben says that it is important to think nutritive life 'as what allows the living to reach the state toward which it tends, as the conatus that drives every being to preserve its being'.[19] It is inseparable from living.

This separation of nutritive life represents a major turning point in Western science.[20] For example, Agamben shows that the French biologist Xavier Bichat, writing in the eighteenth century, uses Aristotle's separation of nutritive life in order to formulate his own thesis on the distinction between so-called animal life and organic life.[21] In *Physiological Researches on Life and Death*, Bichat draws a distinction between the conscious and unconscious functions of the animal, granting the former a higher status than the latter, such that the animal in this sense would be defined by its relation to the external world.[22] It is the latter form-of-life that, according to Bichat, can be considered to be 'animal life'. Bichat goes on to explain that 'the series of the phenomena of these two lives, relate to the individual'.[23] That is to say that these two 'lives' exist together in the human being, though they do not coincide.[24] In this sense, the distinction between animal life and organic life, or 'man' and animal, is also understood to be an *internal* scission, where only by first identifying and defining animal life is the becoming human of the human being made possible, and 'only because his distance and proximity to the animal have been measured and recognised first of all in the closest and most intimate place'.[25] The key question is: how does this internal division, or scission, within man or the human being, play out? For Agamben, the mystery is not the conjunction of both elements, of animal life and organic life, or body and soul, but rather the 'political mystery of separation'. As Agamben says:

> What is man, if he is always the place – and, at the same time, the result – of ceaseless divisions and caesurae? It is more urgent to work

on these divisions, to ask in what way – within man – has man been separated from non-man, and the animal from the human, than it is to take positions on the great issues, on so-called human rights and values. And perhaps even the most luminous sphere of our relations with the divine depends, in some way, on that darker one which separates us from the animal.[26]

For example, for Agamben, a politics of human rights is necessarily predicated upon the division and separation of being into human and non-human. The caesura – that is, occurring within man – is an internal division common to all human beings. That is to say the notion of human rights functions on the premise of a presupposed excluded category, and where something like juridical rights then works to tie them together.[27] For this reason, Agamben proposes a shift in perspective, and for the analysis to turn from the question of how something like a 'body' and a 'soul' could be joined together, to one that asks instead: how was it possible for them to be separated in the first place?

It seems then, that the caesura that characterizes life passes through or within the human being herself. Such that what can be considered human, or not, is dependent upon this internal scission between a so-called vegetative function and the animal within – which then enables, more broadly, the dichotomy between 'man' and other living things to be established and decided.[28] However, such categorizations and delineations have always been arbitrary. For instance, Agamben shows that in France during the Ancien Régime, the boundaries between man and other living things were far more uncertain and ambiguous than they appeared to be later in the nineteenth century with the birth of the human sciences. Indeed, for the former, comparing man to creatures of mythology was not out of the norm, nor was ascribing language to animals, like parrots.[29] This is the operation of the anthropological machine, that each time decides on the moment of division, or separation of what constitutes animality or humanity. Crucially, this is not something that is decided once and for all, nor is it temporally fixed. In this case, Agamben is highlighting the functioning of the machine prior to the advent of modernity. It is a process by which an 'inside' is produced through the inclusion of the 'outside', it is a process of humanizing the animal as with the example of the speaking parrot, or the idea of the *enfant sauvage* (feral child) which was a popular theme during the Ancien Régime.[30] In modernity, as we have seen, the anthropological machine functions by an animalization of the human, that is, where 'the outside is produced through the exclusion of an inside', by 'isolating the inhuman within the human'.[31] It is in this way that the production of something like man necessitates a so-called metaphysico-political operation that enables man to be decided upon and produced by the anthropological machine.[32]

If this is the case, then a usually unfathomable ambiguity concerning our own taxonomical reference – as homo sapiens – becomes not only fathomable but its conception as a simple 'category' shifts to something much more significant, that is, the result of a life-distilling machine, a 'machine or device for producing the recognition of the human'.[33] Moreover, the human and the animal are defined in a functional relationship to each other, such that one is human to the extent that one is not animal, and vice versa. It is this machinic production that encapsulates the notion of anthropogenesis; where the institutions of human culture (for example, religion or law) can be thought of as attempts to organize and establish the becoming human of the living being. This is presented as an originary moment, where man as a human being is recognized as a being opposed to the animal – where the faculty of language, for instance, acts as a marker of difference. While the zoologist and philosopher Ernst Haeckel claimed, through a reconstruction of evolutionary history, to have discovered the missing link between the primate and the human being in the form of the 'ape-man' or *Pithecanthropus alalus*, Agamben argues that this category was only made thinkable through the idea of language as a uniquely human faculty or attribute.[34] In other words, by contrasting an 'ape-man' with a 'man-ape', the leap to a full-fledged man was made possible through the presupposition of language, with language considered as a distinguishing faculty (distinct from animals) which could, in hindsight, function as a marker between our non-speaking evolutionary cousins. As Agamben formulates it: 'in identifying himself with language, the speaking man places his own muteness outside of himself, as already and not yet human.'[35]

Therefore, it would seem that what differentiates Man from animal is language, though Agamben explains that 'this is not a natural given [. . .] it is, rather, a historical production which, as such, can be properly assigned neither to man nor to animal'.[36] Moreover, Agamben shows that if this difference is taken away, then, along with it goes the distinction between man and animal. For this reason:

> We imagine a nonspeaking *man* – *Homo alalus*, precisely – who would function as a bridge that passes from the animal to the human. But all evidence suggests that this is only a shadow cast by language, a presupposition of speaking man, by which we always obtain only an animalization of man (an animal-man, like Haeckel's ape-man) or a humanization of the animal (a man-ape). The animal-man and man-animal are the two sides of a single fracture, which cannot be mended from either side.[37]

This self-referential contradiction was equally recognized by the linguist Heymann Steinthal, who, in attempting to formulate a pre-linguistic stage of humanity, landed on the following conclusion: 'I set man up first and then had him produce language.'[38] For Agamben, a similar contradiction defines the anthropological machine – such that the human is always already presupposed, and hence the production of man through a man/animal dichotomy entails an exclusion which is necessarily included and an inclusion that is already excluded.[39] The anthropological machine (both the modern and the ancient) functions in order to always already produce a zone of indeterminacy, of the missing link. This 'missing link' is, in turn, 'always lacking because it is already virtually present'.[40] The suspension and capture of animal life in the living being in order for 'a rational human being' to occur is the key gesture at play. For Agamben, this means that Western politics has always been biopolitical.

Life and politics

What does it mean for man to be 'a living animal with the additional capacity for a political existence' and 'modern man is an animal whose politics places his existence as a living being in question'.[41] These words by Foucault that we encountered earlier and that feature in the introduction to Agamben's *Homo Sacer* aptly summarize what is at stake in biopolitics. As we saw earlier, Foucault's analysis emphasized the later part of the sentence; that, within a biopolitical paradigm, in modernity, life itself becomes an object of power, power is able to intervene by way of the becoming object of life itself thanks to tools emerging from the human sciences giving rise to the new concept of population. Intervention here is to be understood both as a positive fostering and an extreme exposure to death. Indeed, we had taken the first half of the sentence for granted and did not pause to question it. Yet for Agamben, the first is essential to think through, and the second half is only a logical consequence of the former. By looking more closely at the first part of the sentence we are able to broaden the analysis to consider the fact of the additional capacity for language, recalling an Aristotelian mode of problematization as well as the fact of life itself always being in question in our politics.

The entry of *zoè* into the sphere of the *polis* that constitutes, for Agamben, 'the decisive event of modernity'.[42] We could add that it is not merely the entry of *zoè* as such but more precisely the entry of *zoè* only *following* its identification, and subsequent isolation and splitting through different techniques and technologies of power – such that it is not at all evident where *zoè* ends and *bios* begins. It is this biopolitical horizon, characteristic of the politicization of life, which Agamben seeks to investigate and challenge.

According to Agamben:

> The inclusion of bare life in the political realm constitutes the original – if concealed – nucleus of sovereign power. *It can even be said that the production of a biopolitical body is the original activity*

of sovereign power. [. . .] Placing biological life at the center of its calculations, the modern State therefore does nothing other than bring to light the secret tie uniting power and bare life, thereby reaffirming the bond (derived from a tenacious correspondence between the modern and the archaic which one encounters in the most diverse spheres) between modern power and the most immemorial of the *arcana imperii*.[43]

It is precisely this 'secret tie uniting power and bare life' that Agamben seeks to thematize and eventually critique. In order to do this, Agamben seeks to understand the sense and meaning of Aristotle's definition of the *polis*, as one characterized by 'the opposition between life (*zēn*) and good life (*eu zēn*)'.[44] As we saw earlier, the opposition in question implies the fact that '*zoè*' is included in politically qualified life, such that it is implied that in a politically qualified life, the isolation, exclusion and re-inclusion of '*zoè*' has already taken place. Where, in other words, the isolation, exclusion and re-inclusion of '*zoè*' is the necessary precondition to a politically qualified life as such.

In 'The Human Being without Work,' an earlier chapter of *The Use of Bodies*, Agamben draws an analogy with the place of the slave in the ancient Greek polis as articulated by Aristotle. For Aristotle, although the slave is not considered to be a free person, with social and political rights, they are nonetheless not excluded from humanity. The slave, rather, is who makes possible a properly human life. So that the slave is not conceptualized as something 'other' than human, but one who is 'by nature of another' and that, while being human, 'is equipment, that is, a practical and separate instrument'.[45] The slave appears as being integrally part of the master, part of the 'whole' that constitutes the free person. It is not simply a question of ownership, but an integral part of the free person, 'as an organ is to the body'.[46] So that, in using the body of the slave, the master is effectively using his own body. Unlike the carpenter, whose praxis is defined by the work produced, the slave remains without 'work' – where the slave's praxis is not defined by any work produced but only by the use of the body. Agamben, surprised by this, notes that the classical world never considered human activity from the perspective of labour as such, but only from what was its result. 'Labour' only became recognizable as a juridical reality in contracts for *locatio operarum* in Roman law, or the usufruct of the slave. Indeed, the jurist and legal theorist Yan Thomas shows that Roman law did not necessarily take into account the *process* of work itself; the vocabulary used and multiple categories of what activities constituted work were vast, such that it would not be possible to construct a clear picture of what our concept of labour or work would mean in those terms.[47] In this sense, Thomas shows the incommensurable nature of social representation with juridical constructions. Some contracts adequately illustrated that the productive activity in question served to produce a defined product, while others instead isolated the 'act' of work itself and substantiated it as an entirely separate part treated as a commodity that would be bought and sold. In this sense, the law constructs its own object: labour, of which Roman society did not have a homogenous understanding. Interestingly, Thomas shows that the vocabulary associated with the notion of labour connoted intense suffering, a bodily suffering, rather than a kind of pleasant and productive activity. As Thomas says: 'like the Greek *ponos*, labour designates both work – and particularly toils in the field – and the suffering of soldiers in battle, the suffering of women in labour, in short, the fatigue inflicted on suffering bodies.'[48] Without going into too much detail, it seems that work as such is tied to the body of the slave, a body that is a proprietary object.[49] This work became recognizable in the *locatio operarum*, that is, the form in which an exchange is accomplished, where a certain temporal quantity of work is exchanged for a salary.[50] And, this work is considered unified and abstract – since the work is not tied to a specific result, but rather to a measurable quantity of work. In other words, Thomas shows that something akin to the labour of the slave can only emerge once there has been a conceptual separation between the use (*usus*) and the *fructus*,[51] such that, 'the use of the slave, even when the owner has ceded it to others, always remains inseparable from the use of his body'.[52] In this sense, the reason why something like a 'labour' emerges with the slave before its more traditional conceptualization as emerging with the artisan, precisely because the activity of the slave is not considered to be a proper work of *ergon*, but rather as *argos* and precisely deprived of work.[53] In this sense, one can better understand the status of the slave, as both excluded and included in humanity, 'as those not properly human beings who make it possible for others to be human'.[54] The slave then appears as:

> Both artificial instrument and human being, the slave properly belongs neither to the sphere of nature nor to that of convention, neither to the sphere of justice nor to that of violence. [. . .] The fact is that the slave, although excluded from political life, has an entirely special relation with it. The slave in fact represents a not properly human life that renders possible for others the *bios politikos*, that is to say, the truly human life. And if the human being is defined for the Greeks through a dialectic between *physis* and *nomos*, *zoè* and *bios*, then the slave, like bare life, stands at the threshold that separates and joins them.[55]

The slave then, as not exactly excluded but rather constitutively part of political life, is figured as the condition of possibility for a properly human life. Agamben argues that if Aristotle based the conceptualization of 'the human being' on the model of the free man, then the latter necessarily implies the slave as properly *a part* of him. The slave, then, can be understood as merely an instrument for life; one who is defined 'by means of this "use of the body," is the human being, that living being, who, though human, is excluded – and through this exclusion, included – in humanity, so that human beings can have a life, which is to say a political life'.[56]

This is the conceptualization that Western culture and philosophy has inherited, where the Western idea of the subject is constituted on the model of the 'free man', whose 'freedom' as such is dependent on the use of the slave's body, as an instrument for life and constitutively part of himself. As Agamben puts it:

Aristotle developed his idea of the human being starting from the paradigm of the free man, even if this latter implies the slave as his condition of possibility. One can imagine that he could have developed an entirely other anthropology if he had taken account of the slave (whose 'humanity' he never intended to negate). This means that, in Western culture, the slave is something like the repressed. The re-emergence of the figure of the slave in the modern worker thus appears, according to the Freudian scheme, as a return of the repressed in a pathological form.[57]

It is this idea of a politically qualified life that is dependent on the existence of a lesser, though necessarily still human, life that Agamben firmly rejects and problematizes. The inheritance of this model of the human being has as its necessary correlate the foundation of the *polis*. The *polis* is founded on the basis of the isolation, and exclusion, of bare life, which, in turn, stands as the zone of indistinction between 'natural life' and 'politically qualified life'. Bare or naked life stands at the threshold of *zoè* and *bios*, both separating and joining them together.

The human being must articulate its own *zoè* in some way (simple natural life, or animal voice) in order to *then* become capable of a political life. It is in this sense that there is an operation of 'politicization' of life as such. As Agamben says, 'what we call politics is above all a *special qualification of life*, carried out by means of a series of partitions that pass through the very body of *zoè*.'[58] For this reason, Agamben argues that the Aristotelian division of parts of the soul into nutritive, intellectual and sensitive faculties is not limited to one of psychological significance, but that it is also of an 'ontologico-political' quality. Indeed, it is not possible for these parts of the soul to be separated 'physically' or 'spatially'. These are only separable by the *logos*, and it is precisely 'this "logical" division' exercised on life that then opens the possibility for its subsequent politicization. So that:

> Politics, as the ergon *proper to the human, is the practice that is founded on the separation, worked by the* logos, *of otherwise inseparable functions*. Politics here appears as what allows one to treat a human life as if in it sensitive and intellectual life were separable from vegetative

life – and thus, since it is impossible in mortals, of legitimately putting it to death.[59]

In this sense, one can understand Foucault's characterization of biopolitics as a decision on life that is, at the same time, a decision on death. For this reason, Agamben is concerned with developing a notion of life where such a division is not possible.

Absolute immanence

For Agamben, what remains to be thought is a life conceptualized and lived without the possibility of ground or foundation in a not-yet human, or pre-human, where it is impossible to distinguish *zoè* and *bios*, in other words, a form-of-life. What can this mean? As Agamben puts it, a form-of-life:

> Defines a life – human life – in which the single ways, acts and processes of living are never simply facts but always and above all possibilities of life, always and above all power. Each behaviour and each form of human living is never prescribed by a specific biological vocation, nor is it assigned by whatever necessity; instead, no matter how customary, repeated, and socially compulsory, it always retains the character of a possibility; that is, it always puts at stake living itself. That is why human beings – as beings of power who can do or not do, succeed or fail, lose themselves or find themselves – are the only beings for whom happiness is always at stake in their living, the only beings whose life is irremediably and painfully assigned to happiness.[60]

That is, where one's life is its own possibility of being lived. This is not to say that such a life is immediately good or evil, a success or a failure, but that it simply *is*. Our contemporary moment is characterized by the fact that biological necessities (such as the need for shelter, nutrition and healthcare, among others) are tied to sovereign power, in an administration of life, which increasingly comes to define not just the possibilities of living but how life itself should be lived. Instead, what Agamben seeks to highlight is the possibility of life *as possibility*. That is to say, 'a potentiality that never exhausts itself in biographical facts and events, since it has no object other than itself. It is an absolute immanence that nevertheless *moves* and *lives*.'[61] In this moment, we can glean the profound influence Deleuze has on Agamben, for Deleuze it is precisely this point that marks the distinction between an individuality and a singularity. Agamben explains that 'while decisively rejecting the function of nutritive life in Aristotle as the ground of the attribution of a subjectivity, Deleuze nevertheless does not want to abandon the terrain of life, which he identifies with the plane of immanence'.[62]

Deleuze explains that individual life is tied to facts of life (as Agamben calls it), and as such are tied up with 'empirical determinations'.[63] This is unlike the singular life of infants who, Deleuze says, 'all resemble one another', and can be said to have little individuality as a result. And yet, 'they have singularities: a smile, a gesture, a funny face – not subjective qualities. Small children, through all their suffering and weaknesses, are infused with an immanent life that is pure power and even bliss.'[64] Similarly, Agamben points to the example of infants to illustrate the notion of form-of-life. Indeed, in a child, it is never possible to separate something like a 'bare life', 'it is never possible to isolate in a child something like bare life or biological life'.[65] Agamben explains that this is not because the life of the child is so far removed from reality and reserved to 'fantasy and games'. On the contrary, it is precisely because the child lives its physiological life in the closest proximity that it becomes 'indiscernible from it'. In other words, the child's life adheres uniquely to its own possibilities, 'the child plays with its physiological function, or, rather, *plays it*, and in this way, takes pleasure in it.'[66] In this way, it is an immanence 'that adheres neither to an identity nor to something, but solely to its own possibility and potentiality'.[67] Agamben illustrates this notion of a life inseparable from its form (often, irreparably so) in the life of Helen Grund Hessel, whose life was the subject of François Truffaut's *Jules et Jim* (1962). Here, Agamben refers to Hessel's diaries published nearly a decade after her death, in which 'beyond the extraordinary amorous events that are narrated there, a form of life testifies of itself with an absolutely incomparable intensity and immediacy'.⁶⁸ In other words, there is no distinction as such between the life that one lives, the totality of facts that make up an individual biography, and the 'the life by means of which we live [. . .] that which renders life livable and gives to it a sense and a form'.⁶⁹ There is a continual tension between these two, and yet, a continual striving towards their reunification. However, such a life remains difficult to realize, and examples of such a form-of-life are not evident. Indeed, Agamben says that Foucault had to look to police archives to find precisely lives that are inseparable from their form.⁷⁰ It is not a matter of discovering a life free of all antagonism, one necessarily consigned to success. While that remains a possibility, the possibility or potentiality itself is what is truly in question. Where the possibility exists for 'an experience in which the life that has been lived is identified without remainder with the life by which it has lived' even if, such a life, comes at 'the cost of losing all dignity and respectability'.⁷¹

In the real world

It has been suggested that Agamben and the theory of biopolitics more generally is out of touch with the 'real' world. Philosopher Benjamin Bratton describes Agamben and others as adhering to a dogmatic Heideggerian tradition, where, in the end, 'there is no Human as such, but only *Dasein*'.⁷² Moreover, Bratton denounces what he believes to be an advocacy of the 'foundational distinction between *zoe* and *bios*' so that 'the ones who insult and injure us are those who demand that a realm of supernatural commitments be protected as the zone where the most noble contemplation of the numinous supposedly resides'.⁷³ Bratton writes: 'The cultural and political accomplishments of what Agamben calls *bios* emerge from the physical dynamics of what he calls *zoe*'.⁷⁴ This is interesting since, although Bratton is an advocate of what is called a 'positive' biopolitics, he appears at the same time to be critical of the foundations upon which the concept of biopolitics is based, that is, premised on divisions and caesuras of the idea of 'life'. Though he does not realize this, as it does not seem that he fully grasped what is at stake in the concept, it might be straightforward for us to see why this is the case. Bratton appears to ascribe to Agamben the articulation of life as separable between a biological life and a politically qualified life, *zoè* and *bios*. As we have shown, however, for Agamben, these are inseparable. It is a biopolitical gesture to separate the two, a fictional separation at that since it is not at all clear where one's *bios* begins and *zoè* ends. As we have seen, the point, for Agamben, is to think life inseparably from its form in the manner of a form-of-life. For this reason, Agamben writes: 'In every case, in the idea of a "form-of-life," just like existence and essence, so also do *zoè* and *bios*, living and life contract into one another and fall together, allowing a third to appear, whose meaning and implications still remain for us to deliberate.'[75]

As to the question of the Heideggerian influence, that, Bratton says, 'there is no Human as such, but only *Dasein*',[76] for Agamben, on the contrary, Dasein remains caught up in a biopolitical paradigm and therefore falls short of what is required to think a form-of-life. Indeed, Agamben writes: 'Heidegger's posing again of the problem of being is a revival of Aristotelian ontology will remain up to the very end in solidarity with its aporias.'[77] This is because the 'being there' that Dasein implies is based on a presupposition of a not yet. That is, for Heidegger, the human being is a 'first step' on the path to achieving the truth of Being, a form of being called as 'a throw', 'and from which the throwness of Dasein derives'.[78] In other words, Dasein is something that a human being can *take up* or *assume*. It is a 'burden' that human beings must take up, and therefore is not already present in human beings. Instead, it is 'a task or a test that the human being must take up and endure – and it is an arduous task' that 'remains reserved for the "few and rare"'.[79] Whereas, for Agamben, there can be no such thing: 'how can that in which the very truth of being is in question remain entrusted solely to the uncertainty and contingency of a "test" or a "task"?'[80] As Agamben argues:

> If the human being is truly such only when a simply living being becomes rational, then one would have to presuppose an animal-human

that is not yet truly human. In the same way, if the human being is truly such only when, in becoming Dasein, it is opened to Being, if the human being is essentially such only when 'it is the clearing of Being', this means that there is before or beneath it a non-human human being that can or must be transformed into Dasein.[81]

It is this problem of the foundation or presupposition that Agamben's philosophy seeks to unravel, being intimately linked to the anthropological machine that, each time, seeks to produce, and decide, on the proper *mode* of being of the human being as such. Whereas, for proponents of a positive biopolitics, such as Bratton, this real problem of the presupposition does not figure in the analysis, perhaps believing this to be the hocus pocus of obscure metaphysics with no relation to politics and least of all the real world. Yet, the real world in which we live continues to testify to the consequences of its proliferation. In a chapter entitled 'Resilience and Automation', Bratton writes of the virtues of the private platform, Amazon, whose role during the Covid-19 lockdowns is described as unmatched in managing to employ 'over a quarter of a million people in a matter of weeks, a labour akin to a military draft'.[82] Bratton goes on to say that 'they kept cities going when other means could not', 'the app-to-warehouse-to-driver-to-door cybernetic loop became an emergency public service', 'automation made the lockdown economy possible'.[83] Never mind the immense workload, precarity and humiliating working conditions where workers were denied bathroom breaks and forced to pee in bottles.[84] Never mind to the fact that Amazon actively sabotages workers' attempts at organizing for better working conditions, launching anti-union campaigns and carrying out intrusive measures of surveillance and tracking.[85] The positive biopolitics to which Bratton subscribes cares little for life; it is a worthy sacrifice in his view that refugees in Dabaab and Shatila spend their days labelling videos for little to no pay so that those on other parts of the world might enjoy an un-intelligent intelligence providing answers to bad questions.

This is the positive biopolitics of techno-capital to which Bratton is subscribed, assigning a value to life with some lives necessarily considered more valuable than others, made to work in the service of those whose lives are deemed to be more worthy. No wonder, then, that Bratton situates himself as part of the leadership of any planetary-wide governance to come – being the director of Antikythera, a private research programme studying the future of planetary computation. Figures such as Bratton offer themselves up as the bearers of infinite wisdom best placed to authoritatively answer our epochal question 'What is to be done?' with beliefs like climate change being one example of 'planetary-scale crises of biochemistry'.[86] Such that by simple geo-engineering the effects of climate collapse can be mitigated in a context of global capital's infinite thirst for extractive capacities annihilating the living, both human and non-human, on a path to mutually assured destruction.

4

Juridical artifice

Scribbled across the wall at the *Bidonville de la Folie* in Nanterre, Paris, an inscription reads 'You are living in shit – REACT'.[1] This bidonville, or slum, was the largest of its kind, housing roughly 10,000 people. Since 1951, it was home to workers from North Africa and elsewhere. With no electricity and just one access point for water, the workers and their families lived in self-built cabins made of wood and carton; these were regularly destroyed by the police, who frequently stormed the bidonville and arrested individuals. In one such offensive in 1961, between 100 and 150 migrant workers were killed by the police, many of whom were drowned in the Seine. Commenting on the events of May '68 the Marxist philosopher Henri Lefebvre granted the spatial organization of the University of Nanterre a unique importance. Nanterre, situated in the far West of Paris, was built as an extension of the Sorbonne in the 1960s. Lacking in modes of transportation, students would have to walk through the bidonvilles in order to reach the university campus, and, in a sense, were obliged to confront the material realities of inequality, perhaps even for the first time.[2] It is no coincidence, then, that in 1973, a new train line connecting the University of Nanterre directly to St Germain was made available to commuters and students.

On 13 August 1970, the minister of education, Olivier Guichard, made the demolition of the *bidonville* government priority, believing that their presence encouraged leftist agitation on campus. By 1971 they were demolished and the workers housed in barracks. May '68 now seemed a distant memory, an event that happened where a form of justice seemed to have ensued, in one form or another. The migrant workers, however, continued to be excluded from political life. Many of those migrant workers resided in Paris' 18th arrondissment, in the *Goutte d'Or* neighbourhood. Local residents in the area grew increasingly hostile to the migrants and called for greater government control and security, many even taking to the streets asking citizens to sign petitions for the expulsion of the migrant workers. The killing of Djellali Ben Ali was a defining moment of this history. Djellali was a teenager of Algerian origin who was shot and killed by Daniel Pigot, a driver and delivery worker, on 27 October 1971, on the rue de la *Goutte d'Or*. The Djellali committee was set up by the *Comités Palestine*, working together with local residents and intellectuals, including Michel Foucault, Gilles Deleuze, Claude Mauriac, Jean-Paul Sartre, Jean Genet and others.[3] This support led to the growth of the movement, culminating in a mass demonstration on 7 November of the same year on *boulevard de Barbès* nearby. Activists continued to mobilize in the area in support of both French and migrant families on the issue of inadequate housing, eventually occupying an empty building on the boulevard de la Chappelle. Mobilizations continued, and in June 1972 the Arab and French militants, close to the Maoist movement and the *Gauche prolétarienne* (GP), united in their work on the *Comités Palestine*, established *the Mouvement des travailleurs arabes* (MTA) [Movement of Arab Workers]. They were the first group to consider the material and living conditions of migrant workers as such; motivated by the unequal position they found themselves within the social and economic order of things, the MTA were informed by a pan-Arab and Marxist consciousness. At the time political organizations, including workers' unions, reserved their representations to French nationals. The MTA however sought a common struggle for the migrant worker, who they saw as having:

> Arrived in France for the necessities of industrial modes of production. They broadened their field of actions to the living and working conditions of migrant workers and demanded the condemnation of racist crimes, the transformation of immigrant barracks (a military inheritance of the colonial era), access to decent housing, the receipt of

a stable juridical status that did not depend on an employer's goodwill, the representation of working migrants in unions, etc.[4]

In demanding a wholesale transformation of living conditions the movement was met with fierce resistance from established workers' unions. This resistance was partly due to the so-called 'foreignness' of the migrants themselves and also due to the fact that the unions primarily conceived of class struggle as something that takes place within the confines of the factory. Instead, for the MTA, life itself, the mode of life, was in question: the struggle included problems of inadequate housing and daily racism; oppression and exploitation were seen to be lived not only in the factory but also in cafes and on the street – in everyday life. The conditions of life, including the structural relations of wage labour and the living conditions, held equal importance. In this sense, life and politics could not be said to be separate or distinct spheres. The movement rather encompassed a destituent potentiality incommensurate with the modes of constituent political alignments.

In 1972 and again in April 1973, the MTA mobilized a series of wildcat strikes at Renault-Bilancourt. As reported in the *New York Times* at the time: 'when Renault sneezes, France has the flu.'[5] Half of the 96,000 Renault workers were migrant workers; 'France no longer has colonies where she can send capital and employ cheap labour, so she is importing them from countries with mass unemployment.'[6] The strikes caused angst among official unions given that many of their members also joined in solidarity. The movement's most well-known achievement was the general strike organized in 1973 against racism. This was the first time in French history that a workers' strike took place in order to denounce crimes perpetrated beyond the confines of the factory, concerning the living conditions and everyday life of workers and communities.[7] The strikes started in Marseilles, following a wave of violence against the Arab population, and quickly spread throughout France in factories in different regions. The State's strategy in the face of this growing movement was one of containment by expulsion or imprisonment of the leaders of the MTA, in order to neutralize any capacity they might have had for further mobilizations.[8] As well as threats of deportation and repression made by the French state, the MTA also faced resistance and threats from other organizations with competing interests. The French state encouraged governments in Algeria, Morocco and Tunisia to keep a close eye on their nationals abroad. The countries involved saw this as an opportunity to solidify links with France and to monitor the activities of their citizens. They set up competing associations called the *Amicales* (the irony of the name 'friends' could not have escaped them) with the approval of the French minister of interior so that 'foreign governments – with the encouragement of the French state – dominated the associational life of immigrant communities through the *Amicales*. Postcolonial consular offices used the *Amicales* to assert their control over political activities in France.'[9] Needless to say, the MTA were ideologically and politically opposed to the *Amicales*. They were 'Marxists, oriented toward French politics, highly secular', and, given their desire to target both their countries of origin and France, the MTA 'stressed the distinctive character of the immigrant voice but also emphasized its connections to the general anti-capitalist and anti-imperialist struggles of the French working class'.[10] It is for this reason that the *Amicales* saw the actions of the MTA as posing a direct threat to the imperial political order. While the *Amicales* condemned the racist murders that took place in Marseilles in 1973, in the same breath they urged migrants from the Maghreb to ignore the upheavals and certainly did not support any of the strike actions. In the end, the MTA's activities were infiltrated by the police who gathered detailed information of much of the organizations' activities, whereabouts and key activists. The MTA were finally dissolved in 1976.

Jean Baudrillard, an unlikely commentator perhaps, has some interesting remarks on this subject. In defining class struggle as having both a 'representative historical agency' and a 'political historical agency', Baudrillard claims that the immigrant is precisely the classless, the excluded, the one who falls through the cracks between representation and production.[11] For him, the migrant worker, excluded from all forms of representation, is the one capable of interpreting and calling into question the relation between workers and unions, already falling into disrepute, following the mass protests of '68, since it was the unions who, in the end, facilitated the restitution of the ruling regime. For Baudrillard, the migrant de-structures the process and so-called morality of relations of production which dominates the majority of societies under global capitalism.[12]

While migrants analyse the worker's 'relation to its representative agencies, they analyse the workers' relation to their own labour power, their relation to themselves as a productive force'.[13] From this vantage point, the migrant worker calls into question the idea of *representation*, highlighting imperfections and oddities that it would be more convenient to overlook, as well as workers' position with respect to their incorporeal transformation into providers of labour power and the structural chain and ethical process of production upon which Western societies depend. In other words, the dynamic is one which points a shining light on the very idea of life and politics, their articulation through the medium of political economy, their connections and inseparability. A re-problematization with direct consequences for thinking modes of action and practices of emancipation. As argued earlier, it is not sufficient to engage with problems but to have some manner of control over their formulations. As Derrida notes on Foucault's thought, the point is to attempt to problematize 'the *problematisations* in which a thought of being intersects "practices"'.[14] In the context of sexuality in Foucault's work, the genealogy of the word concerned procedures and problematizations that gave rise to certain practices, and practices of the self.

The difficulties that arise in the process of problematization in our example and context of the struggles of migrant workers are further reinforced in the evolution of the use of the signifiers 'migrants', 'workers', 'immigrants' that, while referring to the same group of individuals, conjure up different meanings, thoughts and, consequently, practices. Indeed, the idea of 'immigration' in France, understood as a separate object of analysis, is a modern one that coincided with a political discourse that emerged alongside increasingly punitive legislation concerning rules of entry into the territory.[15] Through this signifier, the migrant as *worker* is steadily erased, thus progressively transforming the migrant or immigrant into a separate cultural category. The struggle for life becomes a struggle for documents. This is also reflected in the production of knowledge over the precarious lives of the workers; where it was common in the 1970s for studies to focus on 'migrant workers' or 'foreign workers' the 1980s saw the research focus shifting to the idea of national groupings, emphasizing studies on ethnic communities. As the sociologist Laure Pitti says: 'from the mid 80s, in relation to the factory uprisings of the 1970s where workers from abroad played a big role, some historians deployed the category "immigrant" [. . .] whereas the publications at the time described them as "factory struggles" and "a workers' struggle."'[16] The 1973 strike was unlike those that had taken place in previous years. For the first time, the unions were obliged to confront autonomous workers' movements and those who were excluded from official participation, and, as a result, the unions articulated the insurrections as a 'problem of immigration'.[17] Of inadequate documentation, of juridical status, a struggle of a constituent nature. Indeed, the representatives of the CGT, the Confédération Générale du Travail (General Confederation of Labour) at Renault described the workers as anything but workers throughout the strike, with some describing their discontent as 'the chant of black slaves expressing their discontent'.[18]

Denied a political existence in the history of political struggles, the (re)emergence of the migrant workers into the political scene, with the *Sans-Papiers* movement in the 1990s, for instance, apparently took French society by surprise. A mere twenty years later, it was necessary for migrant workers to rearticulate their desire for a life well-lived, only for the rearticulation to be redirected into a discourse stuck between criminality and liberal humanitarianism. What is clear is that the MTA's organizational efforts were more than a demand for this or that right, rights of regularization of status or housing, for instance. What was at stake was a common demand in the history of insurrections, a demand and desire to transform the totality of their social set-up, a transformation of their mode of existence and of living. This is the tension between liberal rights discourse and the language of a people. Deleuze, with a well-known interest in law, knew this very well, distinguishing between rights to life and the Rights of Man. In Deleuze's formulation:

> All the abominations that humans undergo are cases, not elements of abstract rights. These are abominable cases. You might tell me that these cases resemble each other, but these are situations of jurisprudence. . . . To act for freedom, becoming revolutionary, is to operate in jurisprudence when one turns to the justice system. Justice doesn't exist, 'rights of man' do not exist, it concerns jurisprudence. . . . That's what the invention of law is.[19]

What Deleuze is concerned with is the universal application of abstract rules to particular contexts that can only serve to reinforce an existing paradigm, in this case, a context of liberal rights functioning alongside a schema of global capitalism. Granting a kind of regularization to the MTA or *Sans-Papiers*, for example, would certainly alleviate the difficulties and constraints of operating illegally, though this would be insufficient to a broader transformation of their mode of life: having enough to eat, a decent home and good healthcare, to state the bare minimum. Foucault would make similar remarks concerning this deadlock and insufficiency in a comment made in passing during one of his lectures *Society Must Be Defended*:

> When we want to make some objection against disciplines and all the knowledge-effects and power-effects that are bound up with them, what do we do in concrete terms? What do we do in real life? What do the Syndicat de la magistrature and other institutions like it do? What do we do? We obviously invoke right, the famous old formal, bourgeois right. And it is in reality the right of sovereignty. And I think that at this point we are in a sort of bottleneck, that we cannot go on working like this forever; having recourse to sovereignty against discipline will not enable us to limit the effects of disciplinary power.[20]

In a sense, what is in question is the tension between destituent power and constituent power. The latter, premised on the idea of universal rights, is, in truth, a generalization of a mode of thinking and practice incompatible with the universality of a communism to come, where the demand for life comes to be incompatible with the language of power, of sovereignty, of rights. That the superstructures are incompatible with the modes of living is evident, and yet, as Foucault describes, we continue to appeal for their assistance, hoping each time for a benevolent compromise and just outcome. Even when an appeal is non-existent, the discursive appropriation of struggles into a framework of constituent or liberal rights discourse appears unavoidable no matter the theoretical inclination of a particular movement or intellectual articulation. In other words, to use a concept deployed by Laurent de Sutter, the cosmopoetic[21] potential of a struggle over life, over a transformation of relations and the construction of a world are radically interrupted. In order to rethink this problematic, it will be necessary to consider the operations of law, and in turn, the biopolitical operations of rights.

As we have seen, the articulation of life through institutions of human culture, including religion, politics and philosophy, has functioned primarily on the basis of articulating, and re-articulating each time, what constitutes a human being. For Agamben, the concept of anthropogenesis, the becoming human of the human being, is a continual process, separating each time the human from the non-human, in a mechanism that mirrors Spinoza's claim of the metaphysical becoming ethical. For this reason, we now turn to the juridical artifice which, while having roots in being fully cognisant of the impossibility of a complete representation of various contexts, relations and the singularity of human beings, is today a mechanism by which the kaleidoscope of realities are squeezed into their juridical identifications. The articulation of life, as we have argued, rests on an assumption of a certain knowledge of biological life assumed to be distinct from a politically qualified life, an assumption that is not fixed in time and is ceaselessly articulated anew, with the threshold or separation between biological and political life in continual flux. The only certainty, in fact, is the caesura itself. The only certainty then is the sovereign production of the fictional bare or naked life, a life, so-called, without qualities, political or otherwise. As Agamben suggests:

> The very possibility of distinguishing life and law, anomie and *nomos*, coincides in their articulation in the biopolitical machine. Bare life is a product of the machine and not something that pre-exists it.... Life and law, anomie and *nomos*, *auctoritas* and *potestas*, result from the fracture of something to which we have no other access than through the fiction of their articulation and the patient work that, by unmasking this fiction, separates what it had claimed to unite.[22]

How does the production of bare life, a life unworthy of protection or sacrifice, a life abandoned, come to be produced in the first place in the articulation of life and law, in the biopolitical framework of liberal rights discourse? This question is more urgent than ever given the increased juridification of social life, which although in some instances has resulted in the proliferation of subjective rights, so that a form of justice has the appearance of having taken place, the conditions of existence continue to rapidly deteriorate, with every aspect of the living experiencing forms of domination and exploitation in an increasingly uninhabitable planetary environment. Suffering from addictions, depression, epidemics of loneliness, ill health, disease and poverty, genocides, homelessness and dispossession abound; where infringements of secured rights are commonplace, there are few avenues for their recourse both domestically and internationally.

Life and law

The relationship between law and life has a long and disparate history; it has not always been marked by the notion of the individual as a bearer of rights. The law once carried with it an existential element, where any juridical pronouncement or formulation took account of the idea of a mode of life. That is, the juridical potential of instituting life, *vitam instituere*, loosely defined as that which had been composed and articulated together in the city and according to which all live. Thist is because he transmission of law is inseparable from the images, texts, translations, collected authorities and scriptures that make up a particular social set-up: transmitted across time, borders, languages and jurisdictions. Today, our juridical apparatuses are mediated by images captured and disseminated by the spectacle, which, as Debord famously claimed, demands no reply. We no longer have any say in the fabrication of images; our phantasms, the stuff of images and our collective intellect only appear and re-appear as illusions and the unrealistic utopias of infantile projections. What the ancients defined as *modus vivendi*, which differed from the Roman city and the theological interpretations in the Middle Ages, is alien to us, as a law immanent to a plurality of modes of living. What we call the science of law today, following the positivist transformations of the twentieth century, functions as a mirror image to the human sciences affixed to the language of exchange value that we discussed earlier. Though we have little say over the fabrication of our myths, the fact of fiction remains, as Peter Goodrich puts it in *Languages of Law* (1990): 'we live in an artificial universe, in a universe of fiction, defined allegorically and underpinned by the discourse of the inarticulable, of that which can only be formulated ceremonially or poetically.'[23] The effect of the spectacle has convinced us moderns of the irrelevancy of phantasms and images, of the *appearance* of solidity we grant to institutions that only have the appearance of holding up, of remaining in place.

Indeed, the first mark of law, the first division and fiction as it were, the *legis actio*, is that of the person, the mask (persona) of legal personhood. The human being has long been defined and articulated from several differing perspectives, from being born in God's image to the speaking being, political animal, or, in the language of the natural sciences, as *homo sapiens*. The privileging of the question over 'what' the human being is, throughout Western philosophical and scientific thought, and the assumption of its definition as constituting an epistemological consensus in the history of the present, is carried over into the juridical through the institution of legal personality. As is perhaps familiar, legal personhood is the artifice through which citizenship and subjective rights are assigned to the human being, and, without which, within the framework of liberal rights discourse, as Hannah Arendt had most clearly articulated, the human being as such cannot be recognized as being simply human.[24] The work of the jurist Yan Thomas is instructive in this context, whose writings on the legal artefact of the person feature throughout his work, though perhaps most explicitly articulated concerning the *affaire Pérruche*. For Thomas:

> We are still dependent on a formal system that isolates in each of us, a part from what is irreducibly singular, a legal person, where almost nothing of our physical, psychological and social reality is revealed, since it is reduced to a function: our capacity to hold and exercise rights.[25]

With the increased juridification of the social sphere, this significant abstraction, characteristic of law, has, as Thomas writes, largely been forgotten. While the ancient model of Roman law was characterized by jurists attempting to separate natural realities from legal artifices, social facts and norms, the opposite is the case today. Thomas argues that this strictly juridical operation has caused much confusion, to the extent that today its meaning and quality differs significantly from its originally quite narrow function as a legal institution. Through Christian theology and humanism, the juridical person has acquired a new sense and value that, in all respects, is incompatible with its initial utility, as a technical pre-requisite to entering into the language of law. Thomas writes:

> In our legal culture, the person is confused with the human being itself, with the living human being in that which is singular and common to the human species [. . .] Hence, in our contemporary law, regimes of protection attempt to project the individual and generic identity of each person into a double, intimate, and public dimension of the person: personality rights on the one hand, and human rights borne by everyone on the other.[26]

So that the *persona* is a technical artefact of the juridical, a kind of double of the so-called 'real' subject, and this artefact then allows for rights to be conferred onto the subject. There is an abstraction of social particularities in this schema. Indeed, it was common for the human being to hold a number of '*persona*' to suit a number of different roles and a number of juridical relations.[27] Today ours is an inheritance of a theological schema that ties together the inherent nature of the body in the person as such. Since, for theologians, the human person is the unity of two substance: the body generated by man and the soul produced by God, so that the notion of person brings these two together, which, as Thomas writes, 'extended the patristic formula, due to Boethius, of "rational individual substance"'.[28]

Our present is marked by an ever-expanding process of bringing into the fabric of law all aspects of what constitute life with the aim of ostensibly protecting it; where the juridical notion of the dignity of life can, in a sense, be activated and a form of justice apportioned one way or another. It is this understanding of the relation between law and life that gives sense to the idea of extending a form of legal personhood to animals, rivers and ecosystems, so that 'rights of nature' may facilitate a recourse to justice and environmental protections.[29] Yet, for Thomas, extending legal personhood to include nature, while well meaning, is misguided; a case of 'an ill-conceived and dangerous category for men' now assumed to offer protection to 'pelicans and trees'.[30] Importantly, Thomas is not suggesting that subjective rights are an *a priori* negative phenomena, rather, the problem lies elsewhere: in the relationship between law and life. Thomas argues that this is essentially where the notion of biopolitics, as developed by Agamben, can most clearly be elucidated. The shifting limit of legal protection, while including previously excluded elements from the patronage of law, is a simultaneous affirmation of that which lies beyond this limit, beyond the sacredness of life, and therefore unworthy of protection. This logic connecting personhood, rights and justice is the subject of Simone Weil's essay 'Human Personality', where Weil affirms that 'there is something sacred in every man, but it is not his person. Nor yet is it the human personality. It is this man; no more and no less'.[31]

Weil makes a simple assertion, and yet, it is one that is impossible to honour within the framework of rights and juridical personhood. For Weil: 'Justice consists in seeing that no harm is done to men. Whenever a man cries inwardly: "Why am I being hurt?" harm is being done to him.'[32] Weil distinguishes between rights and the impersonal cry of hurt; only an impersonal, non-legal justice can hear the latter. Our juridical institutions, including legal personality, are incapable of hearing this cry of hurt for it is an impersonal cry, and 'the notion of rights, by its very mediocrity, leads on naturally to that of the person, for rights are related to personal things'.[33] Indeed, for Weil, the notion of rights is immediately connected with exchange, it has a 'commercial flavour' being tied up with individual claims.

The problem, then, is twofold: on the one hand, the biopolitical scission characteristic of the legal limit (or prohibition) excludes from the realm of law that which is thought to lie beyond the merits of legal protection. On the other hand, the juridical institution of rights is necessarily tied up with individual, personal claims, and appears to be the only means through which dignity and justice are possible even if, on the whole, ineffective. There are times when what is demanded is not an individual claim for this or that right, but rather the demand and desire to utterly transform one's way of life. Such demands usually go unheard; if they are heard, the only means of redress and response within the juridico-political parameters is brutal repression, as we saw earlier with the *Mouvement des travailleurs arabes*. The juridical separation between a so-called natural and legal reality, or between living being and its juridical person or mask, has been the principal mode of the juridical manoeuvre. The law, in Thomas' descriptions, functions by way of fiction and artifice, managing human relations in the mode of an 'as if' grasping time and space in the life of subjects. These essentially legal set-ups are used to facilitate certain *circumstances* in the life of persons; for example, making out that a living person could be considered dead to facilitate cases of inheritance, or making up that a deceased person were still alive, or acting as if a being to be born was already born, and so on. Importantly, it is not that Thomas was necessarily concerned with the fact that law could, through its fictions and artifices, change the given facts or details of so-called natural life, for instance through the statutory distinction between sex and identity, of sexuality and procreation (nature itself is a fabrication for Thomas). Rather, Thomas writes:

> In the long history of the West, law has been the means par excellence of institutional construction – of these montages made up of words, which, as long as they are uttered by those who have the power to do so, have the ability to promote the existence of what they enunciate.[34]

Indeed, it was the fact that the very distinction between law and fact, between the juridical fiction and the natural reality, could begin to fade away and natural life ends up being articulated, or understood, on simply juridical terms, where *law ends up folding back into life*. The danger, in other words, is that the representation or artifice comes to stand in, or take the place of the kaleidoscopic singularity of human beings. We see this in the case of biometrics, where, should there be an error, there is a greater likelihood that the individual themselves will be detained for further questioning rather than any suspicion arising with the document itself. We see this too in the obsession over juridically inscribing a crude biological essentialism thought to define the complexity of human sexuality and gender. Life is thought to have to match the coordinates of the artifice and live in accordance with it.

When the 1789 declaration of the Rights of Man made the birth of the living subject coincide with its juridical personality, this seemed to him to have produced an ambiguous being, at once natural and juridical, so that the juridical element, when 'folded back onto birth and existence, loses from its precision and utility since it seemed reduced to a description of a natural state without ceasing to be a juridical qualification'.[35] Thomas shows that in juridically defining the dignity of the human person as something that we each have as belonging to a human species, we are obliged to define precisely this part, which means that a third party (the legislator for instance) will each time trace the limit that separates in each subject the indispensable part, that is part of the species, of the dispensable part, that is part of its liberty. This is the biopolitical element, the decision over life and separation of that which belongs or does not belong to it, belongs to or does not belong to the city. A never-ending cycle of law including an exteriority which it had itself originally instituted by way of a sanction, prohibition or limit. As Laurent de Sutter argues, this is the operational character of law, an endless expansion of legal relations.[36]

In the section from *Homo Sacer* entitled "Biopolitics and the Rights of Man" Agamben explores the logic of this articulation of rights, law and life in the context of politics and the nation state. Agamben takes Arendt as a starting point to consider those left out of the paradigm of rights and citizenship, namely refugees. Arendt says: 'The conception of human rights based upon the assumed existence of a human being as such, broke down at the very moment when those who professed to believe in it were for the first time confronted with people who had indeed lost all other qualities and specific relationships – except that they were still human.'[37] That, in other words, stripped of the juridical artifices that enable one to access protection and dignity, the only thing left was the human being paradoxically no longer able to qualify for the humanity the artifices had promised were universal. For this reason, Agamben would say:

> Before the extermination camps are reopened in Europe (which is already starting to happen), nation-states must find the courage to call into question the very principle of the inscription of nativity and the trinity state/nation/territory which is based on it. [...] It is only in a land where the spaces of states will have been perforated and topologically deformed, and the citizen will have learned to acknowledge the refugee that he himself is, that man's political survival today is imaginable.[38]

Agamben, like Thomas, traces this inscription of life, or natural life, into the nation state through law back to the 1789 French Declaration of the Rights of Man and Citizen drawn up after the French Revolution. In the declaration, it is not clear whether the two terms name two separate beings, or, as Agamben argues, instead form a 'unitary system' where the first (man) is always already included in the second. Agamben suggests that the second interpretation is more likely, and that by situating 'man' as always already included in the category of the citizen, natural life is placed as the foundation of the nation state, which immediately vanishes into the figure of the citizen – through whom rights are preserved to the exclusion of non-citizens. For this reason, Agamben says:

> It is not possible to understand the 'national' and biopolitical development and vocation of the modern state in the nineteenth and twentieth centuries if one forgets that what lies at its basis is not man as a free and conscious political subject but, above all, man's bare life, the simple birth that as such is, in the passage from subject to citizen, invested with the principle of sovereignty.[39]

Agamben points out that what constitutes a citizen of a particular nation, for example French or German, had never been a political question but one of social or anthropological curiosities. But once the question of birth or nativity formed the basis of the sovereign nation state it became possible to engage in a process of constant redefinition and rearticulation – so that these questions became political, as is evident in the example of National Socialism. For Agamben:

> Fascism and Nazism are, above all, redefinitions of the relations between man and citizen, and become fully intelligible only when situated – no matter how paradoxical it may seem – in the biopolitical context inaugurated by national sovereignty and declarations of rights.[40]

And,

> One of the essential characteristics of modern biopolitics (which will continue to increase in our century) is its constant need to redefine the threshold in life that distinguishes and separates what is inside from what is outside. Once it crosses over the walls of the *oikos* and penetrates more and more deeply into the city, the foundation of sovereignty – nonpolitical life – is immediately transformed into a line that must be constantly redrawn.[41]

What is in question then are ceaseless decisions over life, over what constitutes it, and a continual potential exposure to death. The balance of power is unmistakably weighed in favour of the whims of sovereignty that, having conceded to include that which had been excluded, can just as easily and without much difficulty or scrutiny reverse the decision. In the UK, this has been evident in the case of Shamima Begum, a British-born young woman, who after being trafficked to Syria in 2019 had her citizenship revoked by the British government, this despite the fact it had been revealed that the Canadian Security Services had facilitated her travels to the region.[42] This highlights the political and juridical relationship that is inextricably tied up with life and living, and the thanato-political potential, the political exposure to death, that co-exist with it. 'The originary structure of Western politics consists in an *ex-ceptio*', Agamben tells us, 'in an inclusive exclusion of human life in the form of bare life.'[43] Importantly, bare life is not to be equated with natural life. Through its division and its capture in the apparatus of the exception, life assumes the form of bare life, which is to say, that of a life that has been cut off and separated from its form, its manner, its mode of living. In other words, the continual reproduction of bare life is an inevitable function of the apparatus. It is for this reason that, for Agamben, as it is for Deleuze, there can be no 'leftist government' as such. Both Agamben and Deleuze articulate this differently while sharing a similar concern. As Deleuze says: 'It's not that there are no differences between governments. The best one can hope for is a government favourable to certain demands from the Left. But a leftist government does not exist since being on the Left has nothing to do with governments.'[44]

This is because Deleuze defines being on the left as being a matter of perception, giving the example of one's locality, that, like a postal address, extends outward from the person: beginning from the street where one lives to the city, the country and other countries further away still. It is a matter of perception, of knowing that global inequalities and the global exploitation of all life on earth cannot go on – much as the analogy with the figure of the slave we saw earlier, acting as the instrument which allows for a properly political or human life to take place, a biopolitical ontological inheritance that Agamben describes. The fact is, nothing justifies that my life would be worthy at the expense of another's. In this way, *whatever being* is being inasmuch as it always matters or, that nobody matters.[45] Since, for Deleuze, just as it is for Agamben, the point is to create new so-called possibilities of life, this does not mean that it is a matter of performing a series of acts to be realized, or choosing this or that hobby or profession. This necessarily presupposes a new manner of life, a new manner of being affected, the power of life. Politics as perception does not mean being able to see into the future. Rather, as François Zourabichvili writes:

> The seer seizes the intolerable in a situation; that is perceptions in becoming or 'precepts', which defeats the ordinary conditions of perception, and which envelop an affective mutation. The opening of a new field of possibilities is linked to these new conditions of perception: the expressible of a situation suddenly irrupts.[46]

This occurs when someone encounters their proper conditions of existence, or those of others, so that it is less a matter of cognition or consciousness than a matter of a new sensibility. The one who is able to see can grasp the un-actualizable in a particular situation, that is, the element that falls out of the edges of the actual situation, the possible as such – seeing the possible is not about elaborating a plan to be accomplished but to seize the actual situation in its potentiality as a field of the possible. By way of a new relation to space and time, a re-composition, a different assemblage is able to be created. We see this in revolutionary movements, which, far from having a plan, image or project to be realized, *make* an image: 'can we see a revolt? Or is it the revolt that sees, and sees itself? The image is fragmentary, and dissipates itself here and there, adequate to the possible as such.'[47] In this way, the possible is what is always left to be created; there is no image adequate to the new sensibility, something exceeds it and no actuality can fulfil it. This is what Deleuze and Guattari call the 'minoritarian universal conscience' that each time exceeds law, being each time an expression of a problematization of existence, like the *Mouvement des travailleurs arabes*, for whom what was in question was a different articulation of life all together. There is, Deleuze and Guattari say, 'a universal figure of minoritarian consciousness as the becoming of everybody, and that becoming is creation'.[48] This has nothing to do with the acquisition of the position of the majority, rather it refers to the opposite position, one that 'oversteps the representative threshold of the majoritarian standard', such that in articulating this minoritarian consciousness 'one addresses powers (*puissances*) of becoming that belong to a different realm from that of Power (*Pouvoir*) and Domination'.[49] This mode of life and power has nothing to do with the alternatives in place, the result of problematizations from above, and it is precisely what the language of power and the language of law can neither tolerate nor understand. For this reason, these singularities concern not law but jurisprudence, not juridical personhood but singularity, not *zoè* or *bios* but form-of-life.

5

Destituent politics

The biopolitical era in which we live functions as a mode, a way of doing things, as much as a rationality: a way of thinking and conceptualizing the world that privileges the idea of hierarchization and consequently of value, with the effect of defining or setting out the parameters of what living itself ought to look like. In *Critique of Everyday Life*, Henri Lefebvre writes: 'in capitalist countries, the superstructures [. . .] are in contradiction with the contents of the living.'[1] This tension between the form-of-life on the one hand and the superstructures on the other hand is evident in different contexts throughout history. From colonial violence to environmental destruction and the annihilation of civilizations, a planetary brutalism ensues, as Achille Mbembe describes it.[2] The question of the form-of-life of the living is fundamental, while it is a shared experience among all life on earth, it remains both a practical and conceptual enigma for us. That each of us is capable of a mode of being is a universality that brings together all species, and yet, it remains out of reach. The conditions of possibilities of the living present one obstacle after another. Our present so-called universal mode of life, if it can be described as such, is one indicative of a planetary world made uninhabitable in our names. What can be described as the tension between the universal and the particular is, in reality, only the forceful, violent, imposition and application on one mode of the particular, one mode of being, among numerous possibilities.

We saw this with the instituting function of law, for example, where what is in question is the transformation of the human being into identity, such that, as Goodrich writes, 'the entry of the individual into the symbolic [. . .] is the condition of institutional existence, the capture of the subject by law'.³ The challenge is, in part, to re-conceptualize our modes of relating, our social relations, that compose the 'theatre of truth' in which we live. In a sense, this is what Antonin Artaud proposed in relation to the theatre of cruelty, recognizing that 'we are not free. And the sky can still fall on our heads'.⁴ The idea, for Artaud, is to overcome the separation between 'the analytic theatre and the plastic world' since 'one does not separate the mind from the body nor the senses from the intelligence'.⁵ Needless to say, there is a risk involved, as Artaud writes:

> In the present circumstances I believe it is a risk worth running. I do not believe we have managed to revitalise the world we live in, and I do not believe it is worth the trouble of clinging to; but I do propose something to get us out of our marasmus, instead of continuing to complain about it, and about the boredom, inertia, and stupidity of everything.⁶

A coincidence between essence and existence, *zoè* and *bios*, living and living well, is difficult for us to achieve and to think in an era founded on their separability, where eventual claims are made for their subsequent unification with farcical and tragic results. It is under global capitalism, our global system of the organization of social life, that a totalizing and generalizing force is in conflict with all modes of living around the world. That this system of social organization is in conflict with the idea of a form-of-life is not to say that it is not compatible with difference and identity. On the contrary, we are faced with a social formation that continually refers to heterogeneous elements which in turn makes possible its continuous proliferation. In *A Thousand Plateaus*, Deleuze and Guattari write that this social formation can be defined as ecumenical, that is, defined in being able to encompass the heterogeneous. It is characterized by its ability to move through and between different and co-existing orders: 'it is not exclusively commercial or economic, but is also religious, artistic, etc.'⁷ That is to say:

> To the extent that capitalism constitutes an axiomatic (production for the market), all States and all social formations tend to become isomorphic in their capacity as models of realisation: there is but one

centered world market, the capitalist one, in which even the so-called socialist countries participate. [. . .] Isomorphy allows, and even incites, a great heterogeneity among states (democratic, totalitarian, and especially, 'Socialist' states are not facades).[8]

The social formations become isomorphic, where heterogeneous states participate irrespective of their political affiliation, or cultural and religious differences. On occasion, a state falls out of favour, and the audacity of self-determination is met with the annihilation of the possibility for living through the imposition of crippling sanctions: a banishment from the world economy where lives are held in permanent suspension and whose cries largely go unheard.[9] In this respect, the social formation knows no compromise, only complicity. If its limit is unreachable it is because it is devoid of any exterior limit, perpetually fulfilling its own immanence. In this sense, we can understand Benjamin's description: 'In capitalism, things gave a meaning only in their relationship to the cult; capitalism has no specific body of dogma, no theology.'[10] While not being a religion as such it is a cult with its own structure of belief and behaviour, law and economy that only it makes sense of. The capital-religion structure guarantees meaning and the meaning of value in relation to it. We can think of the attribution of economic indices to every detail of conduct, as we saw with the gathering of information over minute details of the population, as a part of this structure. Every individual in the cult is the means to an end, a purpose or value, or a meaning. It is permanent, it is a celebration without dream or mercy, only the expansion of despair and for this reason tend to the world's destruction rather than its transformation. The rules of conduct under capitalism, just as cultic and religious structures had done before it, give an answer to 'anxieties, torments and disturbances'.[11] Where there is no atonement, only guilt, the rules of conduct under capitalism systematize deficits without permitting any escape. Its very function is to organize this suffering, through its conjuring and perpetuation, with distraction the only temporary relief. If capitalism as religion is the production of the demonic nexus between debt and guilt, it is because it is first of all a question of freedom. The ambiguity of the demonic leaves man in a position of uncertainty, unable to exercise a decision, left instead at the mercy of forces of domination: subjective, economic and affective. It is not a question of seeking atonement through the guilt-debt nexus, or of seeking reforms here and there, since such reforms will continue to function in relation to the same mechanism. In a sense, when Lenin cautioned against the trap of economism, which would limit any struggle to the immediacy of certain limited economic results, it is this compromise that is rejected.[12] Is an increase in the wage of workers in the Global North that inevitably comes as the result of negotiating cheaper prices for raw materials and lower wages for workers in the Global South an acceptable means of organizing a communism to come? Any communism worthy of the name would think not, no life can be lived at the expense of another. Is there a way of rethinking use, and value, so as to suspend our being caught up in a relation of means and ends, of eternal compromise that is in reality a complicity, and our participation in the nihilism of the present catastrophe? For Agamben, Benjamin and others this necessarily means a move away from constituent power to destituent power. In order to assess the full meaning of a destituent power and what this might mean for a destituent politics, it will be necessary to consider what it means to inhabit a constituent power, what this means for the idea of a people and multitude and the state of exception. First, we will begin with the relationship between people and multitude, in relation to life and singularities.

Subject-to-subject cycle

In the *Grammar of Multitudes,* Paolo Virno writes that there remains an underlying tension and hostility towards the concept of multitude and the singularities that make it up. Virno shows that the distinction between the 'People' and the 'multitude' was the subject of numerous theoretico-philosophical and practical controversies during the seventeenth century. These controversies range from ideas on the formation of the modern State to religious wars and the making of the juridical subject; accordingly, it was the fierce battle between these two concepts that, in the end, shaped the political and social categories of our contemporary politics, with the notion of a 'People' prevailing over a 'multitude'.

Thomas Hobbes, a key thinker of the distinction between these two terms, is well known to have mistrusted the idea of the multitude. On the distinction, Hobbes writes in *De Cive*: 'a *people* is a *single* entity, with a *single will*; you can attribute *an act* to it. None of this can be said of a Multitude.'[13] The key differentiating factor then is the unity of the will in the people. The multitude, for Hobbes, is in a sense something which precedes the 'body politic' and politics proper. Foucault expressed this clearly, stating that the theory of sovereignty characterizes itself through the following formula: a subject-to-subject cycle. In other words, the subject *qua* human being is not thought as immediately political, but rather enters into a body politic by 'giving up' a part of themselves. The biopolitical gesture par excellence. 'Sovereignty', Foucault writes, 'is the theory that goes from subject to subject and establishes the political relationship between subject and subject.'[14] As Foucault says:

> Where, in terms of sovereignty, an assumption exists from the beginning of a multitude whose powers are not-yet political. Instead, these powers: are capacities, possibilities, potentials, and it can constitute them in the political sense of the term only if it has in the meantime established a moment of fundamental and foundational unity between possibilities and power, namely the unity of power.[15]

This 'unity of power' can be said to be embodied in the idea of a single will. As we know, for Hobbes, a '*combination* of several wills' is impractical for the preservation of peace and defence. A single will [*una voluntas*] is required, which can only happen if 'each man subjects his *will* to the *will* of a *single* other [*alterius unius*], to the *will*, that is, of one *Man* [*Hominis*] or of one *Assembly* [*Concilium*], in such a way that whatever one *wills* on matters essential to the common peace may be taken as the *will* of all and each [*omnes et singuli*]'.[16] The multitude, then, cannot be trusted, for it resists political unity, therefore never attaining, as Virno puts it, 'the status of the juridical person', since its own natural rights are never given over to the sovereign.[17] The problem is an ontological one, in that what prevents this transfer from occurring in the first place is the irreparable incompatibility of the multitude with the notions of people and the state. Since, 'it is [the multitude's] very mode of being (through its plural character) and by its mode of behaving'[18] that situates it in an alternate image of thought, rhythm and frequency, than that required by sovereignty.

It is through Hobbes' reading of Aristotle's *Politics*, that this fundamental incompatibility of the multitude with the notions of a people and the state can be most clearly elucidated. Hobbes shows that, for Aristotle, in addition to man understood as a political animal, one can count the ant and the bee. Since, while the insects are lacking in *logos* or reason, they nevertheless direct their actions to a common end. However, Hobbes adds the following caveat: 'their swarms are still not *commonwealths* [*civitates*], and so the animals themselves should not be called political, for their government is only an accord, of many wills with one object, not (as a commonwealth needs) one will.'[19] The conflicting theme rests on the idea of a multiplicity of wills on the one hand and a singular will on the other hand. The latter being a primary qualification to entering into a political community. In this sense, the multitude for Hobbes has no real political significance; instead, it is pre-political and that which must be eradicated for the formation of the State. Instead, in Agamben's words: 'it is the unpolitical element upon whose exclusion the city is founded.'[20] In reality, this 'subject-to-subject' cycle reveals a fundamental paradox: in order for a subject to exist in a political community, they must give up a part of themselves to become counted as part of a people which, in essence, does not exist. Agamben reminds us that the Commonwealth, or political body, does not coincide with the physical 'body' of the city. The Leviathan, after all, is an artificial Man, a 'phantasm', and yet, 'the artifice is effective because it grants unity to a multiplicity'.[21] In this sense, one can understand how 'the unification of the multitude of citizens in a single person is something like a perspectival illusion; political representation is only an optical representation (but no less effective on account of this)'.²² In other words, the optical representation is effective in that it effectuates a transformation of wills to one will, though without erasing the material existence of the multitude itself. The potential of a dissolved multitude continues to exist, albeit in a repressed form. As Agamben argues, the formation of the human species into a political body can only take place through a splitting between 'naked life (people) and political existence (People)' so that:

> The concept of people always already contains within itself the fundamental biopolitical fracture. It is what cannot be included in the whole of which it is a part as well as what cannot belong to the whole in which it is always already included.²³

For Agamben, this is the violence of constituent power, which has had a destructive effect on politics:

> Politics has suffered a lasting eclipse because it has been contaminated by law, seeing itself, at best, as constituent power (that is, violence that makes law), when it is not reduced to merely the power to negotiate with the law. The only truly political action, however, is that which severs the nexus between violence and law. And only beginning from the space thus opened will it be possible to pose the question of a possible use of law after the deactivation of the device that, in the state of exception, tied it to life.²⁴

So, what is constituent power and the state of exception that is tied to life? A brief detour is required.

Constituent power and life

In *Political Theology* published in 1922, Carl Schmitt defines the sovereign as the one who decides on the state of exception. According to Agamben, although Schmitt describes the state of exception, as well as other noted jurists and political scientists, to date there is no theory of the state of exception in public law. It is generally taken as a question of fact or necessity, in certain circumstances of emergency, with little consideration on its juridical form or its status as a juridical problem, with implications for life and for politics. For Agamben, if the law employs the exception, which is essentially the suspension of law, as a means of referring to and including or encompassing life, then a theory of the state of exception is necessary. It is the structure that ties life to law, or life to the juridical order, that the state of exception is concerned with. For Agamben, it is only through understanding the relationship between law and life that one can articulate what it means to act politically.

Over the last few years, in France as in Italy, governance by law-decrees, the executive rather than the legislature, has become more common. In France, this has been the case since before the emergency measures resulting from the pandemic, which has had the effect of limiting the legislature's role to ratifying decrees issued by the executive power. So that, Agamben says: 'At the very moment when it would like to give lessons in democracy to different traditions and cultures, the political culture of the West does not realise that it has entirely lost its canon.'[25] The State of Exception is seen as a figure of necessity, as an 'illegal' but 'juridical and constitutional' measure that is used in the production of new norms, or of a new juridical order. As Agamben says, however, the concept of necessity is a subjective one, and is necessary in accordance with the aims that one wants to achieve. In other words, necessity is the result of a *decision*.

Agamben turns to Schmitt for a technical reason – suggesting that Schmitt's theory on the state of exception articulated for the first time the intricate connection between the juridical order and the exception. Essentially, that what must be included in law must be something external to it – and in that moment, the juridical order is suspended, making an exception to include what the law had up to that point excluded: 'Being-outside, and yet belonging: this is the topological structure of the state of exception.'[26] For Agamben, the state of exception is not a dictatorship but rather a space devoid of law, a zone of anomie where legal determinations are deactivated or suspended. It is not, for

Agamben, a justified exercise of a state's right to its defence – this is the traditional view of the state of exception. Agamben is critical of Schmitt's position that seeks to inscribe the state of exception within a juridical context based on the division we've just mentioned, between the so-called existing norms of law and the norms of the realization of law, the inside and the outside, constituent power and constituted power. The state of exception as the state devoid of law seems – paradoxically – to require *proximity* to law, to assure itself of a connection to law, and, simultaneously, the juridical order needs to maintain itself in relation to this space of anomie, this space of non-law, in order to function:

> On the one hand, the juridical void at issue in the state of exception seems absolutely unthinkable for the law; on the other, this unthinkable thing nevertheless has a decisive strategic relevance for the juridical order and must not be allowed to slip away at any cost.[27]

The force-of-law is the result of this non-place of exception; it is separate from the law. This void is also what is at issue in Benjamin's essay 'Critique of Violence'. Benjamin and Schmitt were in correspondence, notably on the question of the state of exception, between 1925 and 1956. Indeed, Agamben notes that Schmitt had said that his 1938 book on Hobbes was conceived as a response to Benjamin.[28] The 'Critique of Violence' has also been important in thinking the possibility of destituent power, as opposed to constituent power, which Agamben and authors like Marcello Tari have written about as a possibility of creating new worlds of a communism to come. The aim of 'Critique of Violence' is to think the possibility of a non-legal violence, one that lies beyond the law and could therefore shatter the connection between law-making violence on the one hand and law preserving violence on the other hand. This non-legal violence, or violence outside the law, Benjamin calls pure or divine violence, and it is 'revolutionary'. As is self-evident, from the perspective of law, violence beyond its remit and control is intolerable. The characteristic of destituent power, or divine violence, is that it neither makes nor preserves the law – it destitutes it, deposes it and allows for the emergence of a new historical epoch.

This is the opposite position to Schmitt, for whom this space of non-legal violence must be brought back into the juridical context, thereby maintaining the state's violence *de jure*.

For Benjamin there is an inherent tension in relation to state power – in relation to the sovereign's ability to decide: the sovereign, who is responsible for making the decision on the state of exception, reveals, at the first opportunity, that it is almost impossible for him to make a decision.[29] This is significant, and Agamben will develop this in more detail in other works, including the *Kingdom and the Glory* (2011), for instance, which investigates the division between sovereign power and the exercise of that power between God and his kingdom, the sovereign and the police. For Agamben, just like for Benjamin, there is a gap between these two operative notions – between power and its exercise, between law and anomie, inside and outside. So that, for both Agamben and Benjamin, the state of exception:

> no longer appears as the threshold that guarantees the articulation between an inside and an outside, or between anomie and the juridical context, by virtue of a law that is in force in its suspension: it is, rather, a zone of absolute indeterminacy between anomie and law, in which the sphere of creatures and the juridical order are caught up in a single catastrophe.[30]

This new articulation of the state of exception by Benjamin represents for Agamben a different function of the state of exception, which no longer exists as that which guarantees the relation between an inside and an outside as we have discussed, or between anomie and the juridical. Instead, it is a zone of indeterminacy – where it is impossible to tell inside from outside. Agamben suggests that it is in this way that we can understand Benjamin's now well-known eighth thesis on the concept of history:

> The tradition of the oppressed teaches us that the 'state of exception' in which we live is the rule. We must attain a concept of history that accords with this fact. Then we will clearly see that it is our task to bring about a real state of exception, and this will improve our position in the struggle against fascism.[31]

Where for Schmitt the point was to maintain the space of anomie in relation to the law, for Benjamin, instead, the space of anomie must be freed from this legal relation. As Agamben puts it: 'while Schmitt attempts every time to re-inscribe violence within a juridical context, Benjamin responds to this gesture by seeking every time to assure it – as pure violence – an existence outside of the law.'[32] In other words, pure violence is simply human action that neither makes nor preserves the law, 'the task of a critique of violence', Benjamin says, 'can be summarised as that of expounding its relation to law and justice'.[33] According to Agamben, 'Benjamin's thesis is that while mythic-juridical violence is always a means to an end, pure violence is never simply a means – whether legitimate or illegitimate – to an end (whether just or unjust).'[34] It is a violence that does not govern or execute but one that acts and manifests. It is a question of rendering the law *inoperable*, and of discovering a new use of law, of politics and of living. Inoperativity's corresponding political concept is not constituent power but destituent power.

But what would it mean to destitute law, and what is a destituent violence that would no longer seek to constitute and thereby repeat the nexus of the violence of law and the violence that maintains the law? Benjamin located this destituent power in the proletarian general strike – as opposed to the political strike. How can we distinguish between these two modes? Marcello Tari, in *There Is No Unhappy Revolution* (2017), describes it thus:

> The classic strike, which with Benjamin we will call the political strike, has a foreseeable beginning and end, a reactive temporality subordinated to negotiation and, in the best cases, aims at achieving surface-level improvements. It represents a temporality controlled and commanded by an economic logic, a calculation made in the short term in order to indicate a distant future in which everyone is better off, works the right amount for the correct sum, in which citizens no longer need to strike because the law will always be on their side.[35]

This use and manipulation of the future is a capitalist future – an infinite deferral of reconciliation and mystification. The destituent strike, instead, interrupts the now – in an instant calling for another use of this world, and another use of time. It is the realization that the catastrophe is not something that will arrive but that is already here, that it is not something that needs to be warded off through this or that action, this or that policy measure, this or that election, but that capitalism itself is constituted by catastrophes and crises. As Tari says:

> We live in a non-world that *functions* but has nevertheless become *unlivable*, a non-world that continues to *produce* but has become *uninhabitable*. Our subjectivity is not external to all of this; it also functions and produces but is both unliveable and uninhabitable.[36]

How could Artaud have lived in order to think in a world made uninhabitable? Resilience today marks this absence of the possibility of creating a habitable world, and of surviving the uninhabitable. Just as Deleuze distinguished between history and revolutionary-becomings, for Tari, the revolution has no future; it is not a question of means and ends, of instituting this or that law, of accumulating various instruments ranging from the technological to the juridical. Instead:

> It is a process without progress that realises itself, always and forever in each gesture that opens up an exit from the present as organised by domination . . . . Either it is already here, among us, or it is nothing at all. That the distances between us – and, between us and the revolution – can seem insurmountable is another story, one that does not concern the future but rather our own faulty perception of our epoch. It is the difficulty in developing a shared strategic line of thought.[37]

Every politics that seems to preach a constituent power amounts to a promise to delay the catastrophe that has arrived long ago. Is this not the disappointment we see in Chile, that, after a momentous uprising in 2019 culminated in a redrafting of the constitution that was subsequently rejected, with the right gaining power and proposing to redraft it themselves? This world no longer has any meaning, or, as Benjamin would say, only with reference to itself. The political strike, of constituent power, also carves out a subject modelled on a socioeconomic *identity*, so that it is always a substitute for a *representation*, in a party, or nation or government – how these then transform our modes of relation and our system of social relations remains unclear though this is what is called the reality of politics.

Today, the subject is engulfed and folded over by a web of dominations applied through the body and psyche, organizing the possibility or impossibility of encounters, and the scope of action. Communism is the movement that *destitutes* the present state of things, rendering them inoperative; it is a dissolution of the self as self-subject. In a society modelled on enterprise and competition, the only generalized language that exists is that of *managerialism*: the evaluation of projects, the standardization of procedures, the aims of decentralizing various functions, in the name of objectifying individual behaviour and enabling the individual to self-evaluate their supposed progress, or measure their lacks in the context of jobs, careers, wages, health, weight, insurance premium and so on. The subject is invested in their own production quantifying the becoming of their own self – that is at once an invitation to be the best one must become and a commandment, an injunction to participate since living itself is at stake. One's conditions of life and living conditions, one's being and acting, what one is and how one is, collapse into one, directed to survival, experiencing power's positivity and its absolute domination. An ethos of self-evaluation that even if one is successful in relation to the metric scale cannot but reinforce self-alienation, worries and torments. One's life and mode of life are defined and captured, measured and evaluated in relation to the market, in relation to exchange value. This present mode of life does not then lend itself to the possibilities of joyful encounters, of encountering adequate ideas that could form the necessary conditions for a collectivity of thought to emerge, the conditions for a politics of singularity, to use Lazarus' words. That people think is what constitutes politics, and we must ask what our thought makes possible today and, crucially, what it necessarily rules out.

Agamben draws our attention to a remark by Pasolini, who said: 'True anarchy, is the anarchy of power.'[38] Just as Benjamin had noted that 'nothing is more anarchic than the Bourgeois order.'[39] This is because power, as we have seen, constitutes itself through the inclusive exclusion of anarchy – of anomie. For this reason, it is essential to think this contradiction, as well as what Agamben calls the *a-demy*, the absence of a *demos* or people that is the definition of the modern state. Only by exposing power's relationship to anarchy, to inoperativity, can these be made accessible. It is a question of 'releasing oneself from the form they have received in the exception' which for Agamben is necessarily the task of a form-of-life. With the form-of-life, it is no longer a question of asking what 'I' am, with the answers such as: a political animal, a juridical person, a citizen of X or Y, a person of this or that sexuality, this or that gender, this or that political party member, this or that vocation or profession, but instead to ask 'How I am what I am'.[40] The significance of Spinoza's modal ontology cannot be underestimated – it forms the basis of Agamben's development of the notion of form-of-life, a life in which it is impossible to separate *bios* from *zoè*, living from living well, essence from existence.

On the manner of being

Manner has been described as what is most universal among beings. In Agamben's terms, it can be understood as an 'exemplary singularity or a multiple singularity . . . it is an exemplar, in other words a whatever singularity'.[41] The word 'whatever' (*quodlibet*) in this context should not be understood as holding little importance; rather, it is such that it always matters.[42] Agamben explains it thus:

> The Whatever in question here relates to singularity not in its indifference with respect to a common property (to a concept, for example: being red, being French, being Muslim), but only its being such as it is. Singularity is thus freed from the false dilemma that obliges knowledge to choose between the ineffability of the individual and the intelligibility of the universal.[43]

In this way, the whatever singularity is not conditional upon this or that property or particular essence – it is in this sense exemplary, free of any identity. As we have already discussed, Western ontology divides being into an essence and an existence, as a being that is in this *or* that mode, but, with manner, being simply *is* its mode of being, so that, as Agamben writes, 'while remaining singular and not indifferent, is multiple and valid for all'.[44] This being is not an *hypokeimenon*, an existent presupposed, lying under at the base of being. The ontological apparatus, an Aristotelian inheritance, severs 'the pure existent (the "that" it is) from the essence (the "what" it is)' inserting time and movement between these two, the apparatus reactivates the anthropogenetic gesture and thereby 'opens and defines each time the horizon of acting as well as knowing, by conditioning... what human beings can do and they can know and say'.[45] Instead, with manner, the mode is at once identical and different, both terms fall into one another. There is no presupposition or hidden essence of being, being simply *is* its mode, it is *'continually engendered from its own manner'*.[46] Agamben relates this to the idea of a 'free use of the self' and thus a way to think being not as a value or a property, but rather as a *habitus* or an *ethos* that *engenders* us. In this way, being is displaced on the level of the living and generated by the act of living itself, it is a form-of-life. In this way, Agamben is developing a modal ontology that disrupts the Aristotelian ontology premised on the opposition between existence and essence, potential and act. As Agamben describes: 'substance does not "have" but "is" its mode. In every case, in the idea of a "form-of-life," just like existence and essence, so also do *zoè* and *bios*, living and life contract into one another and fall together, allowing a third to appear, whose meaning and implications still remain for us to deliberate'.[47] The significance of this novel approach to the concept of life, being generated by the act of living, and critique of the ontological apparatus that Agamben describes can be seen at play in the well-known Spinozist phrase that 'we do even know what a body can do'. Indeed, there is a reason why Deleuze describes this as a 'war cry'.[48]

The idea of 'what bodies can do' is a direct disruption of the classic ontological presupposition concerning the position of consciousness, or the soul, as having power over the body, that is, directing the course of the body's action. A direct rejection of the idea that the soul must 'command' the body to act, to obey, in accordance with a specific law. This, Deleuze writes, is the traditional moral view of the world. Morality differs from an ethics in its reliance on a transcendental – God, for example – in relation to a specific essence. A command, or moral judgement, derives its authority from morality, whereby an essence is ascribed in accordance with a transcendental. Ethics, on the contrary, is concerned with *how* one is, *what* one is capable of in such a way that the main concern is what beings are capable of and this is not a question of essence. Deleuze gives the example of a bird who is capable of flying, which human beings are not capable of. So that an ethics is principally concerned with the actions and passions that one is capable of rather than *what* one, as such, *is*. For Spinoza, essence is power and this is because there is no essence only power of action: it is the aggregate of what one can do and what one undergoes, what one suffers.[49] Whereas in classical thought, power and action are conceived of separately – this implies that there must be a passage between them. In this model, essence is not something that is realized alone, rather, it is something that must be realized in existence. With potential and action conceived of separately, it is morality, for instance, that is used to bridge the gap, bringing potential *into* action, *realizing* potential and essence. There is no such conceptualization in Spinoza, essence is already power, and existents have more or less power.

Deleuze writes that while the syntagma 'what a body can do' has biological connotations, it is principally juridical and ethical. All a body can do (its power) is also its 'natural right', so that 'if we manage to pose the problem of rights at the level of bodies, we thereby transform the whole philosophy of rights in relation to souls themselves. Everyone seeks, soul and body, what is useful for them'.[50] A slight digression into the main tenets of natural rights theory will help us elucidate the main differences. A principal figure would be Cicero and more specifically his *De Officiis* which would have a substantial influence on Christian philosophers and jurists, including St Thomas Aquinas. Cicero's work on the office and duty would come to shape how life as such is conceptualized in relation to essence. Indeed, Agamben's *Opus Dei* illustrates the dual ontological structure and scission between being and having-to-be, what one is and how one is, essence and existence, through the paradigm of the office and liturgy. Deleuze teases out four main tenets that are of immediate concern for us in this context. The first being the notion that a thing is defined by its essence, so that natural right is that right which conforms to the essence of a thing. As far as the human being is concerned, its essence is being a 'reasonable animal'. Second is the idea that natural right does not refer to a state of nature as such that would be pre-social, but rather that the state of nature would conform to the good society and such a society would be one where the human being can realize its essence. Third, that what is primary is duty, such that it is only through duty that essence can be realized. Lastly, the belief in the practical rule of the figure of the sage who is singularly equipped to know what the essence is and how it can be realized. These principles run counter to Spinoza's effort to conceptualize essence as power. We are better able to see this through Spinoza's reading of Hobbes, an unlikely encounter perhaps. For Hobbes, the propositions just outlined are turned upside down. As Deleuze describes, first, things are not defined by a particular essence but rather by power, so that it is not the essence of a thing that defines its natural right but rather its essence is derived from what it can do, and this is its natural right. Second, that the state of nature is different from the social state whose prohibitions and rules are not natural rights but social. The state of nature is prior to the social state which effectively means that nobody is 'born' social as such. So that the problem for politics will be how to organize so that human beings as such become social and rights take on the function of fulfilling this operation of becoming social. Third, it is not duties that are primary but rather rights, and duties, as secondary, exist to limit rights. Lastly, that the reasonable person and the fool are equal, and are strictly the same, each one doing what is in their power, what they are capable of doing. For Deleuze, the classical theory of natural rights develops a juridical, moral view of the world and the theory outlined by Hobbes develops a juridical concept of ethics where beings are defined by their power. It is this idea that Spinoza will take up from Hobbes though with a few modifications. For Spinoza, we are not simply 'beings' but rather 'manners of being'. As manners of being we are then defined by what each one of us is capable of doing rather than by any fixed essence. Essence becomes that which each one of us is capable of doing, in this way, essence is identical to power and identical to *how* one lives, existence. The theory of natural rights then implies a coincidence between power and its exercise, and of such an exercise of power with a right. As Deleuze writes:

> This is the very meaning of the word law: the law of nature is never a rule of duty, but the norm of a power, the unity of a right, power and its exercise. There is in this respect no difference between wise man and fool, reasonable and demented men, strong man and weak. They do of course differ in the kind of affections that determine their efforts to persevere in existence. But each tries equally to preserve himself, and has as much right as he has power, given the affections that actually exercise his capacity to be affected.[51]

The radical thesis then is that, for Spinoza, power or right is unconditional; there is no life or right distilling machine, it is not something that can be referred to an act that then realizes it in relation to means and ends. This thesis runs counter to biopolitics as a mode of thought premised on scission and division, where life is made governable and assigned a value in relation to means and ends, where life itself is rendered unliveable directed to survival, and where one's capacity to act is conditional and limited by what Agamben would call 'factical vocations' and what Spinoza would call 'affections' and the possibility of encounters.

The point is not to say that all there is to it is to simply randomly multiply encounters, and therefore to live 'at the mercy of encounters'.[52] This would lead to an unbearable scenario, being affected by perpetual fear of encountering that which does not suit us, that affects us nonetheless, while diminishing our power of action, as Deleuze says: 'joys of hate would not eliminate the sadness involved in hatred.'[53]

Instead, if any role is to be given to the state of nature or even to institutions worthy of the name, it is to organize the possibility for encounters, in seeking to organize what might be useful and combined. Needless to say, it would be impossible to avoid all bad encounters, one cannot avoid death, as Deleuze says. So that it would be a matter of forming encounters or the possibility of encounters, to the possibility of being affected in such a way that increases our power of action. This is the ethical vision, where law and right coincide and natural laws are norms of power (in the sense outlined) not duties, and transcendent values are replaced by immanent modes of existence.

How might all this be relevant to the notion of destituent power? First, the disruption of the conventional view of right as being necessarily granted or just as easily withdrawn by a sovereign. As we have seen, the idea in Spinoza is that there is no transcendental value as such ascribing duties to be fulfilled in accordance with a specific essence or task. Second, being is the manner of being, there is a coincidence between essence and existence, *zoè* and *bios*, living and living well; the form-of-life is lived in its acts, generated in living itself. Third, the idea of the free use of the self, and lastly, a rejection of the concept of realization that implies the separation between the possible and the real, between potential and act. While philosophy itself has produced this conceptual and ontological separation it tries to bridge the gap by way of transitions (through morality or duty for example). For Agamben:

> In truth, there is no *transitus* since possibility itself is real, it already contains within itself the force that makes it exist; however, with the sole exception of Spinoza who transforms the *vis existendi* into a *conatus* internal to substance, philosophers have continued to search for this impossible passage toward the north-west in the ocean of metaphysics.[54]

For Agamben, Kant is a key figure in the development of the ontological fracture. In the Kantian critique of the ontological argument and in his doctrine on modality, on the transition from the possible to the real, Kant empties possibility of its *vis existendi* (force of existence, in Spinoza), emptying it of all reality.[55] Such that, 'the two orders of the real and the possible are incommunicable'.[56] While this scission or aporia between the real and possible is taken for granted, it is foundational to the ontological apparatus. As Agamben puts it:

> Essence and existence, potential and act, possibility and reality are the two faces or the two parts of the ontological machine of the West. Ontology is not, in fact, an abstruse artifice without any relation to reality and history: it is, on the contrary, the site where the most epochal decisions are made, with the heaviest of consequences. Without the division of reality (of the human 'thing') into essence and existence, into possibility (*dynamis*) and actuality (*energeia*), neither scientific knowledge nor the capacity to control and permanently manage human actions, that characterises the historic power of the West, would have been possible.[57]

In order for the machine to function, the two parts that are separated are made to be rearticulated, bridged, without much success. What is biopolitics as a system of thought other than the very site of this articulation? The site which defines and governs the boundaries and limits between essence and existence, both defining what is the essence, what is life and how existence should look like and be conducted. Instead, for Agamben, 'the possible is the instance of an unrealisable in every real'.[58] Here we could think of the relation between potentiality to and potentiality not-to that is involved in the act of creation, the basis of inoperativity.

The possible is unrealizable

What characterizes potentiality is that implied in it is a certain mastery over privation. In 'what is the act of creation?' Agamben suggests that the answer to this question cannot be solved by the idea of a transit, that is, from an act to its creation or from potentiality to actuality. It is not a matter of having a potential – artistic talent for example – that one simply realizes and actualizes. This is because, in every act of creation, Agamben writes, there is something that 'resists and opposes expression', that the artist 'can be and do because he preserves a relation with his own not-being and not-doing. In potentiality, sensation is constitutively anaesthesia; thought is non-thought; work [*opera*] is inoperativity'.[59] So that, it is not simply that potentiality is capable of impotentiality, of its opposite, but potentiality always already contains a resistance. For this reason, the act of creation can be thought as a dance between an impersonal element in us, Agamben compares this to Gilbert Simondon's notion of the pre-individual that, importantly, is not to be understood chronologically, and a personal element that resists the impersonal. Each work, in this way, is characterized by an impersonal element understood as the creative potentiality as well as that personal element which resists it. This is not to negate it but to *exhibit it* through its resistance, perhaps even in spite of itself. There is a brilliant illustration of this dance in a work of Kafka that Agamben brings to our attention, concerning the confession of a talented swimmer:

> I have, admittedly, broken a world record. If, however, you were to ask me how I achieved this, I could not answer adequately. Actually, I cannot even swim. I have always wanted to learn, but have never had the opportunity.[60]

Here, the swimmer swims without knowing how to swim, but this not knowing how to swim is not opposed to the potentiality to or ability to swim, rather it results from the deactivation of the dual articulation of potentiality and act; there is an inoperativity – it is, literally, being capable of one's impotentiality. For this reason, inoperativity is not inactivity, or passivity, but is itself a positive act, a rendering or making. As Agamben writes, 'inoperativity is not a suspension of activity but a particular form of activity'.[61] The term 'inoperativity' is essential to Agamben's delineation of destituent power precisely because it obliges us to think differently about the relation between essence and existence, potential and act, as well as that of labour or economic production and use. An example through which to think the latter is the idea of the town festival, which is not a complete suspension of work or activity, since food is still being prepared and gifts exchanged, while productivity as such is suspended. The preparation of food and exchange of gifts are subtracted from their so-called proper economy and put to a new use; they are 'destituted' from their proper or usual significance.[62]

Along with the swimmer who cannot swim, F. Scott Fitzgerald is the writer who cannot write. When the editor in chief of *Esquire* magazine, Arnold Gingrich, went to pay a visit to one of his writers in Baltimore at the end of 1935 to ask why Fitzgerald was no longer sending him any articles. Fitzgerald, ill, in the grips of alcoholism, replied by saying it is just that 'I am no longer able to write.' After some pressure from the editor, Fitzgerald relents and says, fine, 'I will write everything I can on the fact that I cannot write.'[63] This period was a difficult time for Fitzgerald, struggling with his own alcoholism and mental illness, his wife's schizophrenia, in the midst of war, a financial crash and a certain sense of growing older. This life, a process of breaking down as Fitzgerald describes it and writes about it in what would be *Crack-Up*, is composed of a silent crack at the surface, as well as the noisy external pressures which only deepen it and inscribe the body. Put differently, the wound that exists deep within the body can be understood as a pure event, where events are actualized in us. And yet, something happens. Fitzgerald, without being capable of writing, in spite of himself, writes something. To grasp the wound that pre-exists us is the essential question. Not to grasp it as being something unjust, as someone else's fault, for this can only result in *ressentiment* or resentment. Nor is it resignation, of accepting death and war, for example, as this would be another form of *ressentiment*. Rather, it simply means to become worthy of what happens to us. What does this mean? It means, for Deleuze:

> To become worthy of what happens to us, and thus to will and release the event, to become the offspring of one's own events, and thereby reborn, to have one more birth, and to break with one's carnal birth – to become the offspring of one's events and not of one's actions, for the action is itself produced by the offspring of the event.[64]

The challenge then, and it is a challenge as it is certainly no easy thing, is to take the risk of a counter-actualization that, for instance, actors and dancers practice all the time. It is to keep from the event 'only its contour and splendour' all the while acting one's own events. Inhabiting the most instantaneous present, it comprehends the future and the past, an *amor fati*. While the event is composed of the present, its moment of arrival and actualization, the moment of its embodiment in an individual or state of affairs where there is a future and past of the event easily evaluated with respect to it, there is another view. Deleuze says that this new perspective would see the future and the past of the event while sidestepping each present: 'being free of the limitations of a state of affairs, impersonal and pre-individual, neutral, neither general nor particular . . . it has no other present than that of the immobile instant which represents it, always divided into past-future, and forming what must be called the counter-actualisation'.[65]

This testifies for the individual who has cracked, who is not simply tired, but exhausted, where there is no longer any strength to carry out even daily activities. That is, they are no longer able to see what they are capable of. We would be mistaken in thinking that this has anything to do with realizing something, rather it has to do with power, with potential. You may no longer realize anything, though you may accomplish something.[66] Again, this is not passivity, there is a continuation, but towards nothing, the abyss, perhaps. It is the making of an image that dies away, wastes away, a pure intensity, a process of dissipation. From this dissipation emerges a new power, a counter-actualization. Something must happen for this to take place, this something is the crack. The difficulty is not to fall into it, destroyed and impotent, but to find a power or potential in it. This is a risky affair of course, as Deleuze describes, Artaud never managed it, though he made folds, techniques for breathing the unbreathable, he could not manage it.[67] Nor do those who make of what happens to them an instrument of power. One must be capable of living, which is only derived in *engendering*, in living itself, in lines of flight, after all, as Deleuze says, it is a condition of life to be able to break away from death.

6

Collective intellect

Immobility and expression without world

It is not at all self-evident how we would define the state of our contemporary collective intellect, except to say, along with Franco 'Bifo' Berardi, that today 'Everywhere, attention is under siege. Not silence but uninterrupted noise, not Antonioni's red desert, but a cognitive space overloaded with nervous incentives to act: this is the alienation of our times'[1]. We are saturated with symbols of communicability whose empty content can only leave us wanting more in our desperate search for meaning and connection. Our energies and attention are continually mobilized in the service of this saturation on which, and this is not without cruelty, our productive system depends. We are simultaneously producers and consumers of our attentive capture searching for answers and liberation in its captivating reels. Berardi argues that this means the abolition of privacy: that is, beyond its strictly juridical sense. In other words, not simply the rules that protect citizens from being watched but also 'the right to refuse to watch and to be continually exposed to watching and hearing what we would rather not see or hear'.[2] How could we today refuse? When the saturation extends not only from the devices used in our service to wage labour but also beyond, into our leisure time and across towns, cities, homes, in transit, taking over the full dimension of our spatial coordinates. In this way, irrespective of geographic locality or position, there exists a synchronization of affective experience that is, however, immobile and impotent. It is, therefore, expressionless since expression involves and necessitates movement. How are we to understand this injunction to express ourselves without expression?

Over the last few years, just as fierce discussions over both the provision of safe spaces and who has access to them have proliferated in various contexts – women-only spaces, spaces of hygiene, minority spaces among others – the juridico-political assault on communal or public space, indifferent to the commodity form or value of exchange, has strengthened. An illustrative case decided at the European Court of Human Rights in 2002 highlights the urgency of our present predicament. When Eileen Appleby together with other members of the environmental group Washington First Forum gathered in the new town centre in Washington in Tyne and Wear, England, to solicit signatures for a petition from interested parties in the local community, little did she know that this would be prohibited. The petition concerned a campaign against building on the only playing field available in the vicinity of Washington and able to be used by the local community. The trouble was that, by setting up a stall in the entrance of the shopping mall in the centre of town known as "The Galleries," displaying informative posters informing the public of plans to rid the area of the playing field and seeking signatures, Appleby and her group did not realize that they had no right to do so. The town centre now had new owners, a private company, Postel Properties Limited, who had strict rules as to gathering outside the remit of consumption. Once ejected from the town centre, a member of Washington First Forum wrote to the manager of the Galleries asking for permission to set up a stall. The manager replied and refused access, stating that:

> The Galleries is unique in as much as although it is the Town Centre, it is also privately owned. The owner's stance on all political and religious issues, is one of strict neutrality and I am charged with applying this philosophy. I am therefore obliged to refuse permission for you to carry out a petition within the Galleries or the adjacent car parks.[3]

This decision to refuse permission of entry into a privately run town centre is consistent with the common law of England and Wales, where a private owner is presumed to have granted an invitation to members of the public to come onto their land for lawful purposes, though with exceptions. Any such invitation can be revoked, and people ejected, without justification or any test of reasonableness. For Appleby and others this obstruction amounted to a breach of Articles 10, 11 and 13 of the European Convention of Human Rights, that is, respectively, freedom of expression, freedom of assembly and association and the right to an effective remedy. The Court ruled that there had been no violation. Since then, the assaults on expression and assembly have been too numerous to list, culminating in the Public Order Act 2023. This Act builds on the Police, Crime, Sentencing and Courts Act 2022, which gave police further powers to prevent and stop protests deemed disruptive, including any inconvenience to public transport and any activity deemed 'noisy'.[4]

The relative anonymity and impersonal mode of being in common that can be expected in collectively gathering in a public space has been exchanged for a monetized virtual space, a digital commons, predicated on authentication: authenticating the identity of the user, whose persona is held responsible for any utterance and is therefore culpable. In a time where the responsibility and accountability of power is inexistent, and seemingly beyond our reach, the reverse is true for individuals whose thoughts, careless remarks, jokes and outbursts are theirs alone, believed to be expressed in full self-mastery as subjects of will, responsible both for their meaning and for the consequences of their reception, joy or hurt.

The apparent freedom of the so-called digital commons operates much as the analogy of the highway Deleuze uses to describe the society of control – where one drives along the highway experiencing oneself as free all the while observing the rules set out in the highway code. In the digital commons, we experience ourselves as freely communicating within the framework provided by the service provider, as well as following the rules of particular regimes of enunciation. The phrases and statements exchanged are not only without content but order words. Indeed, with respect to content, 'information is only the strict minimum necessary for the emission, transmission, and observations of orders as commands'.[5] As to the order-word it is a language-function while discourse is indirect, there is no single voice in the voice. Deleuze and Guattari write: 'We call order-words, not a particular category of explicit statements (for example, in the imperative), but the relation of every word or every statement to implicit presuppositions, in other words, to speech acts that are, and can only be, accomplished in the statement.'[6] We are immediately plugged in to regimes of enunciation resulting in modes of subjectification and incorporeal transformations.

Take for instance the evolution of the relation between enunciation and culpability in the digital psychosphere mirrors debates in the thirteenth century over the becoming responsible of the human being for their actions; a long and drawn-out process, not at all self-evident. Though this relation was precisely vital to establish for the purposes of culpability and the evolution of the criminal law. When our enunciations in the digital commons – that have increasingly replaced our corporeal engagements – take on the form and language of the juridical, one can expect similar obstacles. It is no coincidence, then, that the primary identities that widely circulate are the victim, the persecutor and the judge. The pre-condition of circulating in the digital commons is, apparently wilfully, to agree to an incorporeal transformation into one of these categories, that are not fixed, of course, indeed these vary depending on the topic of the day. Just as an incorporeal transformation equally occurs when, Deleuze and Guattari remark, a judge delivers a sentence, and the individual becomes a convict. Being a virtual space, not every offence crosses over into the physical courtroom, rather these are self-contained in the spectacle. Much like the scene in Luis Buñuel's 1974 film *The Phantom of Liberty* where, after indiscriminately shooting at random members of society, the sniper faces a trial, the judge reads out the sentence, after which the sniper is free to leave to much applause from well-wishers. Such is the nature of the digital commons that, while having the form of sites of expression, function in relation to their own fulfilment, which is the extraction of value, no doubt a pleasant addition to the historic function of power in managing what used to be the problem of idleness or leisure, putting to work the erratic potential of the passions. In the digital commons these can continue to be regulated, guided and subjugated. The old division between soul and body is in this context replicated at the level of affect, inscribing an artificial separation between feeling and movement that expression necessarily entails. Etymologically, expression is an 'action of pressing out', 'an action or creation', a *use* of the body. For this reason, to describe the encounter, Spinoza uses the word '*occursus*' which is necessarily grounded in movement. Since it is in movement that the possibility for encounters can take place, where the possibility of affection and being affected can occur that necessarily implies a movement and a capacity for action, to do or to *refuse*. As already mentioned, this does not mean being blindly open to every chance encounter but rather learning how to build relations and friendships, being open to the possibility of being affected, moved, changed and developing the courage to act singularly and in common. Here, there is no inherently good or evil encounter, but simply what is good or bad for each person. This view is incompatible with the idea of judgement prevalent in our conceptual image of thought that makes decisions once and for all as to the predicates that make up the good or the bad.

Under these conditions, the soul is under siege. While the body has long been the subject of overt management and discipline, the capture of the soul has not been so evident. By and large, people were left to their own devices after working hours, more or less left to their own thoughts and affects, which did not concern the means of production as such. Today this is no longer the case, and lethargy is a common theme. The collective crisis in our capacity to think and to be affected in such a way that increases our power of action, in our use of the body, is overshadowed by the imperative to act. We are well aware of disasters just around the corner, across the territory, across the road, in our own home, as well as the dangers we could pose to ourselves. How can we not be compelled to act in the face of disaster and the prospect of extinction? So we take action, perhaps sign a petition or put into practice what we learnt at school or university and write think pieces to raise awareness of problems formulated from above, perhaps, with the help of seed funding gathered thanks to our Alumni groups or personal networks, we develop a start-up that manufactures tents not unlike miniature refugee camps to solve the problem of homelessness. Much like the Japanese arcade game "Whac-A-Mole", we stand ready for the next problem and on it goes indefinitely. Everyone, young and old, is an activist; we are not short of activism of one sort or another. These seem to be able to be integrated within our contemporary institutions, which have shown enthusiasm for certain ideas of dissent. While there are signs of integration and appropriation of movements and languages of rebellion and liberation, these should not be taken to be a reflection of the inadequacy of the latter, but the cynicism of the former. What it cannot tolerate, however, under any circumstances is the explosion, the demand for life, as the recent riots in Nanterre, Paris, illustrate. We cannot help but think of the *Mouvement des travailleurs arabes*, for whom it was precisely the demand for a transformation of their mode of living that was at stake, and ignored, returning now as a return of the repressed under similar conditions. The state execution of a young boy, miserable living conditions, except there is no longer any work, a forcible abandonment and designation of a whole section of the population as lives unworthy of being lived, a life of necessity and survival. As Jean-Luc Nancy writes in the *Experience of Freedom* (1988):

> For wickedness wants nothing more than for freedom to disappear into stern necessity, and for commonality to mean nothing but partaking of a common substance, a specific nature, one place of nativity, one nation, a particular race.[7]

A forcible alienation ensues, we can see that the capitalist religion in which we live aims not at transforming the world but at destroying it, and all the contents of the living, both human and non-human. In Christianity, the structure of separation is seen in the passage from the profane to the sacred; this structure of separation is mirrored in the capitalist religion, where it 'assails every thing, every place, every human activity in order to divide it from itself . . . In its extreme form, the capitalist religion realises the pure form of separation, to the point that there is nothing left to separate'.[8] Life is reduced to necessities, wherein the condition of possibility of survival is that nothing is to be profaned, that is, returned to common use. A new use of the self, a use of the body, expression, manner, inoperativity, remain out of reach. All the while, though, the demand persists, the explosive demand to live, of which all the former concepts necessarily entail. These concepts cannot therefore be associated with a quietism and the end of politics, but its being able to take place. For these demands are not to do with reclaiming a juridical right as such but an expression of *refusal* of the current state of things, an expression for a complete transformation of the mode of being of the world. That the people *think* means this: that things can no longer go on as they are, that the destitution of the world can only be, as Marx writes, 'the true resolution of the strife between existence and essence, between objectification and self-confirmation, between freedom and necessity'.[9] This is not to be mixed up with the idea of searching for a more authentic or superior life but rather a life where relations between self, others and the world can be redrawn, where different paths might be able to be traversed.

This is why a form-of-life necessarily coincides with the destitution of the social and biological conditions that it finds itself in. For this reason, it is necessary to challenge our present mode of thought, a biopolitical mode of thought, that already contains within it an articulation of a mode of life premised on value, premised on the separability, no matter how fictional, of the biological from the social, of characterizing life as a series of tasks to be accomplished necessary for survival. A whole series of rationalities are in play that maintain this perspective so that any statement to the effect that 'no one in the world should be left without shelter' appears infantile since we are incapable of thinking this simple truth. Our rationalities do not allow for it, and when the words uttered can never coincide with their intended effect, we cease to believe their truth, or at least take them seriously. This is a natural consequence of the division between the possible and the real, theory and practice, leaving us with the well-known sentiment, that something is all very well in theory but is incompatible with reality. And so the expectation is a certain conformity with a reality that is by all accounts turning unhabitable. And yet, nobody can claim to understand everything, to know everything with the degree of certainty required to believe in the merits offered up by our current reality. As Axelos writes:

> Nobody and nothing understands everything. There is always something to add, remove, change, say and do differently. No method has the ability to contain the course of the world and the course of discourse, and fluidity does not allow itself to be captured by any conceptualisation. Why is it impossible to say everything that comes to mind – would there need to be multiple voices? – and its connection with what is happening on the street? What is the breath of thought? The problem arises when we know that nothing is, nor is said, in its totality. We must schematise in order to speak.[10]

Yet this humble awareness of any limit to our understanding, of the insufficiency of a singular methodology to hold explanatory powers over not simply the contents of the living but its trajectory in the past, present and future, the course of its life, is an oddity if not a direct offence to the current state of knowledge that cannot acknowledge its own fallibility, sweeping schematizations and lacunae. Yet ambiguity and the equivocal exist, not least in language itself through which knowledge is made expressible, communicable and known. While language itself is constructed as a 'real' this construction is only possible by discarding anything that might not be a part of a meticulous order, either of grammar or syntax. This making of language a science representable for calculation and what is called communication. The trouble is that this perceived conceptualization of the real of language as neatly, and tightly, bound together is a mask. The real of language is full of faults. As Jean-Claude Milner writes:

> These lines of fault cross and overlap. Calculation identifies them as what is irreducible to calculation, but it is not another system that they delineate, on which one could construct a new, unheard-of-science [. . .] Yet their nature and their logic can be illuminated by Freudian discourse; in *lalangue*, conceived henceforth as unrepresentable by calculation – that is to say as crystal – they are the recesses where desire flashes and the thrill comes to settle.[11]

In other words, the calculable is retained and assembled into a homogenous whole that we call 'language', all the while excluding from its representation that which is not representable, believing that language has to be whole or one. Furthermore, the demand in question is that language be free from ambiguity, yet the reality of ambiguity, the equivocal, exists.[12] While the linguist strives to retain what is calculable and representable in language, they ignore that there is always something that is not able to be written or said: the not-all. The not-all is not the ineffable, it is on the contrary that which allows the all to be representable in the first place. It is the reference point from which the All is able to distinguish itself, as precisely not not-all. It is the shadow accompanying the real of language, just as the unthought accompanies the real of thought or knowledge. This is precisely what is not able to be thought in our age enamoured with the idea of artificial intelligence. A mirror of that which we call knowledge and intelligence, this mode can only recognize the calculable, recognizing syntax, speak the language of the marketable, without recognizing anything to do with living, which depends on the experience of the body. As Berardi puts it, 'this experience is impossible for a brain without organs. Sensitive organs constitute a source of contextual and self-reflective knowledge that the automaton does not have.'[13] So that while such systems are capable of intelligence they are not capable of thought, since thought necessitates a crossing over into that which is not able to be calculated: the not-all, the unconscious, the unthought, of knowledge and of reasoning. The ungraspable of sensuality, the capacity of being affected, by way of the phantasm and the imagination. While these two have long been expelled from the subject of reason, they persist and accompany our mode of perception even if unrecognized.

To phantasm

What happens to a word or concept that falls out of use? Its banishment or forgetting, like the smoke we see linger long after a candle's flame is extinguished, persists, patiently awaiting the time of its recollection or reconstitution. The word that we have in mind here and that has long ago fallen out of usage is the word *'cogitare'*, cogitate. *Cogitare* is not the same thing as 'think'. When referring to the act of the intellect, medievalists use the verb *'intelligere'*. *Cogitare* is something different. As Jean-Baptiste Brenet writes, first, it is not a fact of the intellect even if it can only be effectuated in its presence. It is an operation of the soul in its body. Secondly, cogitation, unlike intellection, does not have universal notions as its object. It moves from particulars, it proceeds from the animated body's encounters, sensations, with, beings of the external world, of their traces and imprints – their images and their phantasms. Brenet sums it up thus: 'I cogitate means: I phantasm.'[14] Medieval Arab philosophers posed this question, inheriting the Greek *dianoia* and thinkers of a new psychism where the brain is not the centre or site of intelligence or of reason, but became so only through images. Through the idea of *fikr*, possibilities and virtues were situated in this sort of intermediary realm as though the real world was in play in it. As Brenet writes: 'this third middle state is composed of floating representations, neither sensed nor conceived, such that man, before being reasonable, was a cogitating animal by way of its proper phantasms.'[15] Averroës (Ibn Rushd, ابن رشد) develops this idea further, joining the imagination to his doctrine on the intellect. For Averroës, cogitation involves a continual movement between images and memories. Importantly:

> This power of phantasms is ordered by an intellect distinguished by four extreme features: its substantial separation from bodies, its absolute uniqueness, its eternity, and the originary emptiness of its nature since, it is from the beginning pure potentiality. It is in the space opened up by this decentred, unique and omnitemporal mental power that Averroës situates the mediating work of cogitation.[16]

This notion of a third space, where cogitation takes place by way of the phantasms, is unknown in modernity for whom everything comes from the subject; the potential of the phantasm is erased. A forgetting then of the necessary link between the imagination and the intellect, even if, though expelled from the subject, lingers all around it, notably in dreams, where the phantasm still lurks. In *De Insomniis*, for example, Aristotle describes the dream to be a kind of phantasm, belonging to the sense-perceptive part of the soul.[17] Agamben refers to *Roman de la rose* to illustrate this point, an allegorical dream vision where the protagonist's dream provides him with a certain knowledge he would not otherwise have acquired without it, just as the Mohave community, indigenous to the Colorado River, believed that knowledge of myth and skills could only be acquired in dreams. To the extent that anything learnt in a state of being awake remained redundant unless this knowledge was also dreamt. As the anthropologist George Devereux says: 'after allowing me to record his ritual curing songs, a shaman explained that this would not enable me to cure people by singing these songs, because I had not 'potentiated' them by learning them also in dream.'[18] Devereux notes that those songs and myths that are dreamt are so long and detailed, that they would pose great difficulties to psychotherapists seeking to interpret or analyse them. This is because, as Emanuele Coccia tells us, 'dreaming, in fact, means first and foremost to imagine; the image is not just a simple psychic object here, but is in effect the matter or the life from which everything is made and everything is nourished.'[19] That is, it is not a matter of simple cognition to be interpreted, it is a coincidence with the medium of knowing, 'we are made of the same matter as the images that give body and consistency to our desires and our fears, and we have a body which is defined by its sole capacity to be and to become what we are able to imagine'.[20]

Agamben traces the notion of the phantasm to Plato's *Philebus* and a dialogue between Socrates and Protachus, concerning the relation between memory, the senses and truth. A question arises as to where, in the mind, does a painter draw up images of things said, and how does this take place? Socrates answers: 'When a man, after having received from the sight or from some other sense the objects of opinion and discourse, sees within himself in some way the images of these objects.'[21] Agamben says that this artist of the mind who draws the images of things in the soul is what is called the 'phantasy' these images or pictures are then defined as phantasms. For Plato, desire and pleasure are impossible without the phantasy, that a corporeal pleasure, isolated from any other senses or passions, does not exist. Moreover, according to Aristotle, there can be no memory without the phantasm, such that it can be said to be the necessary condition of the intellection and cognition. This mode of thought is foreign to us, Agamben writes, 'perhaps because of our habit of stressing the rational and abstract aspect of the cognitive process' and because of this, we 'have long ceased to be amazed by the mysterious power of the internal imagination, of this restless crowd of "metics" (as Freud would call them) that animates our dreams and dominates our waking moments more than we are perhaps willing to admit'.[22] For Averroës, the eye is a mirror where the phantasms are reflected, as a mirror, it needs to be illuminated for the images to be reflected – the air reflects the 'water' of the eye. Both the eyes and sense are mirror and water that each reflect the form of the object; in Averroës, phantasy is also speculation which can 'imagine' the phantasms without objects. It is Averroës' conception of the phantasm as the point of union between the individual and the unique possible intellect that would be the subject of much controversy in the thirteenth century. For Averroës, the intelligence is something that is both unique and supra-individual, that individual persons simply had the shared *use*. So that, 'the possible intellect is unique and separate: incorruptible and eternal, it is nevertheless joined (*copulatur*) to individuals, so that each of them may concretely exercise the act of intellection through the phantasms that are located in the internal sense'.[23] The image (reflected in the phantasy) is also the union with the supra-sensible. It is situated, then, at the limit between the individual and the universal, corporeal and incorporeal. The material intellect described by Averroës is a power and receiver of thoughts, while there is one intellect for each human being, the material intellect is shared. We have intelligence but only one shared intellect which is accessible to all. By 'one' Averroës does not mean an identifiable person like God, for example, but a power, a human power to think. It is common and not individualizable which is only able to be made use of through the phantasm or images. Beyond a mediating function, the phantasm is also a common power to think the material intellect.

This idea of a communal or collective intellect is also found in Dante's *Monarchia*, which draws heavily from Averroës' conceptualization of the material intellect. The specific power of humanity, Dante writes, is to think the *potentia sive virtus intellectiva*. Unlike God and the angels who think in act, the human being has the *possibility* of thinking, the potential or power to think. Such that what is proper to man is the possible intellect. As Brenet writes, for Dante: 'If, then, the power of human beings as such is intellectuality in potential, its essential operation can only be to activate it, and indeed to actualise it in its entirety simultaneously and all the time, without which a power would exist separate from its act.'[24] In this remarkable formulation we can recognize Spinoza and the conceptualization of essence *as* power, as already being power, so that there is a perfect coincidence between essence and existence, potential and act. How is this feasible for Dante? It is only feasible through the *multitude*. This is because it would be impossible for a single person to entirely and simultaneously put into act this intellectual power, or even for a particular community or village and so it falls to the multitude. The intellection is never a private, individual affair, it can only be realized in common: this is the meaning of *people think*. There is only a multitude because each one carries within themselves a power. For this reason, Agamben writes: 'I call thought the nexus that constitutes the forms of life in an inseparable context as form-of-life. I do not mean by this the individual exercise of an organ or of a psychic faculty, but rather an experience, an *experimentum* that has as its object the potential character of life and of human intelligence.'[25] This is the *experimentum crucis* of Averroism that, by way of the *copulatio*, conjoins the single material intellect and singular individuals, that is, by way of the phantasm.[26] Thinking, for Agamben, is not simply being affected by this or that thing but also and at the same time being affected by one's own receptivity, such that 'thought is, in this sense, always use of oneself, always entails the affection that one receives insofar as one is in contact with a determinate body'.²⁷ In this way, just as for Averroës, Dante and Spinoza, so too for Agamben, the act can never be fully separated from potential, that is, if there is thought, then a form of life can become form-of-life. The point is that this experience of thought can only ever take place as common use and potential, there is a multitude because 'there is in singular human beings a potential – that is, a possibility – to think'.²⁸ Moreover, the existence of the multitude is immediately political since it renders inoperative the mechanism of dividing life into specific functions, values and uses – this mechanism, the inscription of the ontological machine, cannot understand the conjunction of essence and existence but can only know and govern its separability, as something not-yet to be realized even if this means absolute privation and abandonment.

Through the looking glass

Ours is an age of the infinite proliferation of images, everywhere from our so-called public spaces to the devices we carry with us in every corner of the spaces through which we move through and inhabit, our mobile phones; we are saturated with disembodied images, of which we might not know the context or the significance, that mediate and saturate our thoughts, filling them with injunctions and injustices the world over, disasters, war, poverty and looming extinction in the face of which we remain immobile, circulating and exchanging these very same images to each other in the hope that somewhere, somehow, someone will do something. By and large, we remain spectators of our immobility and suffering; this is not to say that acts of sabotage and resistance to injustices do not take place. Indeed 2019 saw a massive explosion of mobilized anger. Everywhere from Baghdad to Santiago, to Paris and Harare, Beirut, Manila and Tehran, people mobilized bringing down leaders as in Lebanon and Iraq, and elsewhere gaining assurances with promises of reform. Yet the suffering and despair remain, with growing disillusionment, entrenched loneliness, famine and exhaustion. While mass impoverishment has taken hold, the number of new billionaires is the greatest since records began, testifying for an unprecedented degree of the transfer of wealth, a heist in broad daylight, a bonanza of the unhinged, with war, misery and impotence as constants.

Such is the cruelty of the spectacle, 'the very heart of society's real unreality', which ensures 'the permanent presence' of justifying the conditions and aims of our regime of social relations.[29] At once the dominant mode of production, it also governs our time spent outside this production process, all the while being informally part of it, participating, under the injunction to belong and be social, as passive recipients of its signs and models. The spectacle presents itself as a vast inaccessible reality that can never be questioned. Its sole message is: 'What appears is good; what is good appears.'[30] The passive acceptance it demands is already effectively imposed by its monopoly over appearances, its manner of appearing without allowing any reply.[31] There is no creative act in the spectacle; the latter can only impose a mode of appearance, it is 'what must be seen but can never be lived'.[32] The cruelty of the spectacle ignores our relation to the image and sensibility, what Pierre Legendre describes through the trilogy body-image-world. Between the self and the world, the potency of imagination tames the void, the abyss in which we dwell. As Legendre writes: 'it is not as if there were the world of things and us, rather there is the generalised theatralisation of man and the world.'[33] With our bodily sensibilities detached from the images, and the capacity to inhabit them eternally postponed, and loneliness becomes a generalized disposition. A loneliness that differs in kind and in form from a necessarily fecund solitude where thought can take place and the imagination flow. Arendt reminds us, however, that even in solitude we will eventually need the presence, solace, of other people, and that:

> the only capacity of the human mind which needs neither the self nor the other nor the world in order to function safely and which is as independent of experience as it is of thinking is the ability of logical reasoning whose premise is the self-evident. The elementary rules of cogent evidence, the truism that two and two equals four cannot be perverted even under the conditions of absolute loneliness.[34]

This kind of strict self-evident logicality has taken over that says nothing of the world. This is the trouble with the spectacle, the expropriation of images and experience, of language and world has left us with a cold determinism and boring causality that is neither inspiring nor comforting. The metaphysical tradition of the West requires a ground, presupposing it, to cover over the abyssal void of origins. In a short intervention concerning this theme entitled *Before the Abyss* Jean-Luc Nancy writes that 'since what is called "the death of God", we – Occidentals or the Western-planetary civilization – are before an abyss ... For the "God" that "died" was nothing other than the ground itself'.[35] This so-called loss of ground leaves us face to face with the abyss that since the beginning of the beginning we have strived to cover over and fill with meaning in the hopes of providing answers to the 'why' of life and living, filling it with stories and myths, images and emblems, that would come to serve as our reasons for living, making life itself worth living. Nancy observes that, today, explanations are offered that, while providing a series of facts concerning this or that phenomenon, end up saying very little. As Nancy writes:

> Today, for example, one can read in a magazine: why do we experience arousals [*Erregnung*] – joyful and sorrowful? And then, there follows a neuroscientific explanation with the brain, neurons, nerves, etc. But with this, we don't get to arousal [*Erregnung*] itself. Through this science we receive knowledge about causalities that have nothing to do with fear, joy, fun, or discontent.[36]

Nothing, then, to do with life and its manifold expressions, emotions, tonalities, affective possibilities and eternal contradictions. While the dominance of the sciences of ultra-modernity is new, the proximity to the abyss characteristic of the human condition precedes the 'death of God' from the seventeenth century. As the human being is the being without essence, answers to its 'what' and 'why' have always been sought and fabricated. For Legendre, this is the characteristic function of the syntagma *vitam instituere*, or instituting life.[37] To *institute*, Legendre says, is 'to establish, construct, in such a way that it holds up'.[38] Referring to Vitruve, a well-known architect from the first century, Legendre adds a crucial caveat: it is not enough for what is constructed or built to hold up, it must also have the *appearance* of being upright, the appearance of solidity. In other words, Legendre says, what is held up is underpinned by a projected image – by the *mise en scene*. Little captures the essence of the fragility of appearance and its disappearance better than Magritte's *La Lunette d'approche* (1963). It is not for nothing that Legendre says that all the images, mirrors and emblems evoke the ungraspable. Yet, the human being ceaselessly interrogates these ungraspable, ephemeral representations. 'We fabricate', Legendre says, 'what Magritte calls the Looking Glass'. We see a window left half open:

> The shutter that opens takes the landscape with it, the clouds and the sky. The looking glass discovers what lies behind the emblems, the images, the mirrors: a void, a chasm, the Abyss of human existence. It is this Abyss that we must inhabit. A reason to live begins here.[39]

The seductive abyss draws us into its emptiness, an abyss that we are compelled to gaze into, manipulate and make our own. From images to myths, emblems and slogans, the collectivity of thought fills the void and renders it meaningful. Gods in mirrors reflecting what we wish to see, a final answer to the '*pourquoi*' being too tempting to forego. And, so we go setting beginning after beginning, foundation after foundation. That we dwell in the dogmatic has long been forgotten; technicity having shunned the mythologemes characteristic of the foundation and ground, purports instead always certain origins. That the enigmatic always plays a role in our encounters is denied, which, for Legendre, shows that the aim is no longer 'an analysis of the human condition, but the legal realisation of the government of subjects'.[40] As Fred Moten and Stefano Harney write in the *Undercommons*:

> Governance is an instrumentalization of policy, a set of protocols of deputization, where one simultaneously auctions and bids on oneself, where the public and the private submit themselves to post-fordist production. Governance is the harvesting of the means of social reproduction but it appears as the acts of will, and therefore as the death drive, of the harvested.[41]

Our modern culture has forgotten its imaginal constitution, and yet, the uncertain persists – the shadow of language and the unthought, the phantasms and dreams that we are incapable of interpreting but precisely for this reason tell us something, all this necessarily accompanies our discursive, textual and evidential certainties. So that while metaphysics has been preoccupied with the presupposition of foundations as conceptual truths, in inadvertently shutting out the imaginal as their very condition of possibility, it brings forth, conjures up, the possibility of its own foreclosure. From the beginning, what has been in question for us is how to 'metabolize' that which for the human condition is precisely impossible to assume, assimilate or represent – this being the abyss and our shared relation to nothingness.[42] If there is to be a universal law that can be said to bind societies the world over, it is the shared dependence on the sensible for crafting an art of living, for the organization of social life; from government to *officio* and form-of-life. This law, Legendre tells us, stems from the encounter with the abyss – the lack of ground or foundation that irreparably envelops all human beings. And it is only through the experience of the sensible that any sense as such can subsequently emerge, or be thought, or constructed and even re-constructed anew. The stakes are high in the 'sensory apprehension of thought' since it is living itself that is in question. This anthropology of the sensible, as Coccia has called it, is not merely a question of cognitively intuiting the meaning of images put forth before us as living beings with so-called sensory faculties. Rather, 'the image and the sensible *give body* to activities of the spirit and give life to man's own *body*'.[43] It is an exercise in proximity, relation, perception of and to the image that brings the spirit to life. The human being can only live through this mediation. More than a faculty, what is in question is the *imaginalis*, which, as Chiara Bottici explains, is an adjective 'used to characterise a *mundus*, a world in itself. It is within this intermediate world – neither material, like the world of pure sensibility, nor immaterial, like that of the intellect'[44] that the imaginal operates. Moreover, 'the imaginal comes before the distinction between "real" and "fictitious"'.[45] More than representation or mirroring, reality and unreality, the imaginal is always an act of creation. In the spectacle, the trilogy image-body-world is effaced. The image is isolated; the body, as the site of politics, can only receive the image in its representative form, without reply and without world, a stunting of the act of creation. Perhaps our present condition is a testament to the consequences of the trilogy's apparent dissolution, a ceaseless confrontation with images that can only be seen, exchanged and presented, but not *lived*. Perhaps despite itself, the imaginal persists, irrespective of our willingness to perceive it or not. This is the quality of the objective unconscious that Coccia alludes to, akin to a medial space that exists externally to us.

What fills the abyss is not permanent, though it has the *appearance* of holding up; it can be imagined and made otherwise. There is no reason why this world might not be other than it is. This ought not to be mistaken for a return to an ideal past, but rather to remember the impermanence and fragility that envelop us. Clouded by the appearance of an unshakeable solidity of our institutions of domination and exploitation, we forget that enigma and the uncertain are always already present here and now. The leap of faith required to construct an unknown horizon is already taken in treading the familiar path, that is, in our familiar world that is itself structurally underpinned by instability and fragility. The void, the abyss, is always shared in common, and in whose void we continually glance even if we do not speak of it out loud. When Fernand Deligny wrote on his experiences working together with autistic children, thought to be entirely outside of language and symbolic reference, a lesson emerged from our eternal concern with the 'why'. The cartographic drawings of the *Lignes D'erre*, lines of errancy, attest to an altogether different relation to the world, a mode of existence specific to the singularity and context of each person living in common with one another. The tracings do not denote a history of the majority, nor a territory, but rather a cartography of life engendered in living. Going beyond the name, the traces exude life, the gestures of daily life. For Deligny, this makes possible a common space for those who speak and those who either do not speak or no longer speak testifying for the uncertainty of our contemporary representations, its ground is always in the process of dissolution. 'What does Lacan say?' Deligny asks, 'the one who takes the door for something real would carry it under his arm to make a draft in the desert'.[46] It will be for us to see that while the door appears to be closed, it can be picked up and put to a different use to make a draft in the desert, to pull apart all that appears as immovable, as a protective screen.[47] To learn to live again, though, this time, without 'why', without *telos*, goal or aim.

Conclusion
Sobriety

'But beautiful too is the time of awakening,' Hölderlin writes, 'so long as we are not awoken at an untimely moment.'[1] 'The grown-ups are back in charge' – who has not heard this sober phrase and not known, with an instinct that is unsettling by virtue of its immediacy, what it stands for – professionalism, efficiency, all of our era's zeitgeist contained in it. This is the time to actualize, to change, to progress and to achieve, to succeed, to turn the possible into a reality, with innovation, creativity and a can-do attitude. With this assurance, we can soberly 'keep calm and carry on', honouring the never-deployed slogan coined by Britain's wartime propaganda department, the Ministry of Information, while the light at the end of the tunnel fades further into the abyss which simultaneously draws ever closer.[2]

But sobriety is not equivalent to being *drunk on water* as Deleuze and Guattari once remarked, to becoming intoxicated on water, wine, poetry, love, laughter, virtue. This is the lesson of Baudelaire's 1869 poem 'Become Drunk' (*ennivrez-vous*):

> One must be drunk always. It's all there: it's the only question. Not to feel the horrible burden of Time that crushes your shoulders and pulls you to the ground, you must be drunk continuously.
>
> But drunk on what? On wine, on poetry, or virtue – to your taste. But be drunk.
>
> And if it should chance, on the steps of a palace, in the green weeds of a ditch, in the dreary solitude of your bedroom, you awake, your drunkenness dwindled or gone, then ask of the wind, of the wave, a star, bird, clock, anything in flight, any that moan, that roll along, that sing, that speak, ask what hour it is; and the wind, wave, star, bird, clock, will reply, 'The hour to be drunk! Not to be Time's martyred

slaves, be drunk; be drunk relentlessly. On wine, on poetry, on virtue – to your liking.'[3]

The actor Serge Reggiani delivers a beautiful reading of this poem adding both love and laughter to the list.[4] Why are love and laughter important for Reggiani, and important for us, too? Both love and laughter are movements in intensities. These are intensities since they are not necessarily of the individual, there is a relation to another intensity, something that escapes the code and what the code wants to translate. Intensities are of the body, being lived only in relation to them. For Deleuze, the intensive and the outside can be said to mean the same thing.[5] The outside is what is furthest away, further even than the external world and no longer mediated by whatever is represented in a diagram – it is impossibility and as impossibility escapes all negativity since it simply is, it is co-constitutive with being. 'Should we then say', Maurice Blanchot asks, 'impossibility is being itself?'[6] The answer is yes, that 'being' on the basis of possibility is at the same time without being. It is to this absolute outside, as impossible, that we must journey to. The outside is an impersonal space, a space of the 'one' and not of the 'I', 'One dies' Blanchot says, this is the line of the outside, the line co-extensive with life and death. The line of the outside is furthest and closest at the same time, and for this reason must be met, a fold must take place, and this would be 'techniques of breathing the unbreathable'.[7] In this way we can say that thinking comes from the outside, the absolute outside, where something prompts us to think, like the crack, it is an exigency for something to take place, of creating new possibilities of life, not as a series of acts to be realized but as a mode of existence. The 'crack' met with a counter-actualization which means and presupposes a new manner of being, a new manner of being affected, not to be re-inscribed in an already given state of affairs. This is why, Deleuze writes:

> If one asks why health does not suffice, why the crack is desirable, it is perhaps because only by means of the crack and at its edges thought occurs, that anything that is good and great in humanity enters and

exits through it, in people ready to destroy themselves – better death that the health which we are given.[8]

The biopolitical era in which we live cannot be thought as being simply the governance of biological life, limited to the politics of biogenetics or surveillance, since it concerns our everyday life, the manner in which we live, the presupposed separation between essence and existence, the possible and the real, living, and living well. To have done with biopolitics means to have done with the rationale of means and ends where the objectification of the living follows the ascription of values justifying that some lives can be lived at the expense of others. Biopolitics, enamoured by the 'what' and knowing nothing of the 'how' can only reinscribe and represent. Harney and Moten articulate the cynicism inscribed in this mode of thought:

> What is the content of (your) (black) technique? What is the essence of the (your) (black) performance? An imperative is implied here: to pay attention to (black) performances since it is left to those who pay such attention to retheorize essence, representation, abstraction, performance, being.[9]

What is missed is the leap into existence of the act of creation, not a project or plan to be realized but to pass through as the swimmer who cannot swim and the writer who cannot write, it is not a question of finding the essence but of experimentation, 'we head for the horizon, on the plane of immanence' Deleuze and Guattari write, 'and we return with bloodshot eyes, yet they are the eyes of the mind'.[10]

Smart Being is the being that has exchanged experimentation for certainty, thinking for information, risk for security. Though besieged by an existential angst which its own name admits it cannot see or perceive the cracks. On the occasions it does see a wound, Smart Being embodies the wound, falls into it, making it the instrument of its power, collapsing into *ressentiment*. It knows nothing of life and of the living, of how there can be love in war, laughter in sadness or life in grief, that is, the gestures of counter-actualization that take place everywhere in all corners of the world, it only knows the appearance of life in the spectacle. It pities modes of living in other parts of the world, the so-called 'primitive societies' who have not yet heard of the Smart mattress and Smart ring, 'intelligent sleep systems', that helps them get to sleep at night.[11] Sleep in a world where 'reality, in all domains, is undone by the processes of realization that are meant to ensure its consistency.'[12] All the while:

> The 'primitive' displays a greater openness, greater *attention* to the COMING INTO PRESENCE OF BEINGS and consequently, a greater vulnerability to its fluctuations. Modern man, the classical subject, doesn't represent a leap beyond the primitive, he is simply a primitive who has been made indifferent to the event of beings, who no longer knows how to heed the coming into presence of things, who is *poor in the world*.[13]

And for this poverty in the world there is no easy cure, no application or training session, despotic rule or masterplan for the 'common good'. Though these continue and will continue to be proposed, entrenching further isolation and atomization, they have the possibility of engendering thought, since 'stupidity (not error) constitutes the greatest weakness of thought, but also the source of its highest power in that which forces it to think'.[14] There is no guarantee in this, only the risk involved in thinking and the possibility of life.

Notes

Preface

1. Guy Debord in a letter to Jaime Semprun, May 4, 1986, https://www.notbored.org/debord-4May1986.html.
2. Jennings Brown, *Many Google Duplex 'AI' Calls are Actually made by Humans*, May 23, 2019, https://gizmodo.com/many-google-duplex-ai-calls-are-actually-made-by-humans-1834976966.
3. *Google Duplex: An AI System for Accomplishing Real-World Tasks Over the Phone*, May 8, 2018, https://ai.googleblog.com/2018/05/duplex-ai-system-for-natural-conversation.html.
4. Mladen Dolar, *A Voice and Nothing More* (Cambridge, MA: MIT Press, 2006), 143. For more on Lacan's concept of lalangue, see Jacques Lacan, *La Troisième, VIIème congrès de l'École freudienne de Paris* (Rome: Patrick Valas, Octobre 31–Novembre 3, 1974), https://www.valas.fr/IMG/pdf/la_troisieme_integrale.pdf.
5. Jean Baudrillard, *The Transparency of Evil: Essays on Extreme Phenomena*, trans. James Benedict (London and New York: Verso Books, 1993), 52.
6. *Forefront Excerpt: Germany's Designer City, Next City*, December 16, 2013, https://nextcity.org/urbanist-news/forefront-excerpt-germanys-designer-city.
7. Phil Jones, 'Refugees help power machine learning advances at Microsoft, Facebook, and Amazon', *Rest of World*, September 22, 2021, https://restofworld.org/2021/refugees-machine-learning-big-tech/.
8. Walter Benjamin, 'Capitalism as Religion', in Walter Benjamin, *Selected Writings Vol.1: 1913-1926*, trans. Rodney Livingston, ed. Marcus Bullock and Michael W. Jennings (Cambridge, MA: Belknap Harvard Press, 1996), 289.
9. Benjamin, 'Capitalism as Religion', 289.
10. Francis Fukuyama, *The End of History and the Last Man* (London and New York: Penguin Books, 2012).
11. Paul Virilio, *The Information Bomb*, trans. Chris Turner (London and New York: Verso, 2005), 9.

12 Gilles Deleuze, 'The Image of Thought', in *Difference and Repetition*, trans. Paul Patton (London and New York: Continuum, 1994), 147.
13 Paul Virilio, *A Landscape of Events*, trans. Julie Rose (Cambridge, MA and London: The MIT Press, 2000), 54.
14 Anne Dufourmantelle, *In Praise of Risk*, trans. Steven Miller (New York: Fordham University Press, 2019), 47.
15 Dufourmantelle, *In Praise of Risk*, 48.
16 Dante Alighieri, *The Divine Comedy: Inferno*, tr. Mark Musa (London and New York: Penguin Books, 1984), Canto IV, 98.

Introduction

1 Antonin Artaud, 'Letter to René Allendy, November 1927', in *Antonin Artaud: Selected Writings*, ed. Susan Sontag, trans. Helen Weaver (New York: Farrar, Straus and Giroux, Inc., 1976), 168–71.
2 Giorgio Agamben, 'What is a Destituent Power (or Potentiality)?', trans. Stephanie Wakefield, Environment and Planning D: *Society and Space* 32 (2014): 65–74, 74.
3 Karl Marx, 'Economic and Philosophic Manuscripts of 1844', trans. Martin Milligan in *Economic and Philosophic Manuscripts of 1844 and the Communist Manifesto* (New York: Prometheus Books, 1988), 102–3.
4 Giorgio Agamben, *L'irrealizzabile: Per una politica dell'ontologia* (Torino: Piccola Biblioteca Einaudi, 2022), 57.
5 Reiner Schürmann, 'Que faire à la fin de la métaphysique?' in *Cahier de l'herne: Martin Heidegger*, ed. Michel Haar, n45 (Paris: Éditions de l'Herne, 1983), 356.
6 Gilles Deleuze, 'The Image of Thought', in *Difference and Repetition*, trans. Paul Patton (London and New York: Continuum, 1994).
7 Deleuze, 'The Image of Thought', 159.
8 Gilles Deleuze, *The Logic of Sense*, trans. Mark Lester with Charles Stivale, ed. Constantin V. Boundas (London: The Athlone Press, 1990), 49.
9 Foucault, *Dits et Écrits*, T.1, 'Foucault', in Dictionnaire des philosophes, ed. Denis Huisman (Paris: PUF, 1984), 631.
10 Sylvain Lazarus, *Anthropology of the Name* (Chicago: Seagull Books, 2015), xvii.

11 Giorgio Agamben, *Homo Sacer: Sovereign Power and Bare Life*, trans. Daniel Heller-Roazen (Stanford: Stanford University Press, 1998), 2.
12 Agamben, *Homo Sacer*, 7.
13 Gilles Deleuze, *Foucault*, trans. Seán Hand (Minneapolis and London: University of Minnesota Press, 1988), 74.
14 Giorgio Agamben, *Karman: A Brief Treatise on Action, Guilt, and Gesture*, trans. Adam Kotsko (Stanford: Stanford University Press, 2017), 44.
15 Olivier Boulnois, *Généalogie de la liberté* (Paris: Seuil, 2021), 475.
16 Lazarus, *Anthropology*, 61.
17 Yan Thomas, 'Sujet concret et sa personne', in *Du droit de ne pas naître: A Propos de l'Affaire Pérruche*, ed. Olivier Cayla and Yan Thomas (Paris: Gallimard, 2002), 125.
18 Gilles Deleuze and Félix Guattari, *A Thousand Plateaus: Capitalism and Schizophrenia*, trans. Brian Massumi (London and New York: Continuum Books, 2004), 106.
19 Giorgio Agamben, *The Coming Community*, trans. Michael Hardt (Minneapolis and London: University of Minnesota Press, 2009), 28.
20 Benedict de Spinoza, *Ethics*, ed. and trans. Edwin Curley (London and New York: Penguin Books, 1996), 71.
21 Gilles Deleuze, *Spinoza: The Velocities of Thought*, Lecture 2, December 9, 1980, https://purr.purdue.edu/publications/2843/1.
22 Franco 'Bifo' Berardi, 'The Premonition of Guy Debord', https://www.generation-online.org/t/tbifodebord.htm.
23 Giorgio Agamben, *Stanzas: Word and Phantasm in Western Culture*, trans. Ronald L. Martinez (Minneapolis and London: University of Minnesota Press, 1993), 83.
24 Giorgio Agamben, *The Use of Bodies*, trans. Adam Kotsko (Stanford: Stanford University Press, 2015), 210.

Chapter 1

1 Foucault, 'Foucault', in Dictionnaire des philosophes, ed. Denis Huisman, in *Dits et Écrits* (Paris: Éditions Gallimard, 1994), tome IV, 631..
2 Foucault, 'Est-il donc important de penser? Entretien avec Didier Eribon' in *Dits et Écrits*, tome IV (Paris: Éditions Gallimard, 1994), 180

3   Foucault, *Dits et Écrits*, 'Foucault', in Dictionnaire des philosophes, ed. Denis Huisman (Paris: Puf, 1984), tome IV, 631.
4   Foucault, *Dits et ecrits*, 180, 'Est-il donc important de penser?' entretien avec D. Eribon, mai 1981.
5   Foucault, *Dits et ecrits*, 180, 'Est-il donc important de penser?' entretien avec D. Eribon, mai 1981.
6   Michel Foucault, *The Birth of Biopolitics, Lectures at the Collège de France 1978–79*, trans. Graham Burchell, ed. Michel Snellart (Hampshire and New York: Palgrave Macmillan, 2008), 219.
7   Kostas Axelos, *Introduction to a Future Way of Thought: On Marx and Heidegger*, trans. Kenneth Mills, ed. Stuart Elden (Lüneburg: Meson Press, 2015), 56.
8   Jean-François Lyotard, *The Postmodern Condition: A Report on Knowledge*, trans. Geoff Bennington and Brian Massumi (Manchester: Manchester University Press, 1984), 4.
9   Lyotard, *Postmodern Condition*, 38.
10 Lyotard, *Postmodern Condition*, 46.
11 Lyotard, *Postmodern Condition*, 4.
12 Lyotard, *Postmodern Condition*, 35.
13 Lyotard, *Postmodern Condition*, 36 [emphasis my own].
14 Lyotard, *Postmodern Condition*, 36.
15 Adolf Berger, *Encyclopedic Dictionary of Roman Law*, Vol. 43, (Philadelphia: The American Philosophical Society, 1991), 403–4.
16 See: *The Compact Oxford English Dictionary*, 2nd ed. (Oxford: Clarendon Press, 1991), 684–5.
17 *The Compact Oxford English Dictionary*, 684.
18 Lazarus, *Anthropology*, 55–6.
19 Lazarus, *Anthropology*, xii.
20 Echoing Agamben's formulation of a people without identity as 'whatever being' – see *The Coming Community* (2009).
21 Lazarus, *Anthropology*, xvii.
22 Lazarus, *Anthropology*, xi.
23 Lazarus, *Anthropology*, xx.
24 Lazarus, *Anthropology*, xx.
25 Lazarus, *Anthropology*, 72.

26 Reiner Schürmann, 'Que faire à la fin de la métaphysique?' in *Cahier de l'herne: Martin Heidegger*, ed. Michel Haar, n45 (Paris: Éditions de l'Herne, 1983), 360.
27 Schürmann, 'Que faire', 360.
28 Lazarus, *Anthropology*, 1–2.
29 Lazarus, *Anthropology*, 64.
30 Schürmann, 'Que faire', 356.
31 Roberto Nigro, 'From Kant's *Anthropology* to the Critique of the Anthropological Question: Foucault's *Introduction* in Context', in Michel Foucault, *Introduction to Kant's Anthropology*, ed. Roberto Nigro, trans. R. Nigro and Kate Briggs (Cambridge, MA and London: MIT Press, 2008), 127.
32 Étienne Balibar, 'Subjection and Subjectivation', in *Supposing the Subject*, ed. Joan Copjec (London and New York: Verso, 1996), 2.
33 Balibar, 'Subjection and Subjectivation', 2.
34 Peter E. Gordon, *Continental Divide: Heidegger, Cassirer, Davos* (Cambridge, MA and London: Harvard University Press, 2012), 2.
35 Gordon, *Continental Divide*. 1.
36 Immanuel Kant, *Lectures on Logic*, trans. and ed. J. Michael Young (Cambridge: Cambridge University Press, 1992), 537.
37 Kant, *Lectures on Logic*, 537.
38 Kant, *Lectures on Logic*, 537 [emphasis in the original].
39 Kant, *Lectures on Logic*, 538.
40 Gordon, *Continental Divide*, 69.
41 Gordon, *Continental Divide*, 69.
42 Gordon, *Continental Divide*, 69.
43 Martin Heidegger, Letter on 'Humanism' (1946), trans. Frank A. Capuzzi in *Martin Heidegger: Pathmarks*, ed. William McNeil (Cambridge: Cambridge University Press, 1998), 252.
44 'Do we in our time have an answer to the question of what we really mean by the word "being" ["seiend"]? Not at all. So it is fitting that we should raise anew *the question of the meaning of being* [*Sein*]. But are we nowadays even perplexed at our inability to understand the expression "being" ["Sein"]? Not at all. So first of all we must reawaken an understanding for the meaning of this question.' in Martin Heidegger,

Being and Time, trans. Jean Stambaugh (Albany: State University of New York Press, 2010), xxix.
45 Jean Greisch, *Ontologie et Temporalité* (Paris: Presses Universitaires de France, 1994), 72.
46 Iain Thomson, 'Ontotheology? Understanding Heidegger's Destruktion of Metaphysics', *International Journal or Philosophical Studies* 8, no. 3 (2000): 297–327, 302.
47 'Metaphysics does indeed represent beings in their being, and so it also thinks the being of beings. But it does not think being as such, does not think the difference between being and beings'. Martin Heidegger, Letter on 'Humanism' (1946), 246.
48 Balibar, 'Subjection and Subjectivation', 2.
49 Heidegger, 'The Age of the World Picture', in *The Question Concerning Technology and Other Essays*, trans. William Lovitt (New York and London: Harper & Row Publishers, Inc., 1977), 130.
50 Heidegger, 'The Age of the World Picture', 132.
51 Manfred Frank, *What Is Neostructuralism?* trans. Sabine Wilke and Richard Gray (Minneapolis: University of Minnesota Press, 1989), 152.
52 Balibar, 'Subjection and Subjectivation', 4.
53 Balibar, 'Subjection and Subjectivation', 4.
54 Indeed, in 1953, Foucault convened a seminar at the École Normale Supérieure on Kant's anthropology and Freud, and between 1954 and 1955 gave a series of lectures entitled *'Problémes de l'anthropologie'*.
55 This could be related to the fact that Heidegger's text *Kant and Problem of Metaphysics,* in which the themes of anthropology and finitude are raised, was only published in France in 1953 by Gallimard.
56 Daniel Defert, François Ewald, and Frédéric Gros, 'Introduction', in Michel Foucault, *Introduction to Kant's Anthropology*, 10. Note that this is also tied up with Foucault's critique of humanism, which should not to be confused with his reflections on the Enlightenment.
57 Michel Foucault à propos de 'Les Mots et les Choses' (1ère diffusion : 01/01/1973) Radio France, Archive Ina-Radio France, https://www.radiofrance.fr/franceculture/podcasts/les-nuits-de-france-culture/michel-foucault-a-propos-de-son-essai-les-mots-et-les-choses-1390104.
58 Michel Foucault, *The Order of Things: An Archaeology of the Human Sciences* (New York and Oxford: Routledge, 2002), 25.

59 Foucault, *The Order of Things*, 60.
60 See, for example, Lucile H. Brockway, *Science and Colonial Expansion: The Role of the British Royal Botanic Gardens* (New York: Academic Press, 1979); and Robert A. Stafford, *Scientist of Empire: Sir Roderick Murchison, Scientific Exploration and Victorian Imperialism* (Cambridge: Cambridge University Press, 1986). Moreover, since any 'specimens' brought back from voyages to Britain were considered to be the property of the Crown, deposited in the British Museum, it was possible to petition for government funds (particularly from military budgets) to conduct studies in comparative anatomy and taxonomy. See Janet Brown, 'A Science of Empire: British Biogeography before Darwin', *Revue d'histoire des sciences* 45, no. 4 (1992): 453–75.
61 Foucault, *Order of Things*, xvi.
62 Marielle Macé, *Styles: Critique de nos formes de vie* (Paris: Gallimard, 2016), 322.
63 Foucault, *Order of Things*, 272–5.
64 Indeed, it is worth noting that with representation, the notion of 'experience' is equally called into question, along with resemblance which is associated with illusions. See Foucault, *The Order of Things*, 57–8.
65 Foucault, *The Order of Things*, 336.
66 Foucault, *The Order of Things*, 336.
67 Foucault, *The Order of Things*, 337. We saw this earlier on with reference to Heidegger and the world 'conceived and grasped as picture'. Heidegger, 'The Age of the World Picture', 130.
68 Foucault, *The Order of Things*, 378. By way of clarification, it is helpful to note that Foucault's use of the term 'positivities' changes to the term 'apparatus' (*dispositif*) in his later work, the latter term derives from Hyppolite's usage and is borrowed from Hegel. For Foucault, both terms aim to understand the relationship between individuals and the set of institutions and processes of subjectivation. An interesting account can be found in Giorgio Agamben, *What Is an Apparatus?* trans. David Kishik and Stefan Pedatella (Stanford: Stanford University Press, 2009).
69 Foucault, *The Order of Things*, 347.
70 Foucault, *The Order of Things*, 338.
71 Foucault, *The Order of Things*, 340.
72 Foucault, *The Order of Things*, 341.

73 Foucault, *The Order of Things*, 341–2.
74 Michel Foucault, *The Order of Things*, 343.
75 Foucault, *The Order of Things*, 343.
76 See Xavier Bichat, *Physiological Researches on Life and Death*, trans. F. Gold (London: Longman, 1815).
77 Michel Foucault, *The Birth of the Clinic*, trans. A. M. Sheridan (London: Routledge, 2003), 144–5.
78 Foucault, *The Order of Things*, 349.
79 Foucault, *The Order of Things*, 349.
80 Foucault, *The Order of Things*, 352.
81 Foucault, *The Order of Things*, 352.
82 Foucault, *The Order of Things*, 353.
83 Foucault, *The Order of Things*, 355.
84 Foucault, *The Order of Things*, 355.
85 Foucault, *The Order of Things*, 356.
86 Indeed, in the late nineteenth and early twentieth centuries, a new interest arose in the notions of glossolalia and aphasia, to the extent that psychiatrists interpellated linguists to aid in formalizing an analysis; asking, for example, whether glossolalia could be considered a language. See Guillaume Sibertin-Blanc, Délires de langue, schizoanalyse de savoir linguistique: *lalangue*, anagramme, homophonie scénique', *Kenose: Revue Philosophique & Politique* (2013–2014): 39.
87 Michel Foucault, *The Order of Things*, 414.
88 Foucault, *The Order of Things*, 407.
89 Foucault, *The Order of Things*, 411–12.
90 Foucault, *The Order of Things*, 413.
91 Foucault, *The Order of Things*, 408.
92 Foucault, *The Order of Things*, 408.
93 Foucault, *The Order of Things*, 409–10.
94 Foucault, *The Order of Things*, 410.

Chapter 2

1 Bruno Karsenti, *L'Homme Total: Sociologie, anthropologie et philosophie chez Marcel Mauss* (Paris: Presses Universitaires de France, 1997), 4.

2   Karsenti, *L'Homme*, 5.
3   Karsenti, *L'Homme*, 5–6.
4   Karsenti, *L'Homme*, 6.
5   On Opus Dei and the notion of Office, see Giorgio Agamben, *Opus Dei: An Archaeology of Duty*, trans. Adam Kotsko (Stanford: Stanford University Press, 2013); on the government of the irrational, see Serene Richards, *Court of Miracles: On the Government of the Passions* (2024).
6   David Garland, '"Governmentality" and the Problem of Crime: Foucault, Criminology, Sociology', *Theoretical Criminology* 1, no. 2 (1997): 177–214, 180.
7   Patrick Zylberman, *Tempête Microbiennes: Essai sur la politique de sécurité sanitaire dans le monde transatlantique* (Paris: Gallimard, 2013).
8   Interestingly, in France, 'statistics' used to be called the 'moral science', that is, the 'science of deviance, of criminals, court convictions, suicides, prostitution, divorce'. See Ian Hacking, 'How Should We Do the History of Statistics', in *The Foucault Effect*, ed. Graham Burchell, Colin Gordon, and Peter Miller (Chicago: The University of Chicago Press, 1991), 182.
9   Giorgio Agamben, *What is Real?* trans. Lorenzo Chiesa (Stanford: Stanford University Press, 2018), 14.
10 Tim Murphy, *The Oldest Social Science* (Oxford: Oxford University Press, 1997), 120.
11 See Ian Hacking, *The Taming of Chance* (Cambridge: Cambridge University Press, 1990); Loraine Daston, *Classical Probability in the Enlightenment* (Princeton: Princeton University Press, 1988).
12 Agamben, *What is Real?* 40.
13 Foucault, *Society Must Be Defended*, trans. David Macey, ed. Mauro Bertani and Alessandro Fontana (London: Penguin Books, 2004), 36.
14 Foucault, *Society Must Be Defended*, 36.
15 Michel Foucault, 'Panopticism', in *Discipline and Punish: The Birth of the Prison*, trans. Alan Sheridan (London: Penguin Books, 1991), 198.
16 Foucault, 'Panopticism', 215.
17 Foucault, *Society Must Be Defended*, 37. The notion of insurance is a good example here, see François Ewald, 'Norms, Discipline, and the Law', in *Law and the Order of Culture*, ed. Robert Post (Berkeley, Los Angeles, Oxford: University of California Press, 1991), 138–61. See also Melinda Cooper, *Life as Surplus: Biotechnology and Capitalism in the Neoliberal Era* (Seattle and London: University of Washington Press, 2008).

18 Foucault, 'Panopticism', 222.
19 Foucault, *Society Must Be Defended*, 38.
20 Foucault, *Society Must Be Defended*, 38.
21 Michel Foucault, 'Truth and Juridical Forms', in *The Essential Works of Foucault (1954–1984), Volume 3: Power*, ed. James D. Faubion (London: Penguin, 2002), 79.
22 François Ewald, 'Norms, Discipline and the Law', in *Law and the Order of Culture*, ed. Robert Post (Berkeley: University of California Press, 1991), 141.
23 Foucault, 'Truth and Juridical Forms', 86.
24 Foucault, 'Truth and Juridical Forms', 87.
25 Foucault, 'Truth and Juridical Forms', 87.
26 Foucault, *Society Must Be Defended*, 39.
27 Ewald, 'Norms, Discipline and the Law', 139.
28 Ewald, 'Norms, Discipline and the Law', 140.
29 Ewald, 'Norms, Discipline and the Law', 140.
30 Ewald, 'Norms, Discipline and the Law', 141.
31 Garland, 'Governmentality', 180.
32 Peter Sloterdijk, *You Must Change Your Life*, trans. Wieland Hoban (Cambridge: Polity Press, 2013), 26.
33 Michel Foucault, 'Right to Death and Power over Life', in *The History of Sexuality*, trans. Robert Hurley (London: Penguin, 1998), 140.
34 Judith Revel, 'Biopolitics', in *Dictionnaire Foucault* (Paris: Éditions Ellipses, 2008), 25.
35 Indeed, for Foucault, the notion of power that had hitherto been developed limited the analysis to an understanding of power in strictly juridical terms. That is to say that power had traditionally been associated with prohibition, such that power could be encapsulated by the formula 'you must not'. For Foucault, this understanding of power is insufficient, and instead seeks to develop a notion of power that is not strictly limited to a juridical understanding, a form of 'negative power', but rather a conception of what can be understood as a technology of power. Shifting the analysis away from an 'ethnology of the rule' or 'ethnology of prohibition' to one concerned with power as a technique, or technology, concerned with the conduct of men and things. See Michel Foucault, 'Les Mailles du Pouvoir', Conférence de Michel Foucault au Brésil, in *Dits et Écrits IV 1980–1988* (Paris: Éditions Gallimard, 1994), 182.

36 Foucault, *Society Must Be Defended*, 24.
37 Foucault, *Society Must Be Defended*, 24.
38 For example, in the struggle between feudal and monarchical power the law functioned as a mechanism of monarchical, or royal, power against rules and institutions characteristic of feudal society. Foucault mentions the re-emergence of Roman law in the West during the thirteenth and fourteenth centuries, which served as a prime instrument for monarchical power to define the sphere of its own potential, its own power, at the expense of Feudal power. See Foucault, 'Les Mailles du Pouvoir', 185.
39 Foucault, *Society Must Be Defended*, 26.
40 Foucault, 'Les Mailles du Pouvoir', 186–7.
41 Foucault, 'Les Mailles du Pouvoir', 187.
42 Foucault, *Society Must Be Defended*, 93.
43 Foucault, *Society Must Be Defended*, 94.
44 Foucault, *Society Must Be Defended*, 94.
45 Foucault, *Society Must Be Defended*, 95.
46 Foucault, 'Right to Death and Power over Life', 136.
47 Foucault, *Society Must Be Defended*, 240–1.
48 Foucault, 'Right to Death and Power over Life', 136.
49 Michel Foucault, 'Governmentality', in *Essential Works, Volume 3: Power* edited by James D. Faubion, translated by Robert Hurley and Others (London: Penguin, 2000), 219.
50 Disciplinary societies can be characterized as a technique of power exercised for the production of docile or productive bodies during, more noticeably, the development of industrial capitalism. For Foucault, discipline is primarily concerned with the subjugation of bodies and control of the population as a whole, where in institutions such as the army, schools and prisons, what was demanded from 'participants' was not simply compliance and observance of a certain set of rules, but more importantly an adjustment in aptitudes and attitudes: the individual being expected to exercise a measure of sovereignty over themselves, eliciting a kind of logic of economic efficiency. A key example of this technique of interiorization is Foucault's analysis of Jeremy Bentham's Panopticon. See Foucault, 'Panopticism', 195–230; and 'Right to Death and Power over Life', 138–41.
51 Foucault, 'Governmentality', 208–9.
52 Foucault, 'Governmentality', 211.

53 Foucault, 'Governmentality', 212–13.
54 Foucault, 'Governmentality', 213.
55 Alain Desrosières, *The Politics of Large Numbers: A History of Statistical Reasoning*, trans. Camille Nash (Cambridge, MA and London: Harvard University Press, 1998), 147.
56 Foucault, 'Governmentality', 217.
57 Foucault, 'Governmentality', 219.
58 Foucault, 'Governmentality', 221.
59 Foucault, *Society Must Be Defended*, 240.
60 Foucault, *Society Must Be Defended*, 87.
61 Foucault, *Society Must Be Defended*, 89.
62 Foucault, *Society Must Be Defended*, 240.
63 Foucault, *Society Must Be Defended*, 242. Essentially, disciplinary techniques focused on the individual body.
64 Foucault, *Society Must Be Defended*, 243.
65 Foucault, *Society Must Be Defended*, 243.
66 Foucault, *Society Must Be Defended*, 254 [Emphasis my own].
67 Foucault, *Society Must Be Defended*, 254.
68 Foucault, *Society Must Be Defended*, 245.
69 Foucault, *Society Must Be Defended*, 254–5.
70 Foucault distinguishes juridical rule from the idea of 'norms', where the former relies on sovereign 'body' or the soul of Leviathan for its authority the latter rather is 'inventive' and have their own discourse, part of a whole mechanics of discipline. 'Disciplines will define node a code of law, but a code of normalisation, and they will necessarily refer to a theoretical horizon that is not the edifice of law, but the field of the human sciences.' See Foucault, *Society Must Be Defended*, 39. See also François Ewald, 'Norms, Discipline, and the Law', in *Law and the Order of Culture*, ed. Robert Post (California: University of California Press, 1992).
71 Foucault, *Society Must Be Defended*, 257.
72 Foucault, *Society Must Be Defended*, 257.
73 Donald A. Mackenzie, *Statistics in Britain, 1865–1930: The Social Construction of Scientific Knowledge* (Edinburgh: Edinburgh University Press, 1981), 33–4.
74 This problem can be situated alongside some of the arguments we looked earlier the effects of evolutionary biology on philosophical and

metaphysical questions about the world and of being as such. What we saw as the growing dominance of scientific explanatory models displacing theoretical, theological and speculative approaches to understanding.
75 Foucault, *Society Must Be Defended*, 257.
76 Foucault, *Society Must Be Defended* 258 [Emphasis my own].
77 For this reason, the question of biopower as technique and technology of the functioning of the state must be inseparable from any mode of political resistance.
78 Agamben, *Homo Sacer*, 122.
79 Agamben, *Homo Sacer*, 122.
80 Matthew Walters, *Death by Poverty: Canada's Assisted Dying Program Exposes Fault Lines in Healthcare*, February 9, 2023, https://www.leftvoice.org/death-by-poverty-canadas-assisted-dying-program-exposes-fault-lines-in-healthcare/.
81 Agamben, *Homo Sacer*, 122.

Chapter 3

1 Agamben, *Use of Bodies*, 263.
2 Agamben, *Use of Bodies*, 272.
3 Agamben, *Use of Bodies*, 272.
4 Agamben, *Homo Sacer*, 2.
5 Giorgio Agamben, *State of Exception*, trans. Kevin Attell (Chicago and London: The University of Chicago Press, 2005), 87–8.
6 Deleuze and Guattari, *A Thousand Plateaus*, 89.
7 Pompeius Festus cited in Agamben, *Homo Sacer*, 71.
8 Agamben, *Homo Sacer*, 71.
9 The peculiarity of the figure of *Homo Sacer* lies in the fact that he can be killed with impunity, that is, the crime of his death would go unpunished, as well as the fact that he is unable to be sacrificed.
10 Indeed, Agamben brings to our attention that Ivan Ilich once described the concept of life as a spectral concept, a fetish. See Agamben, *The Use of Bodies*, 201.

11 Georges Canguilhem, *Knowledge of Life*, ed., Paola Marrati and Todd Meyers, trans. Stefanos Geroulanos and Daniela Ginsburg (New York: Fordham University Press, 2008), xviii.
12 Canguilhem, Knowledge of Life, xix.
13 Agamben, *Use of Bodies*, 195. Elsewhere, Agamben shows how the Latin translations of the expression 'vegetative life' from Greek commentators were passed to modern medicine, so that the latter assumes an understanding and articulation of life whose origins are metaphysico-political, see Agamben, *Use of Bodies*, 201.
14 Agamben, *The Open: Man and Animal*, trans. Kevin Attell (Stanford: Stanford University Press, 2004), 13.
15 Agamben, *The Open*, 14.
16 Aristotle, *De anima*, trans. Christopher Shields (Oxford: Oxford University Press, 2016), 413a 20, 24.
17 Agamben, *The Use of Bodies*, 200.
18 Agamben, *Use of Bodies*, 202.
19 Agamben, *Use of Bodies*, 206. See also: 'the being that desires and demands, in demanding, modifies, desires, and constitutes itself. "To preserve in its being" means this and nothing else,' Agamben, *The Use of Bodies*, 171.
20 Here we can think of Agamben's example in relation to the comatose patient, whose biological life is dependent upon life-support technology; and the boundary between life and death hangs in the balance between progress of medicine and legal decisions. Where, in the case of Karen Quinlan, her body becomes 'a legal being as much as it is a biological being' where 'a law that seeks to decide on life is embodied in a life that coincides with death'. See Agamben, *Homo Sacer*, 186.
21 Agamben, *The Open*, 14.
22 Agamben, *The Open*, 15.
23 Xavier Bichat, *Physiological Researches on Life and Death*, trans. F. Gold (London: Longman, 1815), 23.
24 Moreover, it is on the basis of this distinction that 'power over life' as an essential task of government becomes possible, as biopolitics.
25 Agamben, *The Open*, 16.
26 Agamben, *The Open*, 16.
27 This is the problem of biopolitics and will be further illustrated in the following section. In an article concerning the problem of the subject

and the notion of legal personality, Yan Thomas develops an interesting argument in relation to the idea of ascribing a form of personhood to endangered plants as a technique of conservation. Thomas is critical of this idea, suggesting that it merely reinforces the notion that the human being is the centre of the universe, while purporting the contrary. See Yan Thomas, 'Le Sujet de Droit, La Personne et la Nature: Sur la critique contemporaine du sujet de droit', *Le Débat* 3, no.100 (1998): 85–107.
28 Agamben, *The Open*, 15–16.
29 Agamben, *The Open*, 24.
30 Agamben, *The Open*, 37.
31 Agamben, *The Open*, 37.
32 Agamben, *The Open*, 21.
33 Agamben, *The Open*, 26.
34 Agamben, *The Open*, 34.
35 Agamben, *The Open*, 35.
36 Agamben, *The Open*, 36.
37 Agamben, *The Open*, 36.
38 Agamben, *The Open*, 37.
39 Agamben, *The Open*, 37.
40 Agamben, *The Open*, 38.
41 Foucault, 'Right to Death and Power over Life', 140.
42 Agamben, *Homo Sacer*, 2.
43 Agamben, *Homo Sacer*, 6.
44 Agamben, *Homo Sacer*, 7.
45 Aristotle cited in Agamben, *The Use of Bodies*, 12.
46 Agamben, *The Use of Bodies*, 13.
47 Yan Thomas, 'L'"usage" et les "fruits" de l'esclave: Opérations juridiques romaines sur le travail', the 'Uses' and the 'Fruits' of the Slave. Roman Juridical Operations on Work (1999) *Enquête* 7: 203–30 (electronic edition: http://enquete.revues.org/1578), 4.
48 Thomas, 'L'"usage" et les "fruits" de l'esclave', 4.
49 Thomas, 'L'"usage" et les "fruits" de l'esclave', 5.
50 Thomas, 'L'"usage" et les "fruits" de l'esclave', 6.
51 'It is precisely because the master who places his slave with a third-party conserves ownership [*la propriétée*] over this instrument, that work must be circumscribed as an object dissociated from the servile body. From the

beginning, the juridical category of work is the result of an operation from which is separated the human body the revenue that it is in alignment with, and the usage that remains attached either to the master or to the *usuarius* and, as such, remains subtracted from market circulation. The law here truly constructs an "object."' in Thomas, 'L'"usage" et les "fruits" de l'esclave', 16.

52 Agamben, *The Use of Bodies*, 16.
53 Agamben, *The Use of Bodies*, 17.
54 Agamben, *The Use of Bodies*, 20.
55 Agamben, *The Use of Bodies*, 20.
56 Agamben, *The Use of Bodies*, 23.
57 Agamben, *The Use of Bodies*, 20–1.
58 Agamben, *The Use of Bodies*, 203. [Emphasis my own].
59 Agamben, *The Use of Bodies*, 204.
60 Giorgio Agamben, *Means Without End: Notes on Politics*, trans. Vincenzo Binetti and Cesare Casarino (Minneapolis and London: University of Minnesota Press, 2000), 4.
61 Giorgio Agamben, 'For a Philosophy of Infancy', *Public* 21 (2001): 120–2, 121.
62 Giorgio Agamben, *Potentialities*, ed. and trans. Daniel Heller-Roazen (Stanford: Stanford University Press, 1999), 237.
63 Gilles Deleuze, 'Immanence a Life', in *Pure Immanence: Essays on A Life*, trans. Anne Boyman (New York: Zone Books, 2001), 30.
64 Deleuze, 'Immanence a Life', 30.
65 Agamben, 'For a Philosophy of Infancy', 122.
66 Agamben, 'For a Philosophy of Infancy', 122.
67 Agamben, 'For a Philosophy of Infancy', 122.
68 Agamben, *Use of Bodies*, 191.
69 Agamben, *Use of Bodies*, 226.
70 Agamben, *Use of Bodies*, 226.
71 See Agamben, *Use of Bodies*, 226–7.
72 Benjamin Bratton, *Revenge of the Real: Politics for a Post-pandemic World* (London and New York: Verso Books, 2021), 115.
73 Bratton, *Revenge of the Real*, 115–16.
74 Bratton, *Revenge of the Real*, 116.
75 Agamben, *Use of Bodies*, 223.

76 Bratton, *Revenge of the Real*, 115.
77 Agamben, *Use of Bodies*, 127.
78 Heidegger cited in Agamben, *Use of Bodies*, 182.
79 Agamben, *Use of Bodies*, 177.
80 Agamben, *Use of Bodies*, 177.
81 Agamben, *Use of Bodies*, 181.
82 Bratton, *Revenge of the Real*, 115–16.
83 Bratton, *Revenge of the Real*, 115–16.
84 Michael Sainato, *14-hour Days and No Bathroom Breaks: Amazon's Overworked Delivery Drivers*, March 11, 2021, https://www.theguardian.com/technology/2021/mar/11/amazon-delivery-drivers-bathroom-breaks-unions.
85 https://www.theguardian.com/technology/2021/mar/11/amazon-delivery-drivers-bathroom-breaks-unions.
86 Bratton, *Revenge of the Real*, 142.

Chapter 4

1 Image from Agence Im'Media. Cité de transit Gutenberg, Nanterre.
2 Alison Ross, *May '68 and Its Afterlives* (Chicago and London: University of Chicago Press, 2002), 85.
3 Abdellali Hajjat, 'Alliances inattendues à la Goutte d'Or', in *68: Une histoire collective (1962–1981)*, ed. Michelle Zancarini-Fournel and Philippe Artieres (Paris: La Découverte, 2008), 522.
4 Abdellali Hajjat, 'L'expérience politique du Mouvement des travailleurs arabes', *Contretemps* 16 (2006): 76–85, 83.
5 Nan Robertson, 'Renault Strife Worries France', 4 April 1973, https://www.nytimes.com/1973/04/04/archives/renault-strife-worries-france-a-new-generation-nightmare-of-the.html.
6 https://www.nytimes.com/1973/04/04/archives/renault-strife-worries-france-a-new-generation-nightmare-of-the.html.
7 Hajjat, 'L'expérience politique du Mouvement des travailleurs arabes', 87.
8 Hajjat, 'L'expérience politique du Mouvement des travailleurs arabes', 6.
9 Walter J. Nicholls and Justus Uitermark, *Cities and Social Movements: Immigrants' Rights Activism in the United States, France, and the Netherlands, 1970–2015* (Oxford: Wiley, 2016), 60.

10 Nicholls and Uitermark, *Cities and Social Movements*, 61.
11 Jean Baudrillard, *L'échange symbolique et la mort* (Paris: Gallimard, 1976), 42–3.
12 Baudrillard, *L'échange symbolique*, 46.
13 Baudrillard, *L'échange symbolique*, 46.
14 Jacques Derrida, *The Work of Mourning*, ed. Pascale-Anne Brault and Michael Naas (London and Chicago: University of Chicago Press, 2001), 87.
15 Laure Pitti, 'Grèves Ouvrières versus lutes de l'immigration: une controverse entre historiens', *Ethnologie Française* 31 (2001): 465–76, 466.
16 Pitti, 'Grèves Ouvrières versus lutes de l'immigration', 465–76, 466.
17 Pitti, 'Grèves Ouvrières versus lutes de l'immigration', 467.
18 Pitti, 'Grèves Ouvrières versus lutes de l'immigration', 472.
19 Gilles Deleuze, 'G comme Gauche', in *L'Abécédaire de Gilles Deleuze, avec Claire Parnet,* produced by Pierre-André Boutang (Paris: DVD Editions Montparnasse, 1994).
20 Foucault, *Society Must Be Defended*, 39.
21 Laurent de Sutter, *Hors la loi : Théorie de l'anarchie juridique* (Paris: Les liens qui libèrent, 2021), 106.
22 Agamben, *State of Exception*, 87–8.
23 Peter Goodrich, *Languages of Law: From Logics of Memory to Nomadic Masks* (London: Weidenfeld and Nicolson, 1990), 278.
24 See Hannah Arendt, *The Origins of Totalitarianism* (New York: Harcourt, 1951).
25 Thomas, 'Sujet concret et sa personne', 125.
26 Thomas, 'Sujet concret et sa personne', 125.
27 Thomas, 'Sujet concret et sa personne', 126.
28 Thomas, 'Sujet concret et sa personne', 130.
29 Anastasia Greene, 'Symposium Exploring the Crime of Ecocide: Rights of Nature and Ecocide', Opinio Juris, September 24, 2020, http://opiniojuris.org/2020/09/24/symposium-exploring-the-crime-of-ecocide-rights-of-nature-and-ecocide/.
30 Thomas, 'Le Sujet de droit, la personne et la nature', 85, 97.
31 Simone Weil, 'Human Personality', in *Simone Weil: An Anthology*, ed. Sian Mills (London: Penguin, 2005), 70.
32 Weil, 'Human Personality', 93.

33 Weil, 'Human Personality', 84.
34 Yan Thomas, 'Prefazione a L'artificio delle istituzioni, 250, cited in Xenia Chiaramonte, Instituting: A Legal Practice, HUMANA.MENTE', *Journal of Philosophical Studies* 41 (2022): 1–23, 15.
35 Thomas cited in Giorgio Agamben, 'La vie et le droit', in *Aux origines des cultures juridiques europeenes: Yan Thomas entre droit et sciences sociales*, ed. Paolo Napoli (Rome: Collection de L'École Française de Rome, 2013), 252.
36 de Sutter, *Hors la loi*, 104.
37 Arendt cited in Agamben, *Homo Sacer*, 126.
38 Giorgio Agamben, 'We Refugees', trans. Michael Rocke, *Symposium* 29, no. 2 (1995): 114–19, 118.
39 Agamben, *Homo Sacer*, 128.
40 Agamben, *Homo Sacer*, 130.
41 Agamben, *Homo Sacer*, 131.
42 Shamima Begum: Spy for Canada smuggled schoolgirl to Syria, August 31, 2022, https://www.bbc.co.uk/news/uk-62726954.
43 Agamben, *Use of Bodies*, 263.
44 Deleuze, 'G comme Gauche'.
45 Nathan Moore presents a brilliant formulation of this conceptual gesture in the aptly titled 'Pay it All Back: Paranoid Writing/Writing Paranoia', in *Burroughs Unbound*, ed. S. E. Gontarski (Cambridge: Bloomsbury, 2022).
46 François Zourabichvili, 'Deleuze et le Possible (de l'involontarisme en politique)', in *Gilles Deleuze: Une vie philosophique: rencontres internationales Rio de Janeiro-São Paulo, 10–14 juin 1996*, ed. Éric Alliez (Paris: Institut Synthélabo, 1998), 342.
47 Zourabichvili, 'Deleuze et le Possible', 345.
48 Deleuze and Guattari, *A Thousand Plateaus*, 106.
49 Deleuze and Guattari, *A Thousand Plateaus*, 106.

Chapter 5

1 Henri Lefebvre, *Critique de la vie Quotidienne I* (Paris: L'Arche Editeur, 1997), 58.

2 Achille Mbembe, *Brutalisme* (Paris: Éditions la Découverte, 2020).
3 Goodrich, *Languages of Law*, 278.
4 Antonin Artaud, *Theatre and Its Double* (New York: Grove Press, 1958), 79.
5 Artaud, *Theatre*, 86.
6 Artaud, *Theatre*, 83.
7 Deleuze and Guattari, *A Thousand Plateaus*, 481.
8 Deleuze and Guattari, *A Thousand Plateaus*, 482.
9 See Jessica Whyte, 'The Opacity of Economic Coercion', *Yale Journal of International Law*, June 21, 2023, https://www.yjil.yale.edu/the-opacity-of-economic-coercion/.
10 Benjamin, 'Capitalism as Religion', 288.
11 Benjamin, 'Capitalism as Religion', 288.
12 See V. I. Lenin, *What Is to Be Done?* (New York: International Publishers, 1969).
13 Thomas Hobbes, *On the Citizen* (Cambridge: Cambridge University Press, 2003), 137.
14 Foucault, *Society Must Be Defended*, 43.
15 Foucault, *Society Must Be Defended*, 44.
16 Hobbes, *On the Citizen*, 72.
17 Paolo Virno, *A Grammar of the Multitude* (Los Angeles: Semiotext(e): 2004), 23.
18 Virno, *Grammar*, 23.
19 Hobbes, *On the Citizen*, 71.
20 Giorgio Agamben, *Stasis: Civil War as a Political Paradigm* (Stanford: Stanford University Press, 2015), 47.
21 Agamben, *Stasis*, 41.
22 Agamben, *Stasis*, 41.
23 Agamben, *Means Without End*, 32.
24 Agamben, *State of Exception*, 88.
25 Agamben, *State of Exception*, 18.
26 Agamben, *State of Exception*, 35.
27 Agamben, *State of Exception*, 51.
28 Agamben, *State of Exception*, 52.
29 Walter Benjamin, "The Critique of Violence," cited in Agamben, *State of Exception*, 56.
30 Agamben, *State of Exception*, 57.

31 Walter Benjamin, "Theses on the Concept of History," in Walter Benjamin, *Illuminations,* ed. Hannah Arendt, trans. Harry Zohn (New York: Schocken Books, 1969), 257.
32 Agamben, *State of Exception*, 59.
33 Walter Benjamin, "Critique of Violence," in Walter Benjamin, *Reflections: Essays, Aphorisms, Autobiographical Writings*, trans. Edmund Jephcott, ed. Peter Demetz (New York: Schocken Books, 1986), 277.
34 Agamben, *State of Exception*, 61.
35 Marcello Tari, *There is No Unhappy Revolution: The Communism of Destitution*, trans. Richard Braude (New York: Common Notions, 2021), 55.
36 Tari, *There Is No Unhappy Revolution*, 59.
37 Tari, *There Is No Unhappy Revolution*, 61.
38 Giorgio Agamben, *Création et anarchie*, trans. Joël Gayraud (Paris: Payot et rivages, 2019), 128.
39 Agamben, *Création et anarchie*, 128.
40 Tiqqun in Agamben, *Use of Bodies*, 231.
41 Agamben, *The Coming Community*, 27.
42 Agamben, *The Coming Community*, 1.
43 Agamben, *Coming Community*, 1.
44 Agamben, *Coming Community*, 28.
45 Agamben, *Use of Bodies*, 128–9.
46 Agamben, *Coming Community*, 28.
47 Agamben, *Use of Bodies*, 223.
48 Gilles Deleuze, *Expressionism in Philosophy: Spinoza*, trans. Martin Joughin (New York: Zone Books, 1990), 255.
49 Deleuze, *Spinoza*.
50 Deleuze, *Expressionism in Philosophy*, 257.
51 Deleuze, *Expressionism in Philosophy*, 258.
52 Deleuze, *Expressionism in Philosophy*, 260.
53 Deleuze, *Expressionism in Philosophy*, 260.
54 Agamben, *L'irrealizzabile*, 51–2.
55 Agamben, *L'irrealizzabile*, 59.
56 Étienne Gilson, cited in Agamben, *L'irrealizzabile*, 59.
57 Agamben, *L'irrealizzabile*, 59.
58 Agamben, *L'irrealizzabile*, 85.

59 Giorgio Agamben, "What Is the Act of Creation?" in *The Fire and the Tale*, trans. Lorenzo Chiesa (Stanford: Stanford University Press, 2017) 39 and 40.
60 Kafka cited in Agamben, "What Is the Act of Creation?," 46.
61 Giorgio Agamben, "Vers une théorie de la puissance destituante," https://lundi.am/vers-une-theorie-de-la-puissance-destituante-Par-Giorgio-Agamben.
62 Agamben, "Vers une théorie de la puissance destituante."
63 This anecdote is mentioned by Sheilah Graham in her book *Beloved Infidel*, see Maxime Beaucamp, "Deleuze et La Fêlure de Francis Scott Fitzgerald: de Logique du sens à Mille plateaux," *Klesis: Revue Philosophique* 20 (2011): 104–21, n6 106.
64 Deleuze, *Logic of Sense*, 149–50.
65 Deleuze, *Logic of Sense*, 151.
66 Gilles Deleuze, "The Exhausted," trans. Anthony Uhlmann, *SubStance* 24, no. 3 (1995): 3–28, 4.
67 Gilles Deleuze, *Seminar on Foucault, 1985–1986*, Lecture 20, April 22, 1986.

Chapter 6

1 Franco 'Bifo' Berardi, *The Soul at Work: From Alienation to Autonomy*, trans. Francesca Cadel and Giuseppina Mecchia (Los Angeles: Semiotext(e), 2009), 108.
2 Berardi, *The Soul at Work*, 107–8.
3 Appleby and Others v. The United Kingdom 2002.
4 HM Government. 2022. "Policy paper: Noise-related provisions: Police, Crime, Sentencing and Courts Act 2022 factsheet" https://www.gov.uk/government/publications/police-crime-sentencing-and-courts-bill-2021-factsheets/police-crime-sentencing-and-courts-bill-2021-noise-related-provisions-factsheet.
5 Deleuze and Guattari, *A Thousand Plateaus*, 76.
6 Deleuze and Guattari, *A Thousand Plateaus*, 79.
7 Jean-Luc Nancy, *The Experience of Freedom*, trans. Bridget McDonald (Stanford: Stanford University Press, 1993), xxvii.
8 Giorgio Agamben, *Profanations*, trans. Jeff Fort (New York: Zone Books, 2007), 81.

9 Marx, *Economic and Philosophic Manuscripts*, 102–3.
10 Kostas Axelos, *Vers la pensée planétaire: the devenir-pensée du monde et le devenir-monde de la pensée* (Paris: Éditions Les Belles Lettres, 2019), 15.
11 Jean-Claude Milner, *For the Love of Language*, trans. Ann Banfield (New York: Palgrave, 1990), 52 [Note the English translation uses 'thrill' to denote the term '*jouissance.*'].
12 Milner, *For the Love of Language*, 59.
13 Franco 'Bifo' Berardi, *The Completion, Issue 137*, June 2023, https://www.e-flux.com/journal/137/544269/the-completion/.
14 Jean-Baptiste Brenet, *Je fantasme: Averroès et l'espace potentiel* (Paris: Éditions Verdier, 2017), 10.
15 Brenet, *Je fantasme*, 11.
16 Brenet, *Je fantasme*, 12.
17 Aristotle, *De Insomniis*, in *The Parva Naturalia*, ed. J. I. Beare (Oxford: The Clarendon Press, 1908), 459a, 94.
18 George Devereux, 'Dream Learning and Individual Ritual Differences in Mohave Shamanism', *American Anthropologist*, New Series 59, no.6 (December 1957): 1036.
19 Emanuele Coccia, *Sensible Life: A Micro-ontology of the Image*, trans. Scott Alan Stuart (New York: Fordham University Press, 2016), 65.
20 Coccia, *Sensible Life*, 65–6.
21 Agamben, *Stanzas*, 73.
22 Agamben, *Stanzas*, 77.
23 Agamben, *Stanzas*, 83.
24 Brenet, *Je fantasme*, 83.
25 Agamben, *Means Without End*, 9.
26 Agamben, 'Intelletto d'amore', in *Intellect d'amour*, ed. Giorgio Agamben and Jean-Baptiste Brenet (Paris: Éditions Verdier, 2018), 25.
27 Agamben, *Use of Bodies*, 210.
28 Agamben, *Use of Bodies*, 212.
29 Debord, *Society of the Spectacle*, 13.
30 Debord, *Society of the Spectacle*, 15.
31 Debord, *Society of the Spectacle*, 4.
32 Berardi, 'The Premonition of Guy Debord'.
33 Pierre Legendre, 'The Dogmatic Value of Aesthetics', *Parallax* 14, no. 4 (2008): 10–17, 11.

34 Hannah Arendt, 'Ideology and Terror: A Novel Form of Government'" *The Review of Politics* 15, no. 3 (July 1953): 303–27, 325–6.
35 Jean-Luc Nancy, *Before the Abyss*, April 2021, https://www.philosophy-world-democracy.org/articles-1/before-the-abyss.
36 Nancy, *Before the Abyss*.
37 For a detailed exposition of this phrase and how it related to Legendre's work more broadly see Peter Goodrich and Serene Richards, 'L'Empreinte juridique', in *Introductions À L'Oeuvre de Pierre Legendre*, ed. Katrin Becker and Pierre Musso (Paris: Éditions Manucius, 2023).
38 Pierre Legendre, *L'Inexploré: Conférence à l'École nationale des chartes* (Paris: Ars Dogmatica Éditions, 2020), 1.
39 Pierre Legendre, *Fabrique de l'Homme Occidental* (Paris: Éditions Mille et une Nuits, 1997), 12.
40 Pierre Legendre, 'The Masters of Law: A Study of the Dogmatic Function', in *Law and the Unconscious: A Legendre Reader*, ed. Peter Goodrich, trans. Peter Goodrich with Alain Pottage and Anton Schütz (Hampshire and London: Palgrave Macmillan, 1997), 107.
41 Stefano Harney and Fred Moten, *The Undercommons: Fugitive Planning and Black Study* (Wivenhoe, New York and Port Watson: Minor Compositions, 2013), 80.
42 Pierre Legendre, *Dieu au Miroir: Étude sur l'institution des images* (Paris: Fayard, 1994), 121.
43 Coccia, *Sensible Life*, 5.
44 Chiara Bottici, *Imaginal Politics: Images Beyond Imagination and the Imaginary* (New York: Columbia University Press, 2014), 55.
45 Bottici, *Imaginal Politics*, 56.
46 Fernand Deligny, *L'Arachnéen et autres textes* (Paris: L'Arachnéen, 2008), 198.
47 Schürman, 'Que faire', 363.

Conclusion

1 Friedrich Hölderlin, *Hyperion or the Hermit in Greece*, tr. Ross Benjamin (New York: Archipelago books, 2008), First Book, 3.
2 The Story Behind, 'Keep Calm and Carry On', https://www.london.ac.uk/about-us/history-university-london/story-behind-keep-calm-and-carry.

3 Charles Baudelaire, 'Be Drunk', in *Paris Spleen: Little Poems in Prose*, ed. Charles Baudelaire, trans. Keith Waldrop (Middletown: Wesleyan University, 2009), 71 [translation modified].
4 https://www.ina.fr/ina-eclaire-actu/les-vers-de-charles-baudelaire.
5 Gilles Deleuze, 'Nomadic Thought', in *Desert Islands and Other Texts, 1953–1974* (Los Angeles, Semiotext(e), 2004), 257.
6 Maurice Blanchot, *The Infinite Conversation*, trans. Susan Hanson (Minneapolis and London: University of Minnesota Press, 2003), 47.
7 Deleuze, *Seminar on Foucault*.
8 Deleuze, *Logic of Sense*, 160.
9 Harney and Moten, *The Undercommons*, 49.
10 Gilles Deleuze and Félix Guattari, *What is Philosophy*, trans. Hugh Tomlinson and Graham Burchell (New York: Columbia University Press, 1994), 41.
11 'How the Super-Rich Sleep Well', https://www.thetimes.co.uk/article/mark-zuckerberg-sleep-like-rich-mattress-5rmh67rjt.
12 Agamben, *L'Irrealizabile*, 85.
13 Tiqqun, *This is Not a Program* (Los Angeles: Semiotext(e), 2011), 146–7.
14 Deleuze, *Difference and Repetition*, 275.

Bibliography

Agamben, Giorgio, *Stanzas: Word and Phantasm in Western Culture*, translated by Ronald L. Martinez, Minneapolis and London: University of Minnesota Press, 1993.

Agamben, Giorgio, 'We Refugees', translated by Michael Rocke, *Symposium* 29, no. 2 (1995): 114–19.

Agamben, Giorgio, *Homo Sacer: Sovereign Power and Bare Life*, translated by Daniel Heller-Roazen, Stanford: Stanford University Press, 1998.

Agamben, Giorgio, *Potentialities*, edited and translated by Daniel Heller-Roazen, Stanford: Stanford University Press, 1999.

Agamben, Giorgio, *Means Without End: Notes on Politics*, translated by Vincenzo Binetti and Cesare Casarino, Minneapolis and London: University of Minnesota Press, 2000.

Agamben, Giorgio, 'For a Philosophy of Infancy', *Public* 21 (2001): 120–2,

Agamben, Giorgio, *The Open: Man and Animal*, translated by Kevin Attell, Stanford: Stanford University Press, 2004.

Agamben, Giorgio, *State of Exception*, translated by Kevin Attell, Chicago and London: The University of Chicago Press, 2005.

Agamben, Giorgio, *The Coming Community*, translated by Michael Hardt, Minneapolis and London: University of Minnesota Press, 2009.

Agamben, Giorgio, *What Is an Apparatus?* translated by David Kishik and Stefan Pedatella, Stanford: Stanford University Press, 2009.

Agamben, Giorgio, 'La vie et le droit', in *Aux origines des cultures juridiques européennes: Yan Thomas entre droit et sciences sociales*, edited by Paolo Napoli, Rome: Collection de L'École Française de Rome, 2013.

Agamben, Giorgio, *Opus Dei: An Archaeology of Duty*, translated by Adam Kotsko, 249–258, Stanford: Stanford University Press, 2013.

Agamben, Giorgio, 'What Is a Destituent Power?' translated by Stephanie Wakefield. *Environment and Planning D: Society and Space* 32 (2014): 65–74.

Agamben, Giorgio, *Stasis: Civil War as a Political Paradigm*, Stanford: Stanford University Press, 2015.

Agamben, Giorgio, *The Use of Bodies*, translated by Adam Kotsko, Stanford: Stanford University Press, 2015.

Agamben, Giorgio, *Karman: A Brief Treatise on Action, Guilt, and Gesture,* translated by Adam Kotsko, Stanford: Stanford University Press, 2017.

Agamben, Giorgio, *The Fire and the Tale,* translated by Lorenzo Chiesa, Stanford: Stanford University Press, 2017.

Agamben, Giorgio, *What Is Real?* translated by Lorenzo Chiesa, Stanford: Stanford University Press, 2018.

Agamben, Giorgio, *Création et anarchie,* translated by Joël Gayraud, Paris: Payot et rivages, 2019.

Agamben, Giorgio, 'What Is a Command?' in *Creation and Anarchy,* translated by Adam Kotsko, 249–58, Stanford: Stanford University Press, 2019.

Agamben, Giorgio, *L'irrealizzabile: Per Una politica dell'ontologia,* Torino: Piccola Biblioteca Einaudi, 2022.

Agamben, Giorgio, 'Vers une théorie de la puissance destituante', https://lundi.am/vers-une-theorie-de-la-puissance-destituante-Par-Giorgio-Agamben.

Agamben, Giorgio and Jean-Baptiste Brenet, *Intellect d'amour,* Paris: Éditions Verdier, 2018.

Alighieri, Dante, *The Divine Comedy: Inferno,* translated by Mark Musa, London and New York: Penguin Books, 1984.

Arendt, Hannah, *The Origins of Totalitarianism,* New York: Harcourt, 1951.

Arendt, Hannah, 'Ideology and Terror: A Novel Form of Government', *The Review of Politics* 15, no. 3 (July 1953): 303–27.

Aristotle, *De anima,* translated by Christopher Shields, Oxford: Oxford University Press, 2016.

Artaud, Antonin, *Theatre and its Double,* New York: Grove Press, 1958.

Artaud, Antonin, 'Letter to René Allendy, November 1927', in *Antonin Artaud: Selected Writings,* edited by Susan Sontag, translated by Helen Weaver, 168–71, New York: Farrar, Straus and Giroux, Inc., 1976.

Axelos, Kostas, *Introduction to a Future Way of Thought: On Marx and Heidegger,* translated by Kenneth Mills, edited by Stuart Elden, Lüneburg: Meson Press, 2015.

Axelos, Kostas, *Vers la pensée planétaire: The devenir-pensée du monde et le devenir-monde de la pensée,* Paris: Éditions Les Belles Lettres, 2019.

Balibar, Étienne, 'Subjection and Subjectivation', in *Supposing the Subject,* edited by Joan Copjec, 1–15, London and New York: Verso, 1996.

Baudelaire, Charles, 'Be Drunk', in Charles Baudelaire, *Paris Spleen: Little Poems in Prose,* translated by Keith Waldrop, 71, Middletown CT: Wesleyan University, 2009.

Baudrillard, Jean, *L'échange symbolique et la mort*, Paris: Gallimard, 1976.
Baudrillard, Jean, *The Transparency of Evil: Essays on Extreme Phenomena*, translated by James Benedict, London and New York: Verso Books, 1993.
Beaucamp, Maxime, 'Deleuze et La Fêlure de Francis Scott Fitzgerald: De Logique du sens à Mille plateaux', *Klesis: Revue Philosophique* 20 (2011): 104–21.
Benjamin, Walter, 'Theses on the Concept of History', in Walter Benjamin, *Illuminations*, edited by Hannah Arendt, translated by Harry Zohn, New York: Schocken Books, 1969.
Benjamin, Walter, 'Critique of Violence', in Walter Benjamin, *Reflections: Essays, Aphorisms, Autobiographical Writings*, translated by Edmund Jephcott, edited by Peter Demetz, 253–64, New York: Schocken Books, 1986,
Benjamin, Walter, 'Capitalism as Religion', in Walter Benjamin, *Selected Writings Vol.1: 1913–1926*, translated by Rodney Livingston, edited by Marcus Bullock and Michael W. Jennings, Massachusetts: Belknap Harvard Press, 1996.
Berardi, Franco 'Bifo', *The Soul at Work: From Alienation to Autonomy*, translated by Francesca Cadel and Giuseppina Mecchia, Los Angeles: Semiotext(e), 2009.
Berardi, Franco 'Bifo', *The Completion, Issue 137*, June 2023, https://www.e-flux.com/journal/137/544269/the-completion/.
Berardi, Franco 'Bifo', 'The Premonition of Guy Debord', https://www.generation-online.org/t/tbifodebord.htm.
Berger, Adolf, *Encyclopedic Dictionary of Roman Law*, Vol. 43, Philadelphia: The American Philosophical Society, 1991, 403–4.
Bichat, Xavier, *Physiological Researches on Life and Death*, translated by F. Gold, London: Longman, 1815.
Blanchot, Maurice, *The Infinite Conversation*, translated by Susan Hanson, Minneapolis and London: University of Minnesota Press, 2003.
Bottici, Chiara, *Imaginal Politics: Images Beyond Imagination and the Imaginary*, New York: Columbia University Press, 2014.
Boulnois, Olivier, *Généalogie de la liberté*, Paris: Seuil, 2021.
Bratton, Benjamin, *Revenge of the Real: Politics for a Post-pandemic World*, London and New York: Verso Books, 2021.
Brenet, Jean-Baptiste, *Je fantasme: Averroès et l'espace potentiel*, Paris: Éditions Verdier, 2017.
Brockway, Lucile H., *Science and Colonial Expansion: The Role of the British Royal Botanic Gardens*, New York: Academic Press, 1979.

Brown, Janet, 'A Science of Empire: British Biogeography before Darwin', *Revue d'histoire des sciences* 45, no. 4 (1992): 453–75.
Canguilhem, Georges, *Knowledge of Life*, edited by Paola Marrati and Todd Meyers, translated by Stefanos Geroulanos and Daniela Ginsburg, New York: Fordham University Press, 2008.
Chiaramonte, Xenia, 'Instituting: A Legal Practice', *Humana.Mente Journal of Philosophical Studies* 41 (2022): 1–23.
Coccia, Emanuele, *Sensible Life: A Micro-ontology of the Image*, translated by Scott Alan Stuart, New York: Fordham University Press, 2016.
Cooper, Melinda, *Life as Surplus: Biotechnology and Capitalism in the Neoliberal Era*, Seattle and London: University of Washington Press, 2008.
Daston, Loraine, *Classical Probability in the Enlightenment*, Princeton: Princeton University Press, 1988.
Debord, Guy, *The Society of the Spectacle*, translated by Donald Nicholson-Smith, New York: Zone Books, 1994.
Defert, Daniel, François Ewald, and Frédéric Gros, "Introduction" in Michel Foucault, *Introduction to Kant's Anthropology*, edited by Roberto Nigro, Translated by Roberto Nigro and Kate Briggs, 9–12, Los Angeles: Semiotext(e), 2008.
Deleuze, Gilles, *Spinoza: The Velocities of Thought*, Lecture 2, December 9, 1980, https://purr.purdue.edu/publications/2843/1.
Deleuze, Gilles, *Seminar on Foucault, 1985–1986*, Lecture 20, April 22, 1986.
Deleuze, Gilles, *Foucault*, translated by Seán Hand, Minneapolis and London: University of Minnesota Press, 1988.
Deleuze, Gilles, *Expressionism in Philosophy: Spinoza*, translated by Martin Joughin, New York: Zone Books, 1990.
Deleuze, Gilles, *The Logic of Sense*, translated by Mark Lester with Charles Stivale, edited by Constantin V. Boundas, London: The Athlone Press, 1990.
Deleuze, Gilles, 'G comme Gauche', in *L'Abécédaire de Gilles Deleuze, avec Claire Parnet*, Paris: DVD Editions Montparnasse, 1994.
Deleuze, Gilles, 'The Image of Thought', in *Difference and Repetition*, translated by Paul Patton, 129–67, London and New York: Continuum, 1994.
Deleuze, Gilles, The Exhausted, translated by Anthony Uhlmann, *SubStance* 24, no. 3 (1995): 3–28.
Deleuze, Gilles, 'Immanence a Life', in *Pure Immanence: Essays on A Life*, translated by Anne Boyman, 25–34, New York: Zone Books, 2001.

Deleuze, Gilles, 'Nomadic Thought', in *Desert Islands and Other Texts, 1953-1974*, 252–61, Los Angeles, Semiotext(e), 2004.

Deleuze, Gilles and Félix Guattari, *What Is Philosophy?* translated by Hugh Tomlinson and Graham Burchell, New York: Columbia University Press, 1994.

Deleuze, Gilles and Félix Guattari, *A Thousand Plateaus: Capitalism and Schizophrenia*, translated by Brian Massumi, London and New York: Continuum Books, 2004.

Deligny, Fernand, *L'Arachnéen et autres textes*, Paris: L'Arachnéen, 2008.

Derrida, Jacques, *The Work of Mourning*, edited by Pascale-Anne Brault and Michael Naas, London and Chicago: University of Chicago Press, 2001)

Desrosières, Alain, *The Politics of Large Numbers: A History of Statistical Reasoning*, translated by Camille Nash, Cambridge, MA and London: Harvard University Press, 1998.

de Sutter, Laurent, *Hors la loi : Théorie de l'anarchie juridique*, Paris: Les liens qui libèrent, 2021.

Devereux, George, 'Dream Learning and Individual Ritual Differences in Mohave Shamanism', *American Anthropologist* 59, no. 6 (1957): 1036–45.

Dolar, Mladen, *A Voice and Nothing More*, Cambridge, MA: MIT Press, 2006.

Dufourmantelle, Anne, *In Praise of Risk*, translated by Steven Miller, New York: Fordham University Press, 2019.

Ewald, François, 'Norms, Discipline and the Law', in *Law and the Order of Culture*, edited by Robert Post, 138–61, Berkeley: University of California Press, 1991.

Foucault, Michel, *Dit et Écrits 4 1980-1988*, 180, Est-il donc important de penser ?, entretien avec D. Eribon, mai, Paris: Gallimard, 1994.

Foucault, Michel, *Dits et Écrits 1*, 'Foucault', in Dictionnaire des philosophes, edited by Denis Huisman, 942–4, Paris: Puf, 1984.

Foucault, Michel, 'Right to Death and Power over Life', in *The History of Sexuality*, translated by Robert Hurley, 135–59, London: Penguin, 1984.

Foucault, Michel, *Discipline and Punish: The Birth of the Prison*, translated by Alan Sheridan, London: Penguin Books, 1991.

Foucault, Michel, 'Panopticism', in *Discipline and Punish: The Birth of the Prison*, translated by Alan Sheridan, 195–230, London: Penguin Books, 1991.

Foucault, Michel, 'Les Mailles du Pouvoir', Conférence de Michel Foucault au Brésil in *Dits et Écrits IV 1980-1988*, Paris: Éditions Gallimard, 1994.

Foucault, Michel, 'Governmentality', in *Essential Works, Volume 3: Power*, edited by James D. Faubion, translated by Robert Hurley and others, 201–22, London: Penguin, 2000.

Foucault, Michel, *The Order of Things: An Archaeology of the Human Sciences*, New York and Oxford: Routledge, 2002.
Foucault, Michel, 'Truth and Juridical Forms', in *The Essential Works of Foucault (1954–1984), Volume 3: Power*, edited by James D. Faubion, 1–89, London: Penguin, 2002.
Foucault, Michel, *The Birth of the Clinic*, translated by A. M. Sheridan, London: Routledge, 2003.
Foucault, Michel, *Society Must Be Defended*, translated by David Macey, edited by Mauro Bertani and Alessandro Fontana, London: Penguin Books, 2004.
Foucault, Michel, *The Birth of Biopolitics, Lectures at the Collège de France 1978–79*, translated by Graham Burchell, edited by Michel Snellart, Hampshire and New York: Palgrave Macmillan, 2008.
Foucault, Michel, 'Michel Foucault à propos de "Les Mots et les Choses" (1ère diffusion : 01/01/1973) Radio France', *Archive Ina-Radio France*, https://www.radiofrance.fr/franceculture/podcasts/les-nuits-de-france-culture/michel-foucault-a-propos-de-son-essai-les-mots-et-les-choses-1390104.
Frank, Manfred, *What is Neostructuralism?* translated by Sabine Wilke and Richard Gray, Minneapolis: University of Minnesota Press, 1989.
Fukuyama, Francis, *The End of History and the Last Man*, London and New York: Penguin Books, 2012.
Garland, David, '"Governmentality" and the Problem of Crime: Foucault, Criminology, Sociology', *Theoretical Criminology* 1, no. 2 (1997): 177–214.
Goodrich, Peter, *Languages of Law: From Logics of Memory to Nomadic Masks*, London: Weidenfeld and Nicolson, 1990.
Goodrich, Peter and Serene Richards, 'L'Empreinte juridique', in *Introductions À L'Oeuvre de Pierre Legendre*, edited by Katrin Becker and Pierre Musso, 59–73, Paris: Éditions Manucius, 2023.
Gordon, Peter E., *Continental Divide: Heidegger, Cassirer, Davos*, Cambridge, MA and London: Harvard University Press, 2012.
Greisch, Jean, *Ontologie et Temporalité*, Paris: Presses Universitaires de France, 1994.
Hacking, Ian, *The Taming of Chance*, Cambridge: Cambridge University Press, 1990.
Hacking, Ian, 'How Should We Do the History of Statistics', in *The Foucault Effect*, edited by Graham Burchell, Colin Gordon, and Peter Miller, 181–96, Chicago: The University of Chicago Press, 1991.

Hajjat, Abdellali, 'L'expérience politique du Mouvement des travailleurs arabes', *Contretemps* 16 (2006): 76–85.
Hajjat, Abdellali, 'Alliances inattendues à la Goutte d'Or', in *68: Une histoire collective (1962-1981)*, edited by Michelle Zancarini-Fournel and Philippe Artieres, 491–541, Paris: La Découverte, 2008.
Harney, Stefano and Fred Moten, *The Undercommons: Fugitive Planning and Black Study*, Wivenhoe, New York and Port Watson: Minor Compositions, 2013.
Heidegger, Martin, 'The Idea of a Philosophical Anthropology', in *Kant and the Problem of Metaphysics*, translated by James S. Churchill, 215–20, Bloomington: Indiana University Press, 1965.
Heidegger, Martin, 'The Age of the World Picture', in *The Question Concerning Technology and Other Essays*, translated by William Lovitt, 115–54, New York and London: Harper & Row Publishers, Inc., 1977.
Heidegger, Martin, Letter on 'Humanism' (1946), translated by Frank A. Capuzzi, in *Martin Heidegger: Pathmarks*, edited by William McNeil, Cambridge: Cambridge University Press, 1998.
Heidegger, Martin, *Being and Time*, translated by Jean Stambaugh, Albany: State University of New York Press, 2010.
Hobbes, Thomas, *On the Citizen*, Cambridge: Cambridge University Press, 2003.
Hölderlin, Friedrich, *Hyperion or the Hermit in Greece*, translated by Ross Benjamin, New York: Archipelago Books, 2008.
Judith, Revel, *Dictionnaire Foucault*, Paris: Éditions Ellipses, 2008.
Kant, Immanuel, *Lectures on Logic*, translated and edited by J. Michael Young, Cambridge: Cambridge University Press, 1992.
Karsenti, Bruno, *L'Homme Total: Sociologie, anthropologie et philosophie chez Marcel Mauss*, Paris: Presses Universitaires de France, 1997.
Lacan, Jacques, *La Troisième, VIIème congrès de l'École freudienne de Paris, Rome 31 Octobre –3 Novembre 1974*, Patrick Valas, https://www.valas.fr/IMG/pdf/la_troisieme_integrale.pdf.
Lazarus, Sylvain, *Anthropology of the Name*, Chicago: Seagull Books, 2015.
Lefebvre, Henri, *Critique de la vie Quotidienne I*, Paris: L'Arche Editeur, 1997.
Legendre, Pierre, *Dieu au Miroir: Étude sur l'institution des images*, Paris: Fayard, 1994.
Legendre, Pierre, *Fabrique de l'Homme Occidental*, Paris: Éditions Mille et une Nuits, 1997.

Legendre, Pierre, "The Masters of Law: A Study of the Dogmatic Function", in *Law and the Unconscious: A Legendre Reader*, edited by Peter Goodrich, translated by Peter Goodrich with Alain Pottage and Anton Schütz, Hampshire and London: Palgrave Macmillan, 1997.

Legendre, Pierre, 'The Dogmatic Value of Aesthetics', *Parallax* 14, no. 4 (2008): 10–17.

Legendre, Pierre, *L'Inexploré : Conférence à l'École nationale des chartes*, Paris: Ars Dogmatica Éditions, 2020.

Lenin, V. I., *What is to be Done?*, New York: International Publishers, 1969.

Lyotard, Jean-François, *The Postmodern Condition: A Report on Knowledge*, translated by Geoff Bennington and Brian Massumi, Manchester: Manchester University Press, 1984.

Macé, Marielle, *Styles: Critique de nos formes de vie*, Paris: Gallimard, 2016.

Mackenzie, Donald A., *Statistics in Britain, 1865–1930: The Social Construction of Scientific Knowledge*, Edinburgh, Edinburgh University Press, 1981.

Marx, Karl, 'Economic and Philosophic Manuscripts of 1844', translated by Martin Milligan in *Economic and Philosophic Manuscripts of 1844 and the Communist Manifesto*, 13–168, New York: Prometheus Books, 1988.

Mbembe, Achille, *Brutalisme*, Paris: Éditions la Découverte, 2020.

Moore, Nathan, 'Pay it all Back: Paranoid Writing/Writing Paranoia', in *Burroughs Unbound*, edited by S. E. Gontarski, 71–88, Cambridge: Bloomsbury, 2022.

Murphy, Tim, *The Oldest Social Science*, Oxford University Press, 1997.

Nancy, Jean-Luc, *The Experience of Freedom*, translated by Bridget McDonald, Stanford: Stanford University Press, 1993.

Nancy, Jean-Luc, *Before the Abyss*, April 2021, https://www.philosophy-world-democracy.org/articles-1/before-the-abyss.

Nicholls, Walter J. and Justus Uitermark, *Cities and Social Movements: Immigrants' Rights Activism in the United States, France, and the Netherlands, 1970–2015*, Oxford: Wiley, 2016.

Nigro, Roberto, 'From Kant's *Anthropology* to the Critique of the Anthropological Question: Foucault's *Introduction* in Context', in Michel Foucault, *Introduction to Kant's Anthropology*, edited by Roberto Nigro, translated by R. Nigro and Kate Briggs, Cambridge, MA and London: MIT Press, 2008.

Pitti, Laure, 'Grèves Ouvrières versus lutes de l'immigration : Une controverse entre historiens', *Ethnologie Française* 31 (2001): 465–76.

Richards, Serene, *Court of Miracles: On the Government of the Passions*, 2024.
Ross, Alison, *May '68 and its Afterlives*, Chicago and London: University of Chicago Press, 2002.
Schürmann, Reiner, 'Que faire à la fin de la métaphysique?' in *Cahier de l'herne: Martin Heidegger*, edited by Michel Haar, n45, Paris: Éditions de l'Herne, 1983.
Schürmann, Reiner, *Tomorrow the Manifold: Essays on Foucault, Anarchy and the Singularisation to Come*, Zurich: Diaphanes, 2019.
Sibertin-Blanc, Guillaume, 'Délires de langue, schizoanalyse de savoir linguistique: *Lalangue*, anagramme, homophonie scénique', *Kenose: Revue Philosophique & Politique* no. 0 (2013–2014): 38–62.
Sloterdijk, Peter, *You Must Change Your Life*, translated by Wieland Hoban, Cambridge: Polity Press, 2013.
Stafford, Robert A., *Scientist of Empire: Sir Roderick Murchison, Scientific Exploration and Victorian Imperialism*, Cambridge: Cambridge University Press, 1986.
Tari, Marcello, *There Is No Unhappy Revolution: The Communism of Destitution*, translated by Richard Braude, New York: Common Notions, 2021.
The Compact Oxford English Dictionary, 2nd edn, Oxford: Clarendon Press, 1991, 684–5.
Thomas, Yan, 'Le Sujet de Droit, La Personne et la Nature: Sur la critique contemporaine du sujet de droit', *Le Débat* 3, no. 100 (1998): 85–107.
Thomas, Yan, 'L' "usage" et les "fruits" de l'esclave : Opérations juridiques romaines sur le travail. The "Uses" and the "Fruits" of the Slave. Roman Juridical Operations on Work', *Enquête* 7 (1999): 203–30, electronic edition: http://enquete.revues.org/1578.
Thomas, Yan, 'Sujet concret et sa personne', in *Du droit de ne pas naître: A Propos de l'Affaire Pérruche*, edited by Olivier Cayla and Yan Thomas, Paris: Gallimard, 2002.
Thomson, Iain, 'Ontotheology? Understanding Heidegger's Destruktion of Metaphysics', *International Journal or Philosophical Studies* 8, no. 3 (2000): 297–327.
Tiqqun, *This Is Not a Program*, Los Angeles: Semiotext(e), 2011.
Virilio, Paul, *A Landscape of Events*, translated by Julie Rose, Cambridge and London: The MIT Press, 2000.
Virilio, Paul, *The Information Bomb*, translated by Chris Turner, London and New York: Verso, 2005.

Weil, Simone, 'Human Personality', in *Simone Weil: An Anthology*, edited by Sian Mills, London: Penguin, 2005.
Whyte, Jessica, 'The Opacity of Economic Coercion', *Yale Journal of International Law*, June 21, 2023, https://www.yjil.yale.edu/the-opacity-of-economic-coercion/.
Zourabichvili, François, 'Deleuze et le Possible (de l'involontarisme en politique)', in *Gilles Deleuze: Une vie philosophique: Rencontres internationales Rio de Janeiro-São Paulo, 10–14 juin 1996*, edited by Éric Alliez, Paris: Institut Synthélabo, 1998.
Zylberman, Patrick, *Tempête Microbiennes: Essai sur la politique de sécurité sanitaire dans le monde transatlantique*, Paris: Gallimard, 2013.

Online links

Begum, Shamima, 'Spy for Canada Smuggled Schoolgirl to Syria', August 31, 2022, https://www.bbc.co.uk/news/uk-62726954.
'Forefront Excerpt: Germany's Designer City, Next City', December 16, 2013, https://nextcity.org/urbanist-news/forefront-excerpt-germanys-designer-city.
Google Duplex: An AI System for Accomplishing Real-World Tasks Over the Phone', May 8, 2018, https://ai.googleblog.com/2018/05/duplex-ai-system-for-natural-conversation.html.
Greene, Anastasia, 'Symposium Exploring the Crime of Ecocide: Rights of Nature and Ecocide', *Opinio Juris*, September 24, 2020, http://opiniojuris.org/2020/09/24/symposium-exploring-the-crime-of-ecocide-rights-of-nature-and-ecocide/.
How the Super-Rich Sleep Well', https://www.thetimes.co.uk/article/mark-zuckerberg-sleep-like-rich-mattress-5rmh67rjt.
Jones, Phil, 'Refugees Help Power Machine Learning Advances at Microsoft, Facebook, and Amazon', *Rest of World*, September 22, 2021, https://restofworld.org/2021/refugees-machine-learning-big-tech/.
Robertson, Nan, 'Renault Strife Worries France', April 4, 1973, https://www.nytimes.com/1973/04/04/archives/renault-strife-worries-france-a-new-generation-nightmare-of-the.html.
Sainato, Michael, '14-hour Days and No Bathroom Breaks: Amazon's Overworked Delivery Drivers', March 11, 2021, https://www.theguardian

.com/technology/2021/mar/11/amazon-delivery-drivers-bathroom-breaks-unions.

The Story Behind, 'Keep Calm and Carry On', https://www.london.ac.uk/about-us/history-university-london/story-behind-keep-calm-and-carry.

Walters, Matthew, 'Death by Poverty: Canada's Assisted Dying Program Exposes Fault Lines in Healthcare', February 9, 2023, https://www.leftvoice.org/death-by-poverty-canadas-assisted-dying-program-exposes-fault-lines-in-healthcare/.

Legal Cases

Appleby and Others v. The United Kingdom 2002.

Index

accident   xiii, xiv, 44, 55, 60
Agamben, Giorgio   xv, 11, 43, 44, 65, 69, 77, 119
  anthropogenesis   39, 72–5, 94
  biopolitics   4, 5, 9, 50, 63, 64, 67, 68, 70–2, 75–7, 80, 83, 84, 95, 101–3, 112, 113, 124
  destituent power   110, 115, 121
  ergon   79, 80
  form-of-life   5, 12, 13, 79, 81, 82, 120, 121, 123
  law   98, 113–17
  phantasm   13, 141–3
  potential   10, 12, 13, 104, 120, 121, 125–7, 143, 144
  presupposition   12, 66, 85
Allendy, René   1
Aquinas, St. Thomas   122
Arendt, Hannah   97, 101, 145
Aristotle   9, 24, 50, 67, 70–2, 76, 77, 79, 80, 82, 112, 141, 142
Artaud, Antonin   xiii, 1, 13, 108, 118, 129
artificial intelligence   ix, x
Averroës, Ibn Rushd   13, 140, 142–4
Axelos, Kostas   17, 138

Baghdad   2
Balibar, Étienne   25, 26, 29
Baudelaire, Charles   151, 152
Baudrillard, Jean p.   x, 90–1
Beirut   2
Benjamin, Walter   xii, 109–10, 115–19
Bentham, Jeremy   45, 52, 165 n.50
Berardi, Franco 'Bifo'   131, 139
Bichat, Xavier   35, 72
biometrics   3, 100
biopolitics as a system of thought   3, 6, 14, 126, 153

Blanchot, Maurice   152
Borges, Jorge Luis   31
Bottici, Chiara   148
Bratton, Benjamin   3, 4, 83–6
Brenet, Jean-Baptiste   140, 143
Buñuel, Luis   134

Canada   63
Canguilhem, Georges   69
capitalism   4, 5, 16, 18, 44, 47, 91, 93, 108–10, 118, 165 n.50
Cassirer, Ernst   25, 26
Chile   2, 118
Cicero   122
climate crisis   3, 86
Coccia, Emanuele   141, 148, 149
colonialism   11, 31, 88–90, 107, 161 n.60
  colonizing genocide   63
communism   5, 11, 94, 110, 115, 119
constituent power   11, 89, 92, 94, 110, 113, 115, 117, 118
Cooper, Melinda   163 n.17

Dante   xv, 13, 143, 144
Debord, Guy   viii, 96, 145
Deleuze, Gilles   xiii, 4, 7, 10–12, 88, 103–5, 108, 118, 121–5, 128, 129, 133–4, 152–3
  event   128, 129
  Foucault   10
  immanence   82
  incorporeal   68, 133–4
  jurisprudence   93, 105
  minoritarian universal consciousness (with Guattari)   11–12, 104, 105
  outside   152
  society of control   133

Spinoza 121–5
thinking xiii, 7, 118
Deligny, Fernand 149, 150
Derrida, Jacques 91
Descartes, René 36
Desrosières, Alain 57
Destituent Power 4–6, 11, 12, 89, 94, 110, 115, 117, 119, 125, 127, 128, 137
De sutter, Laurent 94, 101
Devereux, George 141
digital 11, 13, 133, 134
Dolar, Mladen x
Dufourmantelle, Anne 15

ethnology 37, 164 n.35
Eugenics 63
European Court of Human Rights 132, 133
Ewald, François 15, 46, 166 n.70

Fitzgerald, F. Scott 13, 128
Foucault, Michel 4, 88, 91, 94
  anthropology 25, 29, 30, 33, 48, 160 n.54
  biopolitics 8, 47, 49, 50, 53, 54, 58–66, 76, 81
  discipline 44–6, 48, 93, 165 n.50
  governmentality 48, 55
  human sciences 8, 10, 18, 25, 32, 33, 35, 37, 47, 48, 62, 93
  law 45, 51
  management 53, 54, 57, 60, 63
  population 44, 56–8, 61, 65
  psychoanalysis 37, 38
  racism 58–62
  sovereignty 48, 52, 56, 59, 111
  unthought 8, 15–16, 36
Fukuyama, Francis 12

Gauche prolétarienne 88
genocide 2, 61, 63, 95
Goodrich, Peter 96, 107
Google Duplex AI ix, x

Gordon, Peter. E. 25–7
Greisch, Jean 28
Guattari, Félix 68, 104, 108, 134

Harney, Stefano 147, 153
Hayek 16
Hegel, G. W. F. 46
Heidegger, Martin 25, 26, 28, 83, 84, 159 n.44, 161 n.67
Hobbes, Thomas 52, 59, 111, 112, 115, 123, 124
Hölderlin, Friedrich 151
Huisman, Denis 15
Hyppolite, Jean 25, 161 n.68

instrumentalized knowledge 6, 8, 17–18

Kafka 13, 127
Kant, Immanuel 25–7, 30, 125, 126
Karsenti, Bruno 41

labour 34, 85, 89, 91, 92, 131
Lacan, Jacques 150, 155 n.4
lalangue x, xiv, 138, 162 n.86
Law
  European Convention of Human Rights 133
  Rights 11, 22, 45, 51–2, 64, 73, 77, 92–5, 97–102, 112, 122–4
  Roman law 11, 20, 69, 78, 97, 165 n.38
Lazarus, Sylvain xiv, 10, 21–3, 119
Lefebvre, Henri 87, 107
Legendre, Pierre 145–8, 178 n.37
Lenin, Vladimir 6, 110
liberalism 16, 18, 19, 50, 62, 64, 65, 92–5, 97
  and eugenics 62, 63
life-distilling machine 9, 69, 74, 124
Locke, John 46
loneliness 13, 95, 144, 145
Lyotard, Jean-François 17–20

Macé, Marielle 32
Magritte, René 147
Marx, Karl 5, 29, 46, 52, 137
May '68 87
Mbembe, Achille 107
metaphysics 5, 6, 10, 27–9, 34, 66, 67, 74, 85, 94, 125, 146, 148, 160, 166–7 n.74
Microsoft xi
Milner, Jean-Claude 138, 139
morality 4, 10, 41, 91, 122, 125
Moten, Fred 147, 153
Mouvement des travailleurs arabes (MTA) 11, 87–90, 92, 93, 99, 105, 136
  Comités Palestine 88
multitude 13, 110–13, 143, 144

Nancy, Jean-Luc 136, 146
not-all ix, x

Pasolini, Pier Paolo 119
people think 8, 13, 21, 22, 119, 137, 143
phantasm 13, 36, 38, 39, 96, 112, 139–43, 148
Plato 28, 141, 142
positive biopolitics xi, xv, 3, 83, 85
positivism xiv, 8, 10, 18, 21, 35, 96
probability 8, 43, 44, 56

racism 11, 49, 58, 59, 61–3, 88–90
refugee xiv, 11, 85, 101, 136
  'click workers' 85
Reggiani, Serge 152
Revel, Judith 50
risk 14, 36, 43, 44, 50, 62, 129, 153
  of thought xv, 108, 154

Saussure, Ferdinand de x
Scheler, Max 27
Schmitt, Carl 113–17
Schürmann, Reiner 6, 23
Silicon Valley ix–x, xiv
Simmel, Georg 27
smart being viii, ix, x, xi, xii, xiii, xiv, xv, 3, 14, 19, 153, 154
Socrates 17, 141
Spinoza 12, 13, 94, 120, 122–6, 135, 143, 144
statistics 8, 42, 43, 45, 48, 56–8, 60, 62, 65, 66, 163 n.8
surveillance 3, 44, 45, 59, 85, 153

Tari, Marcello 115, 117, 118
taxonomy 6, 24, 31, 74
techno-capital xi, xii, 3, 85
Thomas, Yan 11, 78, 97–101, 168–9 n.27
Truffaut, François 82

value, life xi, 3, 4, 8, 11, 12, 18, 19, 48, 60, 121, 124, 137, 144, 153
  exchange 12, 20, 21, 47, 96, 107, 109, 110, 119, 132, 134
Vermeule, Adrian 3, 4
Virilio, Paul xii, xiii, xiv
Virno, Paulo 110, 112
voice ix, x

Weil, Simone x, 98, 99
Whac-A-Mole 136
what is to be done 2, 6, 31

Zourabichvili, François 104
Zylberman, Patrick 43

www.ingramcontent.com/pod-product-compliance
Lightning Source LLC
Chambersburg PA
CBHW052115300426
44116CB00010B/1676